Invest Outside the Box

Tariq Dennison

Invest Outside the Box

Understanding Different Asset Classes and Strategies

Tariq Dennison
GFM Asset Management
Hong Kong, Hong Kong

ISBN 978-981-13-0371-5   ISBN 978-981-13-0372-2   (eBook)
https://doi.org/10.1007/978-981-13-0372-2

Library of Congress Control Number: 2018943805

Cover Image: © Westend61 GmbH / Alamy Stock Photo
Cover Design by Oscar Spigolon

Printed on acid-free paper

This Palgrave Macmillan imprint is published by the registered company Springer Nature
Singapore Pte Ltd.
The registered company address is: 152 Beach Road, #21-01/04 Gateway East, Singapore
189721, Singapore

PREFACE: HOW BOXES DEFINE INVESTING

This book aims to be one of the most concise introductory guides to investing across many different markets. Many of these investment categories or styles may be outside the comfort zone of non-professionals, or of investment professionals specializing in one of the other "boxes" looking for a refreshing view on another investment "box". Each chapter is meant to be a modular guide to many widely siloed "boxes" of investments, whether boxed by asset class (stocks vs bonds), style (active vs passive, growth vs value), instrument (direct shares vs fund vs ETF vs blockchain), or region (United States vs China), explaining for each of these boxes:

- What each "investment box" is
- Why invest in or avoid investing in that "box"
- Concepts and techniques for understanding and evaluating each "box"
- How to better profit from investing in that box by challenging the conventional wisdom often written on it and by breaking behavioral boxes

There are many books in the field of investing, but this one seemed timely as the post-2009 bull market in stocks and bonds, sometimes termed the "bubble in everything", has been explained by acronyms like "TINA" for "there is no alternative". Not knowing where else to put money is one of the poorest reasons to buy stocks or a piece of real estate and is one of the main reasons many often overlook foreign markets or alternative assets. Investors able to proficiently navigate outside the traditional boxes can expect higher investment returns by buying assets that few competitors are buying at the same time.

This book can be thought of in three parts:

- Part I describes asset classes: stocks vs bonds vs real estate vs currencies vs alternatives. This could be considered the box of "what" to invest in.
- Part II describes different strategies, in other words the "how" boxes of investing.
- Part III surveys several different foreign markets in Chap. 10, and some of the irrational patterns and opportunities seen in the field of behavioral investing in Chap. 11. Part III calls these the "where" boxes and "why break the boxes".

More advanced investors may find some of the topics and explanations basic but are likely to find even "textbook" financial solutions applied in a practical way few academics go into and even fewer funds actually implement. One key example of this is the illustration of how to "beat Berkshire by balancing Berkshire, bonds, and borrowing" in Sect. 7.3 on mean-variance optimization.

Some distinctive goals and features of this book include:

- For readers with no background in finance or investing, each chapter begins with an elementary explanation of each investment "box". Together, the chapters develop a working knowledge across several different types of investments.
- Active investors or investment professionals already focused in one of these investment boxes will find this book a concise and useful introduction to different asset classes, strategies, and regions which may be outside their current comfort zone.
- Unlike many investing textbooks, this book is mostly from the author's own experience with these different asset classes, geographies, and strategies from 1997 to 2017, and answers more of the "why" and "what I do differently" questions rather than just the "what" and "how" of investing in each box.
- This book takes a mostly "outside view" of each investment box, focusing on the bigger questions of diversification and risk/reward, rather than deep analysis on any one type of investment. At times, references are made to other books and sources that go deeper into these topics.

Other than the foundational knowledge in fixed income, asset allocation, and portfolio construction that this book assets as the most important base for almost any investor, the emphasis is on breadth rather than depth with the goal that most readers will be inspired to consider investing in boxes other than ones they were earlier comfortable with.

The first chapter on bank deposits may seem extremely basic for even most non-finance professionals, so is the one chapter many readers may choose to skip or skim through, or use as a guide to the other chapters through the many references there. The second chapter on bonds is one of the longest and most foundational, since in many ways understanding bonds is a base for understanding most other types of investments.

Doing anything "outside the box" may sound like a cliché, but investing uses box terminology in at least three different ways:

- whether an investment is viewed from the inside or outside, and as a "black box" or "white box",
- the "boxes" into which investments are classified, and
- investment processes we use to see if a given investment "ticks the boxes".

First, any investment itself can be viewed as a box into which an investor puts money now with the expectation that the box will return more money at a later time or times. This is a simple but liberating view that helps make clear how $1,000,000 in stock paying $50,000/year in dividends has a lot more in common with a $1,000,000 building paying $50,000/year in rental income than might be obvious to an investor with experience in only stocks or only real estate. To oversimplify the work of Nobel Memorial Prize in Economics winners Daniel Kahneman and Amos Tversky (two of the best known scholars in behavioral finance referenced in Chap. 11), the "outside view" that both boxes paying out $50,000/year can often be both more reliable and less labor intensive than the "inside view" of a stock analyst or property consultant who believes they might have some edge in understanding why their chosen stock or building is likely to outperform other investments.

This "outside view" is one way of understanding the explosive growth of exchange-traded funds (ETFs) in the first two decades of the twenty-first century, as explained in more detail at the end of Chap. 8.

Second, there are boxes defining which investments we will consider for different boxes of our money. For example, we may use bank deposits for short-term cash that has to be kept safe, bonds for long-term income, rental real estate for inflation-protected income, and stocks for long-term growth in a retirement account. Within each of those boxes, there are sub-boxes where we may consider, for example, domestic vs foreign stocks, residential vs commercial real estate, and high-yield corporate taxable vs high-grade municipal tax-exempt bonds. It is well documented that too many investors invest too little outside their home country and/or are too concentrated in one asset class (or even one asset), and so lose out from the benefits of spreading their risk across different boxes.

Thinking of asset allocation in terms of filling and balancing our boxes of needs, Chap. 3 describes an extremely simple inflation-tracking portfolio allocation called a "Four House Pension" made of only four literal houses. 100% property portfolios are practiced by some investors who don't venture into investing in securities or businesses, but a major goal of this book is to help such investors better visualize how to diversify by replacing one or more of the "houses" in their portfolio with a different asset class or investment strategy.

Third, there are the boxes ticked in checklists when deciding whether or not to make an investment, ensuring it meets our requirements for liquidity, transparency, inflation sensitivity, or other factors. Institutional investors are known to have mandates limiting them to investments that "tick all the boxes", but unconstrained investors also benefit from knowing which boxes they tick consciously or unconsciously when making an investment decision. Investment professionals who simply "tick the boxes" are sometimes regarded as inflexible and unsophisticated, but having a checklist to make sure important steps are not overlooked has literally been a lifesaver for pilots, surgeons, and other professionals where consistency is at least as important as intuition or memory.

The parts of this book are mostly organized along four dimensions of the second type of box: asset class, investment style or strategy, instrument or packaging, and geography with illustrations of "ticking the boxes" and taking the outside view of different boxes used throughout. A thorough understanding of each of these different boxes, and how to best apply them, can prevent an investor from getting too concentrated in one comfort zone and instead better find, understand, and more confidently invest in opportunities across diverse markets.

Hong Kong, Hong Kong   Tariq Dennison

ACKNOWLEDGMENTS

This book was a lot of work, and I have many people to thank for helping me complete it.

First of all, I can only thank God and my parents, John and Sue, for having been born, raised, and educated in the late twentieth century in a prosperous and peaceful time and place. It is easy to take for granted the upbringing and privileges that have let me see, do, and learn the things I have been able to do. The many travels my parents took me on as a child implanted in me the desire to see the world, to spend most of my life living outside my home country, and to never stop being curious and fascinated by different people and places.

Second, I thank my wife, Aquin, and children for their amazing support given the time and attention I have had to commit in completing this as my first book. My elder son, Isaac, especially has motivated me with his questions and his desire to go to more countries I've been to, while my younger son, Augusto, challenges me by already speaking better Chinese than I do. My family reminds me I'm still young, still have a lot of work to do, and have a home team that will be proud of the work I do in my time away from them.

I also wish to thank Frank Lavin for his encouragement to write my first book and for the introduction to the team at Palgrave Macmillan, who have been a pleasure to work with.

Many thanks to Professors Emanuel Derman and Terry Odean, to my former Bear Stearns colleague Edward Ho, and my former Bear Stearns and CIBC boss Bill Bamber for initially reviewing the outline and helping this book get started. I especially must thank Bill for his support during the rise of my Wall Street career, where I learned on the job how many of these markets really work.

Also, I owe a debt of gratitude to former HKSFA director Tony Watson, CFA Singapore director Francis Er, and ESSEC professor Peng Xu for providing me the opportunity to share and teach what I've learned in the markets to Asia's current and future money managers.

CONTENTS

LIST OF FIGURES

LIST OF TABLES

Part I

Asset Classes: The "What" Box

The most obvious box classifying an investment is what type of asset the money is being invested in, whether a bank deposit, bond, rental property, stock, foreign currency, or alternative asset like gold, art, or hedge funds. These "asset class" may be the first dimension on where to put money, and generally one of the most natural for investors to think of diversifying between, though in many ways still define how each investment is sold and by whom.

CHAPTER 1

Cash, Bank Deposits, and Interest Rates

Before even beginning to look at buying a stock, bond, or building, an investor is likely to start by depositing money in a bank account. Bank deposits are not so much an investment themselves but rather a convenient place to store money and a platform for using the bank's services to transfer some of that money to other accounts. Usually, a depositor would have to pay a company for storage and other services to take care of personal belongings and valuables, but banks are allowed to invest the money deposited with them into bonds and loans (described in the next chapter), passing on part of the interest from those investments to the customer and keeping the rest as their service fee (rather having to charge direct fees for all of their services). As of 2018, banks and bank deposits are still the main way money moves around from business to business worldwide, and in fast-growing, recently poor countries like China, many first-generation bank customers are switching from banknotes and paper checks to paperless payment systems that move money electronically between bank accounts (like Alipay and WeChat Pay). Over the next decade, there is likely to be a rise in "e-cash" transactions using cryptocurrencies and blockchain technology (described in Chap. 9) and replacing the need for banks to serve as fee-taking and risk-taking intermediaries for the basic functions of storing and transferring money.

© The Author(s) 2018   3
T. Dennison, *Invest Outside the Box*,
https://Doi.org/10.1007/978-981-13-0372-2_1

1.1   What Are the Different Types of Bank Deposits?

The simplest bank deposits are ones that allow money to be withdrawn at any time "on demand", and so are called "demand deposits". These accounts are generally called "checking" or "savings" accounts and are often treated as "cash equivalents", since the customer should be able to withdraw or send out cash from these accounts within a day or two without penalty. These accounts generally pay the lowest rates of interest (if they pay interest at all), since they give the bank the least amount of flexibility to invest that money in longer-term, higher interest bonds or loans, and this lower interest should be viewed as the cost of having that cash available on demand for your immediate use.

Banks also offer "time deposits" or "term deposits", where the depositor agrees to leave a sum of money on deposit for a fixed period of time (say one month, three months, or one year or longer) in exchange for a higher rate of interest, often with a pre-set penalty if the deposit is "broken" or withdrawn before this time period is over. Time deposits can be thought of as an entry-level form of bond investment, and can sometimes pay even higher yields than bonds, as banks often have access to investments most individual depositors so far do not.

1.2   Why Keep Money in Bank Deposits?

In exchange for the lower rate of interest on bank deposits, some of the services and conveniences one should expect from a bank include:

- access to deposit or withdraw cash at branches or automated teller machines (ATMs),
- transferring money to others via check or wire transfer,
- debit cards (for spending directly from the account, using credit card networks),
- currency conversion, and
- bank statements (sometimes used as proof of address or income)

As mentioned earlier, these basic features and services of bank accounts may increasingly be replaced by blockchain technologies (described in more detail in Chap. 9) over the coming decade or two, but as of 2018, the most basic form of savings and wealth is still "money in the bank".

1.3   How Most Money Today Is a Form of Bank Deposit

Accounting 101 teaches that modern money, in the form of bills of cash in a wallet, or cash on deposit at a bank, is a form of debt by a bank to a bearer. Dollar bills, also known as banknotes, are basically a promise by a bank to pay the bearer the face value on demand, as illustrated in Figs. 1.1 and 1.2. This is a historical relic of earlier paper money, which could be redeemed on demand for the face value of gold or silver (precious metals will be introduced in Chap. 6).

When a dollar bill is deposited at a bank, the deposit becomes a debt where the bank is obligated to pay back that dollar on demand, plus interest if the account is interest bearing. The interest rates banks pay can often be adjusted daily relative to prevailing overnight interest rates driven by central banks, or what rates the bank can earn in the market and feels the need to pass on to prevent you from transferring your deposit to another bank. The next section, as well as the following chapter on bonds, describes in more detail how interest rates are driven up and down through economic and market factors.

Banks make their money by borrowing money via deposits at relatively low interest rates and then lending it out to individuals, businesses, and

Fig. 1.1   Series of 1914 US$100 bill, example of an early "Federal Reserve Note" Authorized by the Federal Reserve Act of December 23, 1913, still contains the language "will pay to the bearer on demand" not printed on the 2013 series of US dollar bills. (Photo source: uscurrency.gov; https://www.uscurrency.gov/security/100-security-features-1914-%E2%80%93-1990)

Fig. 1.2   GB £100 banknote issued by the retail bank Royal Bank of Scotland plc Legal tender British pound notes by two other retail banks in Scotland, and by four other retail banks in Northern Ireland, as opposed to by the Bank of England (the central bank) in England, or directly by HM treasury in the crown colonies of Guernsey, Jersey, and Isle of Man. (Photo source: RBS https://www.rbs.com/heritage/subjects/our-banknotes/current-issue-notes.html)

other borrowers at relatively high interest rates. The business model of a bank has been summarized by numbers like "3-6-3" for a bank that pays 3% interest on its deposits, charging 6% on loans, with the bankers having the goal to finish their office work and get out to the golf course by 3 pm. In the second decade of the twenty-first century, when interest rates have been lower and bankers have felt more pressure to work later to keep their jobs, "3-6-3" might be said to have been replaced by "0-3-6", but the simplicity of banks' business models remains the same.

Unlike the deposit side, the loan that banks invest in are usually not payable on demand back to the bank, so the bank needs to keep a certain percentage of your deposit in reserve with the hope that no more than that percentage of their deposits will be withdrawn before the loans are paid back. One of the major roles of central banks like the Federal Reserve and Bank of England is to loan banks the difference if withdrawals ever do exceed the amount held in reserve, but these loans usually charge significantly higher rates of interest than the bank would have to pay on deposits. So one main job of a bank is to keep the balance between deposits, withdrawals, loans, and reserves as tight as possible to maximize profits (called "net interest margin", before subtracting what they pay for their staff, branches, taxes, and other expenses). As a simple illustration, below is a sample balance sheet and income statement for a simple bank funded with $100 of equity capital and $900 in customer deposits, which it uses to make $900 in long-term loans (on which it can earn a higher rate of interest) and $100 in short-term loans (which pay the bank less interest and are paid back quickly enough to provide liquidity for the percentage of depositors wishing to withdraw their funds at the end of the period) (Fig. 1.3):

The $100 in capital serves as a buffer against the first $100 in losses of principal the bank may suffer on its loan investments before the depositors are at risk of the bank rupturing (the origin of the term "bankrupt") and not being able to redeem 100% of the money deposited on demand. Depositors generally have the expectation of being able to withdraw 100% of their money from the bank without having to worry about the capital ratios or loan losses on their bank's balance sheet, so this assurance is provided in

Balance sheet at the start of the bank's first year

Assets		Liabilities & Equity	
Short Term Loans	$100	Deposits from Customers	$900
Long-term Loans	$900	Equity Capital	$100
Total Assets:	$1,000	Total Liabilities & Equity:	$1,000

Income Statement for the bank's first year

Interest income on $900 of LT loans @5%	$45	(+)
Interest income on $100 of ST loans @4%	$4	(+)
Interest expense on $900 of deposits @1%	$9	(-)
Provision for loan losses @1%	$10	(-)
Salaries and other expenses	$20	(-)
Tax on $10 pre-tax profit @30%	$3	(-)
Net Income	**$7**	

Return on Equity = $7 Net Income / $100 Equity Capital = 7%

Fig. 1.3 Balance sheet and income statement for a simple sample bank's first year equity, deposits, assets and income

many banking jurisdictions by bank regulations (often domestic central banks, who have harmonized capital requirement standards in a series of voluntary frameworks so far known as Basel I, Basel II, and Basel III) and reinforced by deposit insurance schemes (e.g. FDIC and NCUA in the United States, CDIC in Canada, FSCS in the United Kingdom, and SDIC in Singapore). These regulators and deposit insurers set the minimum capital ratio requirements (and so the maximum amount of deposits as a multiple of this capital) for banks which limit the amount of risk banks can take in search of profits while keeping deposits safe enough.

The primary objective of commercial banks is to maximize its profitability, which can be measured by this return on equity (ROE) rate to its shareholders (described in more detail in Chap. 4 on equity investing), but must be accomplished by maximizing value to its customers on both ends: depositors willing to accept lower rates in exchange for service, versus creditworthy borrowers able to pay substantially higher rates on loans. Most central banks, unlike commercial banks, have policy objectives centered around macroeconomic goals like maximizing economic growth, maximizing employment, or maintaining stable prices, all unrelated to any objective of maximizing ROE, but both commercial banks and central banks remain focused on one of the most important financial variables described in this book that underlie a large percentage of investment choices across all asset classes: the rate banks pay on deposits.

1.4   What Determines the Rate of Interest Banks Pay on Deposits

Like any other market governed by supply and demand, prices drive and are driven by how willing customers are to deposit more money at a bank versus how motivated banks are to pay higher rates interest to draw more deposits. Banks would maximize their ROE by paying as low an interest rate on deposits as they can to lure enough of a multiple of their equity capital needed to make all the loans they can make at as high a rate as they can find enough qualified lenders to borrow at.

Banks cannot simply set interest rates at whatever level they wish but rather are like oil and sugar companies in having the prices of their primary commodity (which for banks is the cost of borrowing or lending money, priced as an interest rate) determined by larger economic forces. The next chapter describes the multi-trillion dollar bond market, and how bond trading sets and benchmarks the interest.

CHAPTER 2

Bonds, Fixed Income, and Money Markets

Bonds are easily the simplest investment instrument most people claim to not understand. A typical bond is simply a written promise to pay the owner of the bond (the bondholder) fixed amounts of money on fixed future dates, which is why this asset class is also called "fixed income securities". Where bonds begin to differ from bank deposits is that a customer depositing $100 at a bank generally expects to be able to withdraw $100 (plus any interest) no matter what happens in the market, while a bond with $100 face value might be trading in the market at $99, $101, or even at $50 or $150 depending on how far in the future the fixed payments are scheduled and who the issuer promising to pay them is. In other words, although the income is fixed, the value is not.

Understanding fixed income investments is fundamental to really understanding any other class of investment. A bond that pays $10 on each of four fixed dates over the next two years plus $1,000 on a fixed date at the end of those two years is relatively easy to value, since the only variables are the value today of a dollar on each of those four future dates. By contrast, a stock that has been paying a $5 dividend over each of the past several quarters may raise or lower its dividend over the next two years, and there is no promise or guarantee that the stock can be redeemed at any fixed price two years from now or at any future date.

At this point, it would be valuable to define how investment returns from bonds (or most other assets for that matter) can be broken down

© The Author(s) 2018
T. Dennison, *Invest Outside the Box*,
https://doi.org/10.1007/978-981-13-0372-2_2

9

into "income return" plus "price return", which together make up the "total return". Total return minus the cost of financing the investment (or the amount that would have been earned just keeping the money in a bank account over the same period of time) equals the "excess return". As an example, suppose an investor buys a bond for $1,000, holds it for one year to collect $30 in interest cash flows, and then sells it at the end of that year for $1,020. If the investor would have earned 1% keeping the money in a bank deposit over the same year (or, more accurately, would have received or paid 1% as a "repo rate" over the year through a repo trade described later in this chapter), then the investor's returns would be calculated as:

- Income return = +$30, or +3.0% on the $1,000 invested
- Price return = +$20, or +2.0%
- Total return = $30 + $20 = +$50, or +5.0%
- Excess return = $50 − $10 = +$40 or +4.0%

It is likely that many if not most readers of this book will have experience investing in real estate, stocks, or mutual funds, but might have never directly bought a bond for themselves. A large part of this is simply accessibility: bank deposits are available to almost anyone with a bank account, stocks are listed on exchanges that almost any broker can access, but bonds are mostly traded "over the counter" in relatively large denominations and get relatively little direct attention from individual investors. Bonds need not be any more complicated than term deposits or CDs at a bank, but there are some terms and conventions in how bonds are quoted and traded, how interest is accrued and paid, and the difference that the issuer and other features of the bond can make. This chapter will try and explain the most important things to know about how and why to invest in bonds.

2.1   The Basics of How Bonds Work, by Example

Take, for example, the following widely held bond, notated between bond traders with three simple terms:

T	3.000%	5/15/2047
(1)	(2)	(3)

The three parts of this bond identifier are:

1. First, the issuer of the bond, that is, who is actually promising to pay you the money the bond is promising. In this case, "T" is widely understood to represent the US Treasury, the department that borrows money to directly fund the US federal government. More on this and other issuers later in the chapter.
2. Second is the "coupon rate" of the bond, which in this case is 3.000%. This means the bond will pay 3% of its face value to the bondholder every year as a current cash flow. This coupon is a payment of interest only, and does not reduce the face value of the bond to be paid back later.
3. Finally, this bond matures on May 15, 2047 (US bonds typically writing dates as "month/day/year"). This "maturity date" is when the final coupon and the whole face value of the bond will be paid back.

What is not explicit in this bond notation, but is widely understood by traders and investors of US Treasury bonds, includes:

A. Coupon frequency: coupons for US Treasury bonds and notes are paid semi-annually. Other types of bonds may pay coupons annually, quarterly, or monthly.
B. Day count convention: A day count convention clarifies whether more interest needs to be paid in leap years vs conventional years, or in February vs March. US Treasuries trade on an "Actual/Actual" convention, to be described in more detail in Sect. 2.3.
C. Currency: US Treasuries are all in US dollars (perhaps obviously), but many issuers issue different bonds in different currencies.
D. Denomination: US Treasury bonds can be traded in units as small as $1,000, or as large as $1,000,000 per bond.
E. Tax treatment: Interest on US Treasuries is federally taxable income to US taxpayers, but exempt from US state and local taxes. (Source: IRS https://www.irs.gov/taxtopics/tc403.html.) Foreign investors need to be aware of any applicable tax withholding and/or double-tax treaties with their county.

So to finish the short explanation of how a simple bond works: if I buy $100,000 of this bond in July 2017, I will receive my first coupon payment of $1,500 on November 15, 2017, my next coupon payment of

$1,500 on May 15, 2018, and so on every six months until I receive my final payment of $101,500 (face value plus my last coupon) on May 15, 2047.

Bonds are economically the same as loans, and the real difference between bonds and loans is how they are documented and traded. Bonds are meant to be a highly standardized way of borrowing money from investors in a market who often want the liquidity and flexibility of getting their money back before maturity by selling their bonds to other investors, while loans are usually a more direct arrangement between banks and borrowers which may be traded among banks but are not packaged for public trading. Large borrowers like the US Treasury, Apple Inc., and the State of California prefer to borrow from the bond market because large numbers of investors stand ready to compete to lend them large amounts at competitively low interest rates, where banks would not be as diversified source of funding. Most individuals and small businesses, on the other hand, have so far had to do most of their borrowing in the form of bank loans, and banks raise money to make these loans either from the deposits described in the previous chapter or by issuing bonds.

The first thing that may make fixed income securities seem difficult or requiring complex math is that their prices move around in the secondary market and can be well above or well below face value, and there are important mathematical relationships between interest rates and how much I pay or receive when I trade a bond. This will be described in more detail after we discuss some answers to a more basic question "why bother buying bonds at all?"

2.2   WHY BUY BONDS?

Some reasons investors choose to buy bonds include:

- The fixed cash flows from the bond satisfy an investment objective for income or future value accumulation.
- Bonds may pay higher interest rates than a fixed bank deposit of similar term.
- Unlike a term deposit, which may have an early break penalty, bonds may in some cases be sold before maturity for a profit, at prices exceeding face value. This is often a secondary motivation for buying a longer-term or higher-yielding bond, and, together with the previous reason, can be summarized as the search for excess return.

- High-grade bonds often move in the opposite direction of stocks and other risky assets, providing diversification and the occasional hedge, as will be illustrated in Chap. 7.

As an example of the first reason, an investor who has saved up $10,000,000 and can live off a fixed income of $300,000 per year can simply invest the whole ten million into the T 3.000% 5/15/2047 described earlier, as this bond will meet the income need by depositing $150,000 cash into the investor's account every six months, and then returning the $10,000,000 principal in May 2047 to be reinvested or inherited. This single bond investment could be called a "$10,000,000 pension", or perhaps "the world's simplest pension", being even simpler than the "Four House Pension" described in Chap. 3, but exposed to at least the five risks and disadvantages listed below. The "asset liability management" of this "pension" is a simplified version of what many pension funds and annuity providers actually do in managing their bond portfolios to pay out fixed pensions to their beneficiaries (after performing the task of accumulating the pension portfolio, described in Sect. 2.5).

What could go wrong with the above strategy, and why pension funds and annuity providers have a somewhat more difficult job than simply buying the latest long-term bond, includes:

A. The yield may not be enough: you may need $300,000/year but not have $10,000,000, or have $10,000,000 but need more than $300,000/year.
B. Inflation may eat away the value of both your fixed income and your principal by the time you get it back. $300,000 may be harder to live on 2017 than in 1987, and $10,000,000 may seem like a much more meager sum in 2047.
C. If you need liquidity and need to sell the bonds before maturity, the price may have fallen below $10,000,000.
D. When it comes time to reinvest the $10,000,000, or even part of the $300,000/year above your current spending needs, interest rates may be lower and you may earn an even lower rate of return than 3%.
E. The borrower may "default" and not pay back principal and interest in full, on time, as promised.

B and C are actually the opposite problem of D: higher inflation usually means higher interest rates, which lowers bond prices (illustrated in the bond trade in Sect. 2.3), but means that principal and coupons can be reinvested at higher interest rates. The balance between C (interest rate risk) and D (reinvestment risk) is illustrated in Sect. 2.5. E is not considered a serious or likely problem by investors in US Treasuries but is a primary concern for corporate and sovereign bonds described in Sect. 2.7. Problem A seems like the more fundamental problem, especially in a low interest rate environment, and can be solved by diversifying into higher-yielding assets including corporate bonds, real estate, and stocks.

Buying this long-dated bond is more attractive when the yield is higher than on shorter-dated bonds/deposits and in order to lock in that higher rate for the longer period of time.

Besides simply matching future cash flow needs, there are at least three more reasons to buy bonds as an investment:

A. Longer-dated bonds typically earn a term risk premium over shorter-dated bonds, as future rates implied by the yield curve often overestimate how quickly rates will rise. More on this is in Sect. 2.6.
B. Compared with keeping money in a bank, where only $250,000 or so of US-banked deposits are insured by a government-based agency in the event your bank fails, government bonds are direct promises by the government and can give you greater levels of assurance on much larger amounts invested.
C. In the twenty-first century so far, bond prices have often moved in the opposite direction of global stocks and risky assets, making US Treasuries one of the few assets that both pay you to hold them and spike up in value in crises like the crash of 2008. This correlation is described in Chap. 7.

Reasons A and B are why easier electronic access to bond markets in smaller denominations can and should replace term deposits at banks over time.

2.3   Bond Trading, Money Markets, and Repurchase Agreements (Repos)

The most immediate difference between a bond and a bank deposit is in how an investor trades them or puts money into them. Bond trading is highly standardized, but still not as easily accessible to average individuals as bank deposits. Similar to bank deposits or currencies, most bonds are not traded on centralized stock exchanges, but rather over the counter ("OTC") between banks. This means that unlike an exchange-traded stock or futures contract, bond trading requires a step of *price discovery*, where a customer must generally get quotes from three or more banks for the same bond in the search of the best price. Traditionally this price discovery was done by calling bank desks sequentially by telephone and asking for their bid and offer price on a particular bond, but electronic communications systems are increasingly making the distribution of prices and search for highest bid and lowest offer price more and more similar to how stocks trade on an exchange. Price discovery and transparency has greatly improved in the US corporate bond market (both investment grade and high yield) since the 2002 launch of the NASD (now FINRA) Trade Reporting and Compliance Engine (TRACE), which widely disseminates the prices of OTC bond trades as an exchange would. Expansion of TRACE-like systems to other bond markets around the world is likely to improve the depth and liquidity of debt markets in other countries and currencies.

The examples here of US Treasuries are mostly similar to how most major bond markets around the world trade (with a few exceptions that will be noted) and fall into one of three categories: short-term bills, long-term bonds or notes, and repurchase agreements (repos).

Short-term treasury bills ("T-bills") are similar to term bank deposits, except that they are issued in much larger blocks, are actively traded on a secondary market (where the investor cashes out by selling the T-bill to another investor rather than "redeeming" it like a bank deposit), and are issued at a discount to face value. The last point is a subtle difference between treasury bills and bank deposits: while you would simply deposit $10,000,000 at a bank and get this amount back plus interest in three months, $10,000,000 of 13-week T-bills may be trading at a "discounted price" of "99.737111" (percentage of face value), so you would invest the same amount of money by buying $10,026,000 face value of these T-Bills for $9,999,642.65 and keeping the remainder in a bank deposit or money market account (Fig. 2.1).

Longer-term notes and bonds differ from bills in that they often (but not always) make cash interest payments in the form of coupons periodically (often semi-annually or annually, sometimes monthly or quarterly). In the case of US Treasuries, "Notes" are issued with a maturity of longer than one year and up to ten years, while "Bonds" refer to

Fig. 2.1 Auction history of the US Treasury bill maturing on October 12, 2017 Prices shown are for three different auctions on the same bill at maturities of 13 weeks, 26 weeks, and 52 weeks. (Source: TreasuryDirect.gov)

government obligations longer than ten years, although they otherwise trade almost identically (Fig. 2.2).

If Tracy the trader wanted to buy $1,000,000 face value of the bond "T 3.000% 5/15/2047" on August 1, 2017, she might have seen a market price of "102-31/103-00", meaning the market would offer to sell her the bonds at a "clean price" of 103 0/32% of face value or buy them from her at 102 31/32% of face value. (It is important to note that in the US Treasury market, US Treasury notes and bonds are still quoted and traded in 1/32nds of a point, rather than in decimal cents like most other bonds, where the 16 following dash in "101-16" means "16/32nds", and should not be confused with a decimal place like the one in the equivalent decimal price "101.50".) "Clean price" means that the quoted price does not include accrued interest, so Tracy will also need to calculate and add the 3% per year interest accrued on the $1,000,000 from the issue/last coupon date (in this case, the issue date on May 15, 2017) until the settlement date when the bond and purchase funds actually change hands (for US Treasuries, this is "T+1" or one business day following the trade date, in this case, August 2, 2017). The clean price and accrued interest add up as follows:

$1,000,000 face value × 103-00 offer price =	$1,030,000
+3.00% * $1,000,000 face value * 79/365 days =	$6,493
Total "dirty price" =	$1,036,493

Accrued interest for US Treasuries is calculated according to an "Actual/Actual" or "Act/Act" *day count convention*, meaning the percentage of

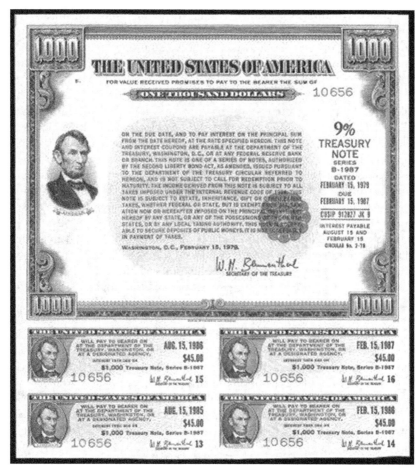

Fig. 2.2 US $1,000 9% treasury note due February 1987
Historically, bond certificates had paper coupons that could be clipped and redeemed
for cash, often at a bank. The coupons on this certificate could be redeemed for $45
each on the 15th of February and August, 1986 and 1987. (Image source: https://
www.quora.com/How-is-the-coupon-rate-of-a-bond-calculated)

the annual interest rate accrued is calculated by dividing the number of
days accrued divided by the actual number of days in the year. Other commonly
used day count conventions include "30/360" (where each month
is rounded off to having 30 days and is divided by a 360-day year, which

simplifies calculations for many fixed rate corporate bonds, but means the same amount of interest accrued in February as in January or July) and "Actual/360" or "Act/360", which is more commonly applied to floating interest rates based on indices like the London Interbank Offered Rate (LIBOR).

At this price, the bond has a "yield to maturity" of 2.85% (which can be calculated by putting these numbers and dates into the Microsoft Excel "YIELD()" function), meaning that the combination of 3.00% per year coupon interest offset by the loss of the 3% premium over the 30 years (as the $1,030,000 price paid converges to the $1,000,000 face value that will be repaid at maturity, also known as "pull to par") adds up to an average rate of return of 2.85% per year assuming: (1) The bond is held to maturity. (2) The bond does not default. (3) If reinvestment is considered in the rate of return, all coupons are somehow reinvested at the same 2.85% yield.

One of the first relationships students of fixed income often learn is this inverse relationship between yields and prices: rising yields mean falling bond prices and vice versa. This makes sense considering the total rate of return from paying more than $100 receive $3 per year in interest plus $100 at maturity must be less than 3%, while paying less than $100 for the same $3 per year plus $100 at maturity would have a rate of return greater than 3%. The amount that a bond would actually change in value for a given change in yield depends mostly on the tenor (or time to maturity) and coupon rate of the bond, combined into a metric called "duration" described in Sect. 2.5.

If, instead of holding the bond to maturity, Tracy has only a four-month trading time horizon and plans to sell the bonds on December 1, 2017, the risk/reward can be projected in two possible profit/loss scenarios: (A) interest rates rise, with the yield on this bond rising to 3.00% (a yield increase of 15/100ths of a percentage point or "15 basis points", "15bps" for short) and its clean price falling to 100-00, or (B) interest rates fall, with the market yield on this bond falling to 2.75% and its clean price rising to 105-00. Either way, Tracy will receive a $15,000 coupon on November 15, 2017, and accrue another $1,562 in interest from November 15 to the settlement date on December 4 (the Monday following the December 1 trade date) for a total "interest return" of $10,069 (=$1,562 accrued interest received + $15,000 coupon received − $6,493 accrued interest paid). Scenario A would mean a "price return" loss of $30,000, while scenario B would mean a "price return" gain of $20,000, adding up to "total returns" of −$19,931 and +$30,069, respectively.

2.4   REPURCHASE AGREEMENTS (REPOS): LEVERAGE, FINANCING, AND A SECURED MONEY MARKET

Sale and repurchase agreements, also called "repos" for short, are the money market based on the trading of liquid bonds (generally government bonds), and on which the financing of those bond trades are based. In the above example of a bond trade, it is assumed the Tracy would fund the whole $1,036,493 due on the settlement date with cash sitting in her account, but there are many cases where an investor or trading desk would either want to minimize the amount of cash and capital tied up in a bond position, which is commonly done in institutional bond markets through repo financing.

Suppose Tracy buys same bond on August 1 as above, but finances $900,000 of the bond price (almost 90%) using an "overnight" repo trade with Reba, a repo trader at a bank's repo desk. The steps are:

A. On August 1, Tracy buys the $1,000,000 of T 3.00% 5/15/2047 at 103-00.

B. On the same day, Tracy "repo sells" the same bonds to Reba for $900,000, with the bundled agreement to buy back the same bonds for $900,027 the next day.

C. On August 2, Tracy receives $900,000 from Reba and uses $136,493 from her account to settle the purchase of the bonds, which Reba then holds as collateral.

D. On August 3 (the maturity date of the "overnight" repo), Tracy pays Reba the $900,027 and receives back the bond as agreed.

E. Tracy may have raised this $900,027 by either:

a. Selling the bond at a profit or loss, or
b. Refinancing the trade by rolling into a new repo, or
c. With funds from other sources

The $27 difference between the price at which Reba "repo buys" the bond and sells it back to Tracy the next day is effectively Reba's interest charge for lending Tracy the $900,000 for one day (or "overnight", as one-day repos are often called) and holding the bonds as collateral. This is equivalent to an interest rate of 1.095% per annum, and repos are often quoted in terms of the interest rate a repo buyer would effectively lend at against a specific bond or against a "general collateral" pool of acceptable bonds. The other term that needs to be understood before trading the repo is the "haircut", or percentage below the market value of the bonds that the repo buyer will pay. From Reba's point of view, regardless of likely Tracy is to go bankrupt or run away with the $900,000 in the next 24 hours, Reba has $1,036,493 worth of bonds as collateral, which would have to fall over 10% in value overnight (an extreme move even for 30-year bonds) before Reba would be at risk of not recovering 100% of her money from the collateral. This is why repos with proper haircuts generally trade at or below "risk-free" benchmark rates of interest like the federal funds rate, LIBOR, or treasury bill yields. Fed Funds, LIBOR, and other money markets are described in Chap. 5.

Counterparties that frequently trade repos with each other generally have Global Master Repurchase Agreement (GMRA) documentation detailing how exactly all the terms of the repo quoted on a phone call or Bloomberg screen (such as the repo rate and haircut) will translate into exact amounts of money (including coupons paid during the repo) to be transferred back and forth, and terms of the "margin call" (where Reba can require Tracy to send extra cash or bonds, or terminate the repo early, in cases where the value of the bonds moves too close to the hair-cut and Reba needs to protect the value of her loan versus the collateral).

Tracy's gross profit and loss (P&L) is calculated the same way as in the bond trade example in the previous section, but adding the repo means factoring in the repo interest cost and effect of leverage to calculate the total rate of return on the trade. In this case, assume Tracy holds the bonds for only one day and cashes out the position the same day the repo matures on August 3, with the following two scenarios of the price return being positive or negative (Fig. 2.3):

Note that, regardless of whether the bond market goes up or down:

A. Tracy accrues $83 in interest from owning the bond,
B. Reba accrues $27 in interest from Tracy on the repo, and
C. Tracy's is exposed to the price volatility of $1,000,000 face value of bonds with only $136,493 of cash invested, a leverage multiple of about 7.5×

The difference between A and B shows that Tracy would accrue $56 per day in net interest from accruing 3.000% on the long bond position while paying 1.095% for the repo financing, making this a "positive carry trade". So long as the repo rate remains below the coupon rate (or

Scenario 1: Yield falls and price rises on the bond, price return is positive

	August 2nd	August 3rd
Clean Price of Bond	103-00	103-16
Accrued Interest	$6,493	$6,575
Cash Flow (bond trade)	($1,036,493)	$1,041,575
Cash Flow (repo)	$900,000	($900,027)
Net flow (whole trade)	($136,493)	$141,575

Net P&L on trade: **$5,082 profit**

$5,082 profit / $136,493 cash investment = +3.70% return over one day

Scenario 2: Yield rises and price falls on the bond, price return is negative

	August 2nd	August 3rd
Clean Price of Bond	103-00	102-16
Accrued Interest	$6,493	$6,575
Cash Flow (bond trade)	($1,036,493)	$1,031,575
Cash Flow (repo)	$900,000	($900,027)
Net flow (whole trade)	($136,493)	$131,575

Net P&L on trade: **$4,918 loss**

$4,918 profit on $136,493 cash investment = -3.62% return over one day

Fig. 2.3   Sample profit and loss calculations on a $1,000,000 bond trade

yield to maturity, if the bond is held long enough for the pull to par effect to be significant), this positive carry can represent a substantial share of the profits from a financed bond position, which can be described as "borrowing short, lending long". This positive carry also provides some support against rising interest rates, as the price of this bond would have to fall by more than $56 per day in order for the return on this trade to be negative.

Why would Reba want to lend cash in a repo like this? There are two primary motivations for a repo seller (also known as a "reverse repo", if Reba is the client of a bank's repo desk):

A. Reba may be running a money market fund, and needs to invest the money on an overnight basis in something more secure than a bank deposit. The treasury bond collateral provides this additional security.
B. Reba may need to sell the bond short to profit from rising interest rates, and the cash serves as collateral for Reba to borrow the bond.

In case B, where Reba is using the repo to borrow the bond to sell short, the haircut will often (but not always) be in the direction where Reba posts more cash than the face value of the bond to protect the repo counterparty from not having the bonds returned if they become more valuable than the cash collateral. The direction and amount of haircut in a repo depend on who the two counterparties are and what they negotiate in their GMRA or on a specific trade. High demand to sell a specific bond short can also drive down repo rates to negative, effectively requiring the short seller to pay to borrow the bond.

Here is an illustration of how the repo and short sale would work from Reba's perspective as a short seller of the bond, posting $1,100,000 as cash collateral (Fig. 2.4):

Note that, regardless of whether the bond market goes up or down:

A. Reba earns $33 in interest on her cash collateral posted on the repo,
B. Reba effectively pays the $83 accrued interest on the bond to the repo counterparty. This is a straight pass-through if Reba held the bond during the course of the repo, but since Reba sold the bond one day and bought it back the next, she is out of pocket this one day's accrued interest, and
C. Having sold the bonds "short", Reba is exposed to the price volatility of $1,000,000 face value of bonds with only $63,507 of cash invested, a leverage multiple of about −15× (minus because unlike a "long" bond position, Reba makes money when rates go up/the bond price goes down and vice versa).

So in summary, while repo selling a bond is primarily used as a financing tool, to borrow money at low rates to own a long position in a bond that is posted as collateral, the trader repo buying the bond (or doing a "reverse repo") may be motivated to either (a) earn a low interest rate on a short-term

Scenario 1: Yield falls and price rises on the bond, Reba loses money

	August 2nd	August 3rd
Clean Price of Bond	103-00	103-16
Accrued Interest	$6,493	$6,575
Cash Flow (bond trade)	$1,036,493	($1,041,575)
Cash Flow (repo)	($1,100,000)	$1,100,033
Net flow (whole trade)	($63,507)	$58,458

Net P&L on trade: **$5,049 loss**

$5,049 profit / $63,507 cash investment = -7.95% return over one day

Scenario 2: Yield rises and price falls on the bond, Reba makes money

	August 2nd	August 3rd
Clean Price of Bond	103-00	102-16
Accrued Interest	$6,493	$6,575
Cash Flow (bond trade)	$1,036,493	$1,031,575
Cash Flow (repo)	($1,100,000)	($1,100,033)
Net flow (whole trade)	($63,507)	$68,458

Net P&L on trade: **$4,951 profit**

$4,951 profit on $63,507 cash investment = +7.80% return over one day

Fig. 2.4 Sample profit and loss calculation of a "short sale" trade on a bond borrowed on repo

cash investment, secured by bonds as collateral, or (b) sell a bond short, borrowing the bond by posting cash as collateral.

2.5   THE SIMPLEST ASSET LIABILITY MATCHING PROBLEM: DURATION MATCHING

Assume that on February 22, 2006, Penny the pension fund manager has been given one specific job: turn $10,000,000 into no less than $20,000,000 in 16 years (so by February 22, 2022) by buying only plain, vanilla, coupon-paying US Treasuries. Penny needs to achieve this $20,000,000 account balance whether interest rates move up, down, or not at all. She will not receive any bonus for ending up with any more money, but will have no excuse for ending up with any less. Which bond(s) should Penny buy?

February 22, 2006, was chosen for this example, because on that date the US Treasury yield curve was almost perfectly flat with any treasury bill, note, or bond of any tenor from three months to 30 years offered at a yield around 4.50%. $10,000,000 invested at a compound annual growth rate of 4.5% per year over 16 years would grow to just over $20 million, which would just be more than enough to reach Penny's goal. Penny takes a look at the market, and all available bonds with a coupon of 4.5% trade at prices near par, as expected from the yield curve.

Penny's first thought is to buy a 16-year bond with a 4.5% coupon to match the maturity of the asset with the maturity of the liability, but she immediately notices that this would expose the portfolio to the risk that if interest rates fall, the coupons would have to be reinvested at lower rates. In that case, the assumption of compounding at 4.5% for 16 years won't hold, and Penny would end up with less money than required at the end of 16 years. On the other hand, falling rates would also mean that Penny's bond would go up in price (as explained earlier, bond prices fall as bond yields rise and vice versa) and that might lead to some capital gains. Conversely, rising rates would mean coupon cash flows could be reinvested at higher rates of interest, but the market value of the bonds would have fallen in value. Thinking of it this way, Penny balances the trade-off between reinvestment risk from the interim coupons and interest rate risk affecting the market value of the bond position, and runs scenarios to see which bond maturity would best meet the objective.

Penny runs scenarios using an unrealistically simple but useful assumption: she assumes that right after she buys the bond, the whole yield curve will instantly shift up or down from the 4.5% initial rate to a new level, and then stay at that level for the remaining 16 years. Figure 2.5 shows that buying 10- or even 20-year bonds can produce a massive surplus if rates rise (and coupons can be reinvested at higher rates), but with the risk of a multi-million dollar deficits if rates fall (and returns from reinvesting those coupons end up being significantly lower than expected). Conversely, if Penny could buy a 40-year bond (theoretical, as the US Treasury has not issued bonds longer than 30 years as of this writing), she could end up with a multi-million dollar surplus if rates fall (and she ends the 16-year

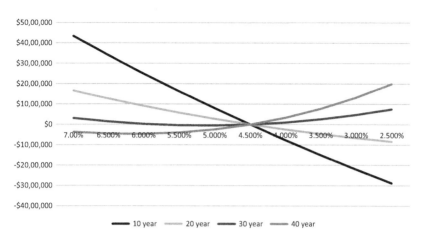

Fig. 2.5   Surplus/deficit (y-axis) of holding and reinvesting a 10-, 20-, 30-, or 40-year 4.5% bond for 16 years over different interest rate scenarios (x-axis)

period with a 24-year 4.5% fixed rate bond in a sub-3% rate environment), but would risk having the bond being worth less than she needs if rates rise. Right in the middle, she finds that a 30-year bond happens to balance the effect of rising and falling rates on coupon reinvestment versus the market value of the bond, and in this analysis would produce small surpluses if rates rise or fall significantly, with smaller surpluses if rates remain around 4.5%.

The key metric in this case is called the *duration* of the bond. As opposed to tenor or maturity date, which is the time until all the cash flows from the bond are eventually due to be paid, **duration measures the weighted average amount of time the bondholder waits to receive the "center of gravity" of the bond's cash flows**. Two duration formulas often introduced in many fixed income textbooks are: (a) Macaulay duration, the original and more pure "average time to get paid" metric, and (b) modified duration, which divides Macaulay duration by a factor that makes the measure useful for estimating the interest rate sensitivity of a bond. In Microsoft Excel, modified duration is calculated with the MDURATION() function.

In the days before fast and ubiquitous computers and bond calculators, duration calculations were valuable to keep handy as a way to quickly estimate how much the price of a given bond would change given a certain change in the bond's yield, and vice versa. Using the example of the T 3.000% 5/15/2047 bond used throughout this chapter, the duration is calculated using Excel's MDURATION() function as follows:

MDURATION("8/2/2017",   "5/15/2047",   3.00%,   2.85%,   2)
             Settle date   Maturity   Coupon   Yield   2=semi-annual

On that particular date and yield, this formula calculates that the bond has a duration of 19.66 years. This means that if the yield to maturity in the market were to rise by one basis point (from 2.85% to 2.86%), the price of the bond should fall by 0.01% per year × 19.66 years = 0.1966%. Conversely, the price of the bond should rise by 0.1966% if the yield were to fall from 2.85% to 2.84%. In rougher terms, the 19.66 could also be rounded to 20 to roughly estimate that this bond will rise or fall 1% in value for every 5bp (0.05% per year of yield) the yield falls or rises. This makes sense given that yield to maturity is a percentage return per year and that a change of 0.01% per year affects a bond with a duration of ten years five times more than it would affect the price of a bond with a duration of two years.

Back to Penny's asset liability matching problem, the durations of the different bonds considered both initially (the 16-year bond) and in the scenario analysis (10, 20, 30, and 40 years) would have been as follows (Fig. 2.6):

When looking at the list of bonds by duration rather than by term to maturity, it becomes clear that the 10-year, 16-year, and even 20-year bonds paid back more of their present value before the 16-year target date, and would leave Penny with an extra 8.0, 4.7, and 2.9 years of reinvestment risk, respectively. At the other extreme, the 40-year bond has a duration 2.5 years too long, and would mean Penny still has a relatively long-dated bond at the end of the 16 years when the portfolio needs to be cashed out. The duration of 30-year bond fortunately seems "just right", with its 16-year duration closely matching the duration of the 16-year liability.

Fig. 2.6 Duration values for 10- to 40-year 4.5% bonds	Tenor of 4.5% bond	Duration
	16 years	11.3 years
	10 years	8.0 years
	20 years	13.1 years
	30 years	**16.4 years**
	40 years	18.5 years

Asset liability management often starts by matching the duration of assets with the duration of liabilities. Many life insurers, pension funds, and annuity providers have exactly this challenge in having promised retirees a certain level of retirement income in the future calculated based on today's interest rates, and these providers need to deliver this promised income whether interest rates rise or fall before and during their clients' retirement. These long-term income providers therefore regularly seek and buy "long-duration assets" to match their long-duration liabilities.

Some useful guidelines applying to duration include:

a. Duration of a zero-coupon bond (i.e. a pure promise to deliver the whole cash flow at maturity) is roughly equal to the tenor of the bond.
b. The higher the coupon rate of a bond, the lower its duration (since on average, a larger share of the cash flow will be paid back sooner).
c. The higher the yield to maturity, the lower the duration (this lowers the present value of the principal at maturity relative to the coupons as a percentage of the value of the bond)

Point (a) above answers one of the metrics of Penny's job that has so far been overlooked: her liability was essentially a zero-coupon "bullet" to pay out $20,000,000 in 16 years, and so this liability also has a duration of 16 years. Real pension funds of course have liabilities that are not simple zero-coupon bullets but rather are obligations to pay out obligations of income, either now or later, perhaps at an escalating scale, and perhaps conditional on the longevity of beneficiaries, and those liabilities also have durations which are calculated in the same way as for bond assets.

Although fast computers make it less necessary to calculate durations to match assets and liabilities or to estimate interest rate sensitivities, understanding the concept of duration is important to understanding why a longer or shorter bond may be more appropriate for a given portfolio or situation before plugging it into the computer.

Related to duration is a different metric applied to bonds and bond portfolios called "PV01" (present value of 1 basis point, or 0.01% per year change in rates), also known as "DV01" (dollar value of 1 bp) in dollar-denominated bond markets. Using the same bond as an example, the $1,000,000 face value of T 3.000% 5/15/2047 trading at 103-00 (yield to maturity of 2.85%) settling on August 2, 2017, has a PV01 of about $2,040, calculated by repricing the bond at a yield-to-maturity shifted by 1 bp and taking the price difference. PV01 is measured in dollars (or other currency the bond may be denominated in), as opposed to duration, which is measured in years. To estimate how much the bond would move in value if the yields were to rise (or fall) by 5bp, simply multiply the PV01 by 5 to see how much the market value of the bond would fall (or rise). This makes PV01 a more immediately useful measure for risk management in summarizing the size of interest rate sensitivity in one metric, but has the disadvantage in making it hard to tell the difference between $5,000,000 of bonds with a duration of two years vs $1,000,000 of bonds with a duration of ten years, which would have roughly the same PV01 but would of course react differently on a day when two-year yields rise and ten-year yields fall (a "flattening", described in more detail in the next section on yield curves).

PV01 and duration estimates are only accurate for small shifts in yields. If the yield of the above bond were to rise to 3.85% (a rise of 100bp), the bond would not fall by $204,000 in value (100 × the $2,040 PV01), but by $179,860. Conversely, if the yield fell 100bp to 1.85%, the bond would rise in value by $232,471, over $28,000 more than estimated by the PV01. This feature where fixed rate, non-callable bonds gain more and lose less than is estimated by their PV01 is called "convexity", and used to be more important for estimating larger moves in bond prices for given shifts in yields, but can now be seen directly in computer calculations.

As an example of how two different strategies with roughly equal amounts of face value x duration, suppose Penny was operating in a market that did not have any bonds with a tenor longer than 15 years (Australia announced plans to issue a 30-year bond only in 2016, and as of 2017, Hong Kong bonds still have a maximum tenor of 15 years). The 15-year 4.5% bond has a duration of only 10.8 years, but if Penny could buy $15,000,000 of the 15-year bonds with her $10,000,000 plus $5,000,000 from repo financing, how similar would the result be? Figure 2.7 shows the scenario analysis for applying this 1.5× leveraged strategy to 5-, 10-, 15-, and 20-year bonds:

In contrast to the unlevered strategy, where a sharp rise in rates after buying the bond would mean coupons could be reinvested and compounded at higher rates from early on, the leverage would mean an initial lag as Penny has to pay higher the $5 million repo financing while only earning 4.5% on the $15 million of bonds, but then the excess cash would also be reinvested at these higher rates after the coupons pay off the borrowing (around year 9) and after the bond matures (after 15 years). This would result in a slight deficit in a rising rate scenario, as shown on the left end of the green line in Fig. 2.7. Falling rates, on the other hand, would

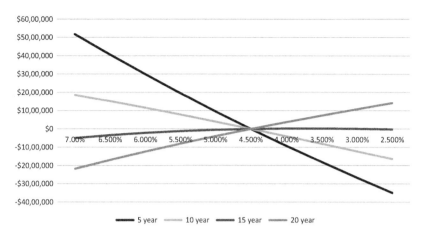

Fig. 2.7   Surplus/deficit (y-axis) of holding and reinvesting a 1.5× levered 5-, 10, 15-, or 20-year 4.5% bond for 16 years over different interest rate scenarios (x-axis)

mean a positive carry trade in the early years as Penny earns 4.5% on the bonds and pays a lower rate of interest on the repo, but then the excess cash would also be invested at lower rates later. Although the scenario of rates shifting significantly once after Penny's bond trade and remaining flat for 16 years is unrealistic, this levered strategy shows how "path dependent" real-world bond portfolio management can be, so the next section begins the examination of the shape and dynamics of yield curves.

2.6   Yield Curves, and the Future Interest Rates They Imply

Real-life situations are rarely satisfied simply by buying a single bond, and conversely there are usually multiple different bond investing strategies that can each satisfy a given investment goal. Also, as has been the case on most dates in the past decade other than February 22, 2006, bond yields (even by the same government issuer) can differ significantly between those maturing in 2 years and those maturing in 10 or 30 years, and yields often move by different or opposite amounts rather than in parallel. So rather than tracking the yields and movements of hundreds of different bonds individually, it is useful to have a consistent framework to describe how "interest rates" or "the" bond market are doing through a few key metrics. Stock investors (more in Chap. 4) are accustomed to seeing updates on how "the market" for stocks is doing by watching broadly followed indices like the Dow Jones Industrial Average, S&P 500, Nikkei, or Hang Seng indices (more on these indices in Sect. 2.1), and similarly US dollar bond investors often start by looking at the "10-year" treasury yield as a benchmark, and from there perhaps the "2-year", "30-year/long bond", or a given credit spread is moving by comparison.

If an investor's bond portfolio is promised a cash flow of $1,000 on November 15, 2018, from a US Treasury, it should not matter to the price whether that cash flow is coming from a maturing treasury bill, the principal of the 2-year note due that day, or one of the coupons of a 30-year bond paid out that day. If $1,000 from that treasury bill is worth $990 today in the market, then the 2-year note's principal and 30-year bond's coupon should each also be worth $990 in the market. So a first calculation many bond computers start with is to line up all bonds of a given issuer by the calendar of cash flows scheduled to be paid out on each date, and solving for the present value or market price of each of those cash flows in a technique known as *bootstrapping*. For example, consider the following three bonds quoted on May 12, 2017 (settling on May 15, 2017) (Fig. 2.8):

Bond A only has one more cash flow of $1,021.25 scheduled on November 15, 2017, with no other coupon payments before then, so it is straightforward to divide the $1,015.85 price today by the $1,021.25 to be received at maturity to calculate that the present value ("PV") of $1.000000 paid on November 15, 2017 is worth $0.994712 as of this bond quote.

Bond B has one coupon payment of $5.00 due on November 15, 2017, plus the final coupon plus principal payment totaling $1,005.00 due on May 15, 2018. Since the present value of the November 15, 2017, cash

#	Bond	Dirty Price of $1,000 face value
A	T 4.250% 11/15/2017	$1,015.85
B	T 1.000% 5/15/2018	$998.28
C	T 1.250% 11/15/2018	$1,000.00

Fig. 2.8 Three example bonds for bootstrapping

flow was already calculated from bond A, the 0.994712 × $5.00 = $4.97 PV of that coupon can be subtracted out to determine the PV of the May 15, 2018, cash flow must be $998.28 − 4.97 = $993.31. Dividing the present value by the future value of the cash flow paid out on May 15, 2018, gives a discount factor of $993.31/$1,005.00 = 0.988368.

Similarly, bond C has two coupon payments of $6.25 each due on November 15, 2017, and May 15, 2018, respectively, and the final coupon plus principal cash flow of $1,006.25 on November 15, 2018. The present value of the first coupon is 0.994712 × $6.25 = $6.22, and the present value of the second coupon is 0.988368 × $6.25 = $6.18, so subtracting these from the present value of the whole bond means the present value of the final $1,006.25 paid at maturity was $1,006.25 − ($6.18 + $6.22) = $993.85. Dividing the present by the future value of this last cash flow yields a discount factor of $993.85/$1,006.25 = 0.987677.

This bootstrapping calculation produces a function or table sometimes denoted PV(Date) or D(t) (the latter being short for "the discount factor D of a cash flow due to be paid at time t") which serves as an unambiguous curve of what the benchmark bond yields up to any given date. Unlike yield-to-maturity or other rates which can vary depending on day count convention, compounding frequency, or reinvestment assumptions, this discount factor is always a single number between two dates.

This bootstrapping calculation can be done instantly by organizing the cash flows from the above bonds into a matrix algebra problem, which may seem complicated to non-math lovers, but here is an attempt at one of the simplest illustrations of this matrix calculation (Fig. 2.9):

Mathematical matrix notation allows the organization of each cash flow on each of the three different dates into a 3 × 3 matrix, the 3 PVs into a 1 × 3 matrix, and the three dirty bond prices in a 1 × 3 matrix can be written as follows (Fig. 2.10):

The advantage of organizing this calculation in matrix notation is in the ability to calculate all the PV values simultaneously, and in a fraction of a

$1,021.25 x PV(11/15/2017)   = $1,015.85

$5.00 x PV(11/15/2017) + $1,005.00 x PV(5/15/2017)   = $998.28

$6.25 x PV(11/15/2017) + $6.25 x PV(5/15/2017) + $6.25 x PV(11/15/2018)   = $1,000.00

Fig. 2.9 Bootstrapping three bonds as three equations with three unknown PV values

$$\begin{bmatrix} \$1{,}021.25 & 0 & 0 \\ \$5.00 & \$1{,}005.00 & 0 \\ \$6.25 & \$6.25 & \$1{,}006.25 \end{bmatrix} \begin{bmatrix} PV(11/15/2017) \\ PV(5/15/2018) \\ PV(11/15/2018) \end{bmatrix} = \begin{bmatrix} \$1{,}015.85 \\ \$998.28 \\ \$1{,}000.00 \end{bmatrix}$$

Fig. 2.10   Bootstrapping the same three bonds, written as a matrix equation

#	Bond	Dirty Price of $10,000,000 face value
A	T 4.250% 11/15/2017	$10,158,500
B	T 1.000% 5/15/2018	$9,982,800
X	Strip due 5/15/2018	$9,863,000

Fig. 2.11   Example of three bonds whose prices present an arbitrage opportunity

second, using matrix functions like those available in Excel or Matlab. In Excel, the cash flows of 60 bonds (maturing semi-annually over the next 30 years) can be laid out in a 60 × 60 matrix (say, A1:BH60), and the bond prices arranged in a 1 × 60 column (say BJ1:BJ60), enabling the PVs to be calculated through the single formula:

$$MMULT\big(MINVERSE(A1:BH60), BJ1:BJ60\big)$$

This formula solves for the 1 × 60 matrix of PVs by multiplying both side of the above equation of the inverse of the cash flow matrix, by computing it as the product of the two known matrices.

The US Treasury market developed the ability to separate coupon and principal payments of a US Treasury into separate "zero-coupon" bonds that can be traded independently, through a program known as the "Separate Treasury Registration of Interest and Principal Securities" or "STRIPS", where the individual securities are simply called "strips". For example, bond B above can be broken up into three strips: (a) the coupon due on November 15, 2017, (b) the coupon due on May 15, 2018, and (c) the principal due on May 15, 2018.

Equivalence between the prices of strips, T-bills, and the coupon and principal cash flows paid out on the same dates are kept in line by traders seeking profits from *arbitrage* opportunities if these cash flows ever get out of line. Assume that alongside bond A and bond B, the following price for strip X appeared in the market (Fig. 2.11):

Although the bootstrapping shows in theory that the strip should be worth PV (May 15, 2018) × $10mio = 0.988368 × $10,000,000 = $9,883,680, it seems to be available in the market at a discount of greater than $20,000 versus this calculated price. An arbitrage trade to capture this $20,000 would be to:

A. Buy strip × for $9,863,000
B. Post strip × as collateral for a repo to borrow and sell short $9,950,000 face value of bond B, proceeds = $9,932,386
C. Buy $5,000 of bond A for about $5,080

No matter what happens to interest rates, this trade will net about $25,000 of cash up front, the maturing principal plus coupon from bond A will pay off the coupon owed on the short position from bond B, and on the final maturity date of May 15, 2018, the $10,000,000 in principal from the maturing strip will just about cover the maturity value of bond B which was sold short. In other words, this arbitrage trade would net about $25,000 of cash profit up front with no risk due to rising or falling bond yields, and most of the exposure to short-term interest rates also offset because the repo posts one bond as collateral for another only a fraction of the face value as cash collateral to cover any haircuts. The only major risk of this trade would be if the repo were not a term repo, and had to be rolled over, and effective repo rate difference between the strip and bond X were enough to eat up all or more of the $25,000 up-front arbitrage spread. Of course, such nearly risk-free profit opportunities are highly sought after by traders who can act on them, and competition between these traders almost instantaneously pushes the price of the strip up and the price of bond B down until this arbitrage trade is no longer profitable. If the reverse were true, and the strip traded in the market for more than the bootstrap price, arbitrage traders would simply execute this trade in reverse, again until the prices were all in line and no arbitrage profit remained possible. This competition for arbitrage is essential to keeping bond prices in line so that most investors need not worry about getting a fair price for most liquid bonds they would consider trading.

In addition to calculating the present and future values of individual cash flows, and exposing any arbitrage opportunities, the bootstrapped PV curve can also be used to calculate what the current yield curve implies about the entire future yield curve one, three, or ten years in the future. This implied future yield curve, also known as the *forward curve*, can be used as a baseline to against which to decide which bonds to buy/

sell based on an investor's forecast of what the future curve is actually likely to be.

A frequently asked interview question is "if a 1 year bond yields 1% and a 2 year bond yields 2%, what is the 1 year rate 1 year forward?" This is a long way of saying "if a 1 year bond yields 1% and a 2 year bond yields 2%, what would 1 year rates have to be one year from now so that there is no difference between buying the 2 year bond now or buying the 1 year and rolling to another 1 year next year?" The short answer is "about 3%" and can be understood this way:

- The 2% two-year bond would pay 2% interest per year for the two years, or $4 total interest on $100
- The 1% one-year bond would only earn 1% of $100, or $1 of interest after one year, so
- In order to add up to the same total of $4 of interest over the two years, the one-year interest rate must rise from 1% to 3% over the course of the year.

A flip side of this interview question on forward rates is "if an investor bought the 2 year bond, and one year later the 1 year rate rose to 3%, what would be the investor's total return?" No matter how interest rates moved, the investor still would have earned the $2 of interest per $100 of bonds, but a one-year 2% bond in a market with one-year rates at 3% would only be worth about 99 cents on the dollar (since another investor would only buy this bond if they could earn the market rate of 3% on it =2% from the coupon +1% from the appreciation from 99 to 100), so the investor would have gotten back $101 ($99 from selling the bond +$2 in interest) per $100 invested, or a 1% return. In other words, the return from a two-year bond over one year if one-year rates move to the forward rate is the same as the return from a one-year bond.

Below are the forward interest rate curves calculated from the boot-strapped US Treasury curve as of May 15, 2017. Understandably, the upward sloping yield curve implies that the "breakeven" yield curve one year forward is higher than the current one, about 30bp higher for one- to seven-year maturities and narrower at longer maturities. The five-year forward curve may be a little harder to imagine or estimate without doing the calculation work, but implies that the breakeven yield curve is almost flat at 3% five years forward.

This "breakeven" view of yield curves and forward curves is not only a useful way to visualize how far rates can rise before a bond investment will underperform cash or treasury bills, but also can help decide which bonds offer the greatest expected upside versus expectations. In many cases, forward curves more than a year or two out can look quite unrealistic and unlike any yield curves experienced rate watchers have seen, so economic forecasters can contrast the forward curve implied by the market against a more realistic forecast of what the curve might actually look like in the future, and position a bond portfolio accordingly. For example, the May 2017 curves in Fig. 2.12 show the ten-year bond yields 2.4%, and the five-year yield five years forward is 3.0%. Suppose that rather than the forward curve being realized, the yield curve in May 2022 ends up looking exactly the same as it did in May 2017 (black line), with the five-year yield at 2.0% and the ten-year yield at 2.4%. The total return from buying the ten-year 2.4% note in this scenario could be estimated one of two ways, using 4.5 as the estimated duration of the five-year 2.4% bond:

A. Selling a five-year 2.4% bond at a yield of 2.0% produces a price return calculated as duration × (change in yield) = 4.7 × (2.4% − 2.0%) = +1.9%, plus the interest return of 2.4% per year for five years = +12.0%, for a total return of 13.9%.

May 2017 UST Yield Curve 1 and 5 years Forward

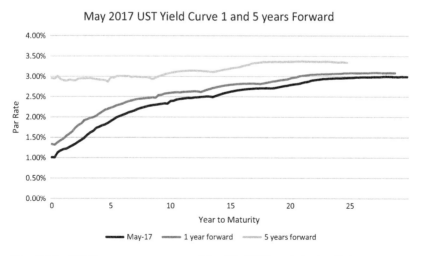

Fig. 2.12 US Treasury par curve on May 15, 2017, and the implied curves one year and five years forward

B. Locking in a five-year yield of 3.0% five years forward would have a value in five years at a 2.0% yield of duration x (change in yield) = 4.7 × (3.0% − 2.0%) = +4.7%. Meanwhile the money would have been invested at a five-year note at 2.0% interest, with an interest return of +10.0%, for a total return of 14.7%.

Method B is more descriptive of how bond investors earn their return by buying and rolling bond futures instead of cash bonds, a technique described in more detail in Sect. 7.3.

Buying a longer-dated bond when the curve is upward sloping; selling that bond when it becomes a shorter-dated bond at a lower-, nearer-term yield on the curve; and using the proceeds to buy another longer-dated bond is a strategy called "rolling down the curve" and works when rates do not rise as quickly as the forward curve implies. Rolling down the curve is one of the main ways bond investors often earn total returns higher than the initial yield-to-maturity rates on their bond portfolios.

In March 2003, the ten-year Japanese government bond (JGB) yield was 0.705%, while the ten-year yield on Australian government bonds was 5.17%. Over the following decade, Japanese ten-year yields fell only 14bp to 0.56%, while Australian yields fell 167bp to 3.50%. When asked which bond market had the better risk-adjusted returns over cash over that ten-year period, many bond investors, including many professional single-currency bond fund managers, have mistakenly answered that Australia must have produced better returns. Australia, they would reason, started with higher yields with more room to fall, and knowing that Australian rates did fall almost 12× as much as Japanese rates must mean Australian bonds performed better, no? The important missing data point in this "trick question" is that although Japanese ten-year rates were con-sistently far lower than Australian rates over this period, the Japanese curve remained steep (with short-term rates often ranging between 0.0% and 0.3%), while the Australian curve remained relatively flat (with short-term rates averaging almost 5%). The effect of rolling down the steep JGB curve meant buying and rolling ten-year JGBs between 2003 and 2013 produced an average annual excess return over cash of 2.3%, while Australian ten-year bonds (with almost no roll-down pickup) averaged only 1.8% per year over cash, despite Australian bond yields being 4× higher than Japanese bond yields on average. When it is further factored in that the Australian bond market was almost twice as volatile as the Japanese market (rates tend to move more when they are higher than when they are lower), the risk-adjusted excess return of Japanese bonds was over twice as high as those down under, as measured by the Sharpe ratio (described in Chapter [7]).

2.7 SOVEREIGNS, SSAS, MUNICIPALS, CORPORATES, AND STRUCTURES: FIVE CATEGORIES OF CREDIT RISKY ISSUERS

So far, six sections have been devoted to thoroughly understanding benchmark government bonds, like US Treasuries, that generally have the greatest liquidity and lowest yields, because they are widely accepted as being free from any risk of not being paid back on time and in full. This risk-free assumption may be somewhat debatable, especially for bonds issued by the governments of countries whose currencies have independent central banks, but a widely understood assumption is that a country let its currency devalue to a level it could keep paying its own currency debts rather than to technically defaulting on those debts. This is the case with US Treasury bonds issued in US dollars, Japanese government bonds (JGBs) issued in Japanese yen, Government of Canada bonds issued in Canadian dollars, and Korean treasury bonds (KTBs) issued in Korean Won, but no longer applies as soon as either (a) that central government issues bonds in a currency other than its own or (b) the issuer is not that central government. Bonds other than those issued by central governments tend to be less liquid and higher-yielding than benchmark bonds of the same tenor and currency, but the higher yield is exactly why many bond investors take time to study and lend to these issuers.

This section outlines five categories of issuers of credit risky bonds.

The first category of credit risky bonds are bonds issued by the same national governments and treasuries as would issue bonds in their own currencies, but instead are bonds issued in a foreign currency. Canada, the Republic of Korea, and the Russian Federation, as three examples, have issued bonds in US dollars. These foreign currency-denominated bonds are called "sovereign" bonds as opposed to the local currency bonds which are often called "treasury" or "government" bonds. Unlike with their own currencies, the Canadian, South Korean, and Russian governments have no power or influence to devalue the US dollar, and so these bonds have a very real chance of not being paid back in full and on time if these governments run out of US dollars, as Russia demonstrated when it defaulted on its US dollar bonds in 1997. A different group of examples of sovereign bonds are euro-denominated bonds issued by members of the European common currency, including the German Bund, French OAT, Italian BTP, and Greek bond. The common currency, described in more detail in Chap. 5, locked the Eurozone countries into not being able to devalue their way out of a debt crisis like the one in 2011–2013, as Greece and Italy were frequently able to do before the euro was introduced (one reason interest rates were significantly higher in Italian lira and Greek drachma than in German marks).

A second category of issuer with credit risk are government agencies or other issuers often compared directly to national governments in ability to repay, but technically these bonds are not directly issued by any national government. A broad definition of this category would include both Supranationals and Sovereign Agencies (together known as "SSAs" on many bond desks). Supranationals include organizations like the International Bank for Reconstruction and Development (IBRD, aka the "World Bank"), European Investment Bank (EIB), African Development Bank (AfDB), Asian Development Bank (ADB), and more recently the Asian Infrastructure Investment Bank (AIIB), each formed and capitalized by multiple highly creditworthy national governments working together. Supranational bonds tend to have the highest credit ratings and yields often very close to the benchmark bonds of their respective currencies. Sovereign agencies, on the other hand, issue bonds to fund a specific role on behalf of a single national government. For example, Export Development Canada (EDC) and the Japan Bank for International Cooperation each issue bonds in foreign currencies (often US dollars) to fund or insure the export trade of Canadian and Japanese companies, respectively, while the United States's Government National Mortgage Association (GNMA or "Ginny Mae") guarantees home mortgage loans. Supranational and sovereign agency bonds may be explicitly or implicitly guaranteed by one or more national governments, or just widely assumed that a national government would not allow them to default on any of their bonds, so are generally considered to be as creditworthy as the respective national governments.

Below the level of national governments is a third category of credit risky bond issuer: sub-national municipalities including city, state, or provincial governments. The US municipal bond market is one of the world's largest, in no small part due to the interest from many such bonds being exempt from US federal (and, in many cases, also state and local) income taxes for US taxpaying bondholders. This tax exemption is why many US municipal bonds may actually trade at lower yields than their benchmark (same maturity or duration) US Treasuries, since 2% tax-free is still better to an investor than 2.5% from the US Treasury taxable at 28% or higher rates. US tax-exempt issuers include the State of California, the City of Chicago, the Seattle Transit Authority, and the Commonwealth of Puerto Rico. In 2017, Puerto Rico effectively defaulted on its bonds, resulting in large losses for investors in US tax-exempt bonds. In an attempt to expand the appeal of the US municipal market beyond its tax advantages, in 2009, the US federal government started the "Build America Bonds" program, which paid tax credits to US municipalities that issued bonds with taxable interest, and many of these bonds were bought by foreign investors attracted by the higher yields. Municipal bonds may also differ in what exactly backs the promise to repay principal and interest: for example, State of California "general obligation bonds" are backed by the full faith and credit of the State of California, while Seattle Transit Authority "revenue bonds" are only backed by collections from bus fares, parking fees, and other revenue without recourse to the city's general funds. Outside the United States, sub-national bond issuers include Canadian provinces like Ontario and Quebec, French cities including Paris and Lyon, the Indian state of Karnataka, and the Malaysian state of Sarawak. The credit quality of these municipal issuers can vary greatly within as well as between countries.

While this may seem like a lot of emphasis on bonds issued or guaranteed by various levels of governments, bonds issued with some level of government involvement understandably give investors some level of assurance their money will be paid back that most private company issuers cannot provide. Governments effectively have a monopoly (or, in the case of national vs sub-national governments, overlapping monopolies) on collecting taxes from residents of, citizens of, or activities within a given territory. The comfort may come from the observation that territories don't just disappear, and even the dissolution or overthrow of currently functioning governments is either difficult to imagine, or hard to worry beyond. When the Tsarist government was overthrown in the Russian Revolution of 1917, the new Soviet government repudiated the prerevolutionary debt, and only at the end of the century did Boris Yeltsin agree to compensate French bondholders for some of these losses (http://www.nytimes.com/2000/11/19/world/russia-redeeming-czar-s-bonds.html?mcubz=0).

Beyond government issuers, a fourth category could broadly include "corporate" issuers, generally thought of as including both banks and non-financial corporations like iPhone maker Apple Inc. or Chinese property developer Country Garden. Companies issuing publicly traded debt are generally required by their governments to publicly file audited financial statements, which are often not required of nor exactly the same as the financial fundamentals underlying the different types of government debt. While government debt is generally backed by the power to tax, private issuers are limited by their power to generate cash from their own assets or business acumen to pay back their debts, hopefully with profit left over above that to pay their shareholders. Between the third and fourth categories listed here might be placed the list of "government-owned", "government-sponsored", or otherwise closely government-related issuers, which could include national oil companies like Mexico's Pemex or Malaysia's Petronas, or Singapore's sovereign investment fund Temasek.

A fifth and final category of bond issuers to be boxed off here would be "structured" or "special purpose" issuers that don't technically fit in any of the above boxes, though they might be most similar to municipal revenue bonds. Structured notes are sometimes issued by a bank or other seasoned issuers with a special payoff formula, but this category is meant to focus on special purpose companies specifically set up to issue a specific series of debt, often backed by a specific pool of assets or cash flows. Mortgage-backed securities (MBS) own a portfolio of mortgages and pass their cash flows on to different classes of investors in a specific order, and a large share of planes operated by airlines are owned by bankruptcy remote issuers of enhanced equipment trust certificates (EETCs). The term "bankruptcy remote" means the pool of mortgages or airplane leases could fail to pay the bondholders without the sponsoring bank or airline going bankrupt, and the bank or airline could go bust without the MBS or EETC missing a payment.

The one common question when considering investment in any bond by a credit risky issuer is the probability of not getting paid back in full and on time, versus the extra yield that bond pays to compensate for that risk. Many issuers are assigned credit ratings by widely recognized credit rating agencies (the global "three majors" as of 2017 being S&P, Moody's, and Fitch) that categorize the issuer, and in some cases specific bonds, on their respective default risks. These credit ratings could be listed as (Fig. 2.13):

The next section goes beyond credit ratings and explains a framework for calculating and assessing credit risks.

S&P / Fitch	Moody's	2017 Example	Meaning
AAA	Aaa	Canada	Top-quality credit
AA+	Aa1	Apple, US Treasury	Default extremely unlikely
AA	Aa2	France, Korea	
AA-	Aa3	HSBC, Qatar	Traditional LIBOR rating
A+	A1	PepsiCo, Japan	
A	A2	ICBC, Iceland, Malaysia	
A-	A3	JP Morgan, Latvia	
BBB+	Baa1	Hungary, Trinidad & Tobago	
BBB	Baa2	Panama, Philippines,	
BBB-	Baa3	Italy, Indonesia	Lowest "Investment Grade"
------	------	------	------
BB+	Ba3	Gazprom, Portugal	Highest "Junk" grade
BB	Ba3	Brazil, Bolivia	
BB-	Ba3	Vietnam, Honduras	
B+	Ba3	Sri Lanka, Sharp Corporation	
B	Ba3	Angola, Argentina	
B-	Ba3	Ukraine, Mongolia	
C- to CCC+	C3 to Caa1	Venezuela, Del Monte Foods, Distressed Names	
	D	"D" refers to names in default	

Fig. 2.13 List and explanation of major credit ratings
Sovereign ratings source: S&P ratings/CapitalIQ (https://www.capitaliq.com/CIQDotNet/CreditResearch/RenderArticle.aspx?articleId=1894456&SctArtId=433731&from=CM&nsl_code=LIME&sourceObjectId=10199471&-sourceRevId=1&fee_ind=N&exp_date=20270804-21:15:37)
Corporate ratings source: Company websites

2.8   CREDIT RISK: CALCULATING THE CHANCE AND COST OF NOT BEING PAID BACK IN FULL ON TIME

With benchmark government bonds, calculations and forecasts are usually not of if or how much a future cash flow will be, but of the present value of those certain future cash flows today, and the changes in this time value of money, known as interest rate risk. For most other types of investments, including the credit risky bonds illustrated here, but also for real estate and equity investments (public and private), the uncertainty of whether a future cash flow will be paid and how much it will be is added to the uncertainty of its present value, and these all need to be combined to calculate a current price of the asset. Of these different asset classes, credit risky bonds are a good one to start with, since at least two highly likely future values a high-yield bond's cash flows are known with a good degree of confidence: the amount paid if the bond doesn't default, and an estimate of the value of the bond if it does default. Probability-scenario analysis of this credit risky bond can be extended to valuing real estate or equity investments in the exact same way, using different scenario assumptions illustrated in Chaps. 3 and 4, respectively.

As an example, assume a two-year credit risky bond issued by XYZ pays an annual coupon of 6.0%, when the bootstrapped present value of a "certain" cash flow in one year and two years calculated as 0.990 and 0.975, respectively. Three scenarios can then be modeled with respective present values of each scenario:

- **Scenario A**: The bond is repaid on time, in full without defaulting. The present value of this scenario is $6.0 \times 0.990 + 106.00 \times 0.975 = 109.29$.
- **Scenario B**: The first coupon is paid, and then the bond defaults before maturity, with an assumed recovery rate/defaulted FV of **20**. The present value of this scenario is $6.0 \times 0.990 + 20.0 \times 0.975 = $ **25.44**.
- **Scenario C**: The bond defaults before the first coupon is paid, and the assumed recovery rate/defaulted FV is **20**. The present value of this scenario is $6.0 \times 0.990 + 20.0 \times 0.975 = $ **19.80**.

If the bond is currently trading at par (100.00), and it is assumed that there is an equal probability of scenarios B and C, the market and our assumptions imply that scenario A has an 89.3% probability, as:

$$\left(\text{Prob of A} \right) \times \left(\text{PV of A} \right) + \left(\text{Prob of B} \right) \times \left(\text{PV of B} \right)$$
$$+ \left(\text{Prob of C} \right) \times \left(\text{PV of C} \right) = \text{Price}$$
$$\left(0.893 \times 109.29 \right) + \left(0.0536 \times 25.44 \right) + \left(0.0536 \times 19.80 \right) = 100.00$$

The main assumptions are recovery rate and timeline of default probabilities, but this math of scenarios and present values unambiguously links these two assumptions with a price and vice versa. If an investor calculates that a bond is less likely to default, or likely to have a higher recovery rate/ defaulted value than the price implies through this formula, then the investor should buy the bond, and conversely, if the investor assumes a higher default probability or lower recovery value, the investor should sell the bond or buy credit protection. This same formula framework can be extended to bonds of any maturity or credit quality, as well as to other assets with risky future cash flows. In this example 20 was chosen at random as the recovery rate, and in practice recovery rates range from almost zero to over 80% depending on the nature and asset quality of the issuer and seniority and security of the debt.

A probability weighted expected value of a future cash flow is also known as a certainty equivalent, and is what allows these probability-adjusted cash flows to be discounted back to present value using the same PV factors as for "risk-free" treasury bonds. This certainty equivalent valuation method can be applied to valuing almost any asset with cash flows, including stocks, real estate, royalty trusts, and private equity investments, and has several advantages over IRR or other discounted cash flow (DCF) approaches that require an input of an arbitrary discount rate other than the unambiguously bootstrapped discount factors from treasuries.

There are whole books written on the topic of credit analysis and how to assess the probability that a given borrower will go bankrupt or otherwise fail to pay, but there is only room in this chapter for the highest level overview of these techniques.

The most obvious method is sometimes called the *structural method*, which involves projecting the cash flows of the issuer versus the debts on its balance sheet and considering the relatively likelihood of scenarios where those cash flows would or would not cover those debts. Metrics like the interest coverage ratio, debt to equity, debt to free cash flow ratio, and debt to EBITDA ratio are commonly used numbers for comparing relative creditworthiness vs financial distress, but a full and thorough projection of cash flows and balance sheets is more useful than any single metric.

The structural method covers at least two of what are often called the 5 *Cs of credit*, traditionally listed as: (1) cash flow (is the issuer bringing in enough cash to service its debt), (2) capital (how much equity and subordinated debt is junior to the one in question), (3) conditions (trends in the overall economy and other external factors which may influence future cash flows), (4) collateral (if the debt isn't paid out of current cash flows, are there assets which can be sold to pay back the debt, and do the debtors have security over these assets?), and (5) character (does the management in charge of paying back the debt actually have the willingness to repay, or will they try and benefit other stakeholders at the expense of creditors?).

Continuing the example of the Simple Sample Bank from Sect. 1.3, suppose the bank wanted to "lever up" its balance sheet and supplement its equity capital borrowing $900 from the bond markets in the form of a 2% senior note, and expand its deposit and asset base accordingly. The figure below shows a balance sheet and income statement for the bank with this added debt capital (Fig. 2.14).

The structural approach to evaluating the credit risk of the 2% notes involves looking at how the cash portion of the income below, plus the assets on the left side of the balance sheet, would "waterfall" to the creditors and owners on the right side of the balance sheet. The first priority is to pay principal plus interest to the depositors, followed by principal plus interest to the 2% noteholders. The more capital provided by the equity holders, the more of a "cushion" these senior debt creditors have against short falls in cash flows or asset values.

Note that income statements like the one above show economic profits and losses, especially the earnings before interest, tax, depreciation, and amortization (EBITDA) number of interest to creditors, but are only a proxy for the cash flows which must come in to cover debt payments. Withdrawals from deposit accounts do not directly show up on the income statement, but are cash flows and reductions to the balance sheet that would have to be funded by current cash flows from loan assets, or by short-term borrowing from other banks or the central bank. By raising debt capital in the form of the 2% note, this bank has not only levered up its return on equity (doubling it from 7% to 14%), but also reduced its dependence on deposits from 90% to 50% of its total liabilities and shareholder equity. Another way of saying this is that the bank has reduced the liquidity of its liabilities by replacing demand deposits with more expensive term debt that can't be redeemed on demand, and in doing some

Balance sheet at the start of the bank's second year, with $900 2% Note

Assets   Liabilities & Equity

    Short Term Loans $500   Deposits from Customers $1,000

    Long-term Loans $1,500   2% Senior Note $900

                                Equity Capital $100

Total Assets: $1,000   Total Liabilities & Equity: $1,000

Income Statement for the bank's second year

Interest income on $1,500 of LT loans @5% $75 (+)

Interest income on $500 of ST loans @4% $20 (+)

Interest expense on $1,000 of deposits @1% $10 (-)

Interest expense on $900 senior debt @2% $18 (-)

Provision for loan losses @1% $20 (-)

Salaries and other expenses $27 (-)

Tax on $20 pre-tax profit @30% $6 (-)

Net Income $14

Return on Equity = $14 Net Income / $100 Equity Capital = 14%

Fig. 2.14   Balance sheet and income statement for Simple Sample Bank's second year, with bond debt

comes closer to matching the liquidity of its assets with its liabilities, and reducing the risk of a "run on the bank". A run on the bank can leave the bank unable to pay its debts, even with assets worth more than the total value of its debts, because those assets are not liquid enough to keep current on debt payments. This is the risk of the issuer defaulting due to lack of *liquidity*, rather than due to lack of *solvency*, and might be best understood by example through studying and contrasting the 2008 collapse of Bear Stearns (liquidity) versus the collapse of Lehman Brothers (solvency).

In addition to cash bonds, credit markets also trade a pure instrument of whether or not a particular issuer or borrower will default on its debt called a *credit default swap* (*CDS*). In exchange for an annual premium, the buyer of credit protection through a credit default swap has the right to exchange defaulted bonds for face value in the event of default. For the same issuer XYZ above, suppose two-year credit protection on $100 worth of bonds costs $5 per year for each of the two years, with the bootstrapped value of cash flows in one year and two years calculated as 0.990 and 0.975, respectively. Three scenarios similar to the ones above can then be modeled with respective present values for the credit default swap for each scenario:

- **Scenario A**: XYZ does not default in the next two years. The present value of this scenario is $(-\$5.0 \times 0.990) + (-\$5.0 \times 0.975) =$ **-$9.825**.
- **Scenario B**: XYZ defaults right after the first year and after the first premium payment, with an assumed recovery rate/defaulted FV of **20**. The present value of this scenario is $(-\$5.0 \times 0.99) + (((\$100.0 - \$20.0) \times 0.975) =$ **+73.05.**
- **Scenario C**: XYZ defaults before the first premium payment, and the assumed recovery rate/defaulted FV is **20**. The present value of this scenario is $((\$100.0 - \$20.0) \times 0.990) =$ **+79.20**.

In these scenarios, the −$5.00 are the premium payments the protection buyer has to make (which, as with many insurance policies, stop when the insurable event happens), while the positive ($100.0 − $20.0) cash flows are the value of putting the defaulted bonds to the CDS counterparty in exchange for full face value. As with the bond scenario probability calculation above, the price of the CDS (which in this case is assumed to be zero up front, with all the $5/year premiums payable over time) is calculated as follows:

$$\left(\text{Prob of A}\right) \times \left(\text{PV of A}\right) + \left(\text{Prob of B}\right) \times \left(\text{PV of B}\right)$$
$$+ \left(\text{Prob of C}\right) \times \left(\text{PV of C}\right) = \text{Price}$$

$$\left(0.886 \times \left(-\$9.825\right)\right) + \left(0.057 \times 73.05\right) + \left(0.057 \times 79.20\right) = 0$$

As with the cash bond calculation, a trader who believes the probability of default is higher than 12% should buy this CDS, while a trader who believes default is far less likely should consider selling credit protection on this name.

Users of credit default swaps include:

- Banks and bond portfolio managers who need to **buy** credit protection
- Hedge funds who **buy** credit protection to "sell short" a credit, in the hopes of profiting if a given name does default (unlike insurance, CDS buyers can go "naked" and buy protection on names in which they have no insurable interest).
- Investors, insurance companies, and special purpose issuers may **sell** credit protection as a way of earning premium by taking credit risk on a name they may not be able or interested in lending to in the cash market.

Just as banks run their business on the asset side by taking both liquidity and credit risk in exchange for the higher interest rates they charge on loans, insurance companies are in the business of taking risk by collecting premiums in exchange for the probability of having to pay out larger amounts if the insured event occurs, so in many ways an insurance company is like a portfolio of short CDS positions, but mostly linked to risks other than credit risks.

Like a bank or insurance company, an investor considering buying a credit risky bond notices the highly skewed risk/reward profile, where there is perhaps a 95% probability of earning 6% higher rate of return than bank deposits or government bonds, balanced with a 5% probability of losing 80% or more of the amount invested. This is why diversification is critical to bond investors and is explained in detail in Chap. 7.

One specialized type of debt instrument that became famous (and infamous) in the 2008 mortgage bond crash is the collateralized debt obligation ("CDO"). CDOs have been called "complicated" and "financial weapons of mass destruction", but in fact they are simplified and specialized versions of what banks do. CDOs hold fixed income assets (mostly bonds or loans, known as the "collateral") and issue debt in "tranches" ranked so that senior tranches must be paid in full before any junior tranches are paid. These tranches are often designed to achieve specific credit ratings such as "AAA" for investors who seek bonds with such ratings, and consider CDOs as a way of earning a higher spread compared to bonds with the same rating. In the below example, the assets are a diversified pool of 100 different bonds or loans, and these have been funded by issuing a "AAA senior", "BBB mezzanine," and "Equity" tranches of securities to investors. The AAA has priority in that it must be paid back in full before the BBB or equity tranches receive back any of their principal, and the high rating is assured by the condition that the AAAs will only be at risk of losing money if losses on the asset portfolio exceed 30%. The BBB tranche is subordinated to the AAA, but is protected by an equity tranche that only exposes the BBB tranche to losses of the portfolio greater than 20%, but risks losing 100% of principal if portfolio losses exceed 30%. The equity tranche is the most junior and is immediately exposed to any defaults on the asset portfolio, but is attractive for the leverage provided by the senior tranches. As in the example of the bank, assume the asset portfolio generates a gross yield of 5%, the AAA senior tranche bonds pay 2%, and the BBBs pay 4%, then the equity tranche has the potential annual upside of:

$$(\$10,000 \times 5\%) - (\$7,000 \times 2\%) - (\$1,000 \times 4\%) = \$320$$

On a $2000 equity investment, this $320 is gross return of 16%. For every 1% loss in the asset portfolio, the return to the equity holders will be reduced by 4%, until portfolio losses add up to over 20% and wipe out 100% of the equity capital. This "first loss" exposure of the equity piece protects the BBB tranche from a large percentage of likely losses, and the BBB in turn protects the AAA tranche (sample balance sheet in Fig. 2.15).

The next section described features common to many credit risky bonds that make their payoff structure more complicated, but possibly also more attractive to issuers and investors.

Sample balance sheet of a CDO

Assets		Liabilities & Equity	
Bond or loan #1	$100	AAA Senior Tranche	$7,000
Bond or loan #2	$100	BBB Mezzanine Tranche	$1,000
Bonds or loans #3-100	$9,800	Equity Capital	$2,000
Total Assets:	$10,000	Total Liabilities & Equity:	$10,000

Fig. 2.15   Sample balance sheet of a CDO

2.9   CALLABLE BONDS, AND OTHER FEATURES TO WATCH OUT FOR

So far, it has been assumed that bonds simply pay interest in the form of fixed periodic coupons, with the final coupon and full principal amount repaid on a fixed maturity date, but many bonds may vary their coupons, maturity dates, or other features:

- Amortization
- Callability or prepayment options
- Floating interest rates
- Caps or floors on floating coupons
- Inflation indexing

Amortization means "to death" and refers to fixed income instruments that pay not only interest but also a portion of principal back with each coupon payment. Many loans are structured this way, so that the borrower pays off the entire loan through equal monthly installments rather than through interest-only payments with a large "bullet" payment of principal at maturity, which may require refinancing or an asset sale to pay off. Mortgages (with the same root word "mort" meaning death) are one of the largest and most familiar of these markets, both to borrowers who use mortgages to buy homes and to investors who buy mortgages for their relative yield vs safety, but shorter-term installment loans work very similarly. As an example, suppose an airline finances a $115,000,000 aircraft with a $20,000,000 cash down payment and payments of $10,000,000 per year for 12 years. The effective yield to the lender calculates out as 3.791% per year, and the annual payments break into interest and principal payments as follows (Fig. 2.16):

Besides amortization, what also makes mortgages (and mortgage-backed securities) different from many bonds is the right, but not obligation, of the borrower to prepay the loan early without penalty. This prepayment feature, also known as a call feature, is a valuable option in the hands of the borrower, in that the borrower retains the right to continue paying the original locked-in rate even as rates rise, but the ability to refinance and lock in a new lower rate if rates fall. To compensate the investor for the risk of having to earn a lower rate for longer while having any relatively high rate cut short from investing in callable debt, the borrower must pay a higher yield for this right to call or prepay.

Year	Beginning Balance	Payment at Year End	Interest	Principal
1	$ 95,000,000	$ 10,000,000	$ 3,601,450	$ 6,398,550
2	$ 88,601,450	$ 10,000,000	$ 3,358,881	$ 6,641,119
3	$ 81,960,331	$ 10,000,000	$ 3,107,116	$ 6,892,884
4	$ 75,067,447	$ 10,000,000	$ 2,845,807	$ 7,154,193
5	$ 67,913,254	$ 10,000,000	$ 2,574,591	$ 7,425,409
6	$ 60,487,845	$ 10,000,000	$ 2,293,094	$ 7,706,906
7	$ 52,780,940	$ 10,000,000	$ 2,000,925	$ 7,999,075
8	$ 44,781,865	$ 10,000,000	$ 1,697,681	$ 8,302,319
9	$ 36,479,546	$ 10,000,000	$ 1,382,940	$ 8,617,060
10	$ 27,862,485	$ 10,000,000	$ 1,056,267	$ 8,943,733
11	$ 18,918,752	$ 10,000,000	$ 717,210	$ 9,282,790
12	$ 9,635,962	$ 10,001,261	$ 365,299	$ 9,635,962
13	$ 0			

Fig. 2.16 12-year amortizing loan breakdown into interest and principal

Readers familiar with bonds or mortgages that charge floating rather than fixed rates of interest will note that having a floating rate removes any need or incentive to prepay and refinance at lower rates but instead leaves the uncertainty of having interest payments rise and fall with interest rates. This uncertainty was one of the triggers of the 2008–2009 global financial crisis ("GFC"), when borrowers who could afford floating rate mortgages at lower rates were unable to keep up with payments as rates rose. Floating rate debt effectively provides long-term financing at short-term rates, and since the rate can rise or fall like that on a rolling bank deposit, the market price of a floating rate bond or loan usually remains close to face value, barring changes in the borrower's perceived credit quality. There is an entire market of "interest rate swaps" where one counterparty pays a fixed rate of interest on an agreed-upon notional amount, while receiving a floating rate of interest on the same notional amount, without the notional amount of money ever actually changing hands. For example, ABC Corp may trade a $1,000,000 notional interest rate swap with DEF Bank where ABC pays DEF the three-month LIBOR floating rate on the $1,000,000 (which could be $7,500 this quarter and more or less next quarter) while receiving 3.0% per year fixed on the $1,000,000 (equal to $30,000 per year).

Floating interest rates on bonds or loans can sometimes be subject to "caps" or "floors", limiting how much a floating rate can rise or fall, either in one period or overall. These caps or floors sometimes have a "ratchet" feature, meaning the coupon interest payment from one period to the next may be allowed to rise but not fall, or vice versa, rather than being subject to a fixed cap or floor. Understandably, caps and ratchet-down features are valuable to the borrower (and so would require the borrower to pay a spread above the floating rate they would otherwise pay), while floors and ratchet-up features are valuable to the lender.

One special type of floating rate note is one where the coupon and often the principal are indexed to a broadly recognized indicator of inflation. In the United States, the Treasury has issued Treasury Inflation-Protected Securities (TIPS) since 1997 (https://www.treasurydirect. gov/instit/marketables/tips/tips.htm), where the principal amount is adjusted up or down in proportion to changes in the Consumer Price Index for Urban Consumers (Non-seasonally Adjusted) Index (CPI-U, or CPI), while the coupon is paid as a fixed percentage of this indexed principal amount. For example, if an investor purchases $1,000 of a ten-year 1% TIPS in 2030, and the CPI increases by 20% over the next ten years, the final principal amount will be $1,200 and the final semi-annual coupon would be $6 (1% annual rate on the $1,200 for six months). US TIPS have a floor on the principal that the principal amount cannot be lower than the original face amount, even in the event of long-term deflation.

Inflation-indexed bonds have been issued by several other governments and private issuers in Europe, Asia, Australia, and Latin America. Mexico and Chile have gone a step further by creating legally defined currencies called the "Unidad de Inversion" ("UDI") and "Unidad de Fomento" ("UF"), which act as inflation-indexed versions of the Mexican peso and Chilean peso, respectively. UDI and UF are not only used to denominate bonds but also in long-term leases, salary agreements, and other long-term contracts requiring inflation indexing. Several other governments also issue inflation-indexed bonds linked to their own inflation indices, and Argentina has even issued bonds indexed to its gross domestic product (GDP).

Varying the tenor to maturity or coupon interest rate on a bond or loan may have advantages to some borrowers or lenders, but simplicity, standardization, and the broad need for assets to match fixed liabilities explain why many publicly traded bonds are relatively simple fixed rate instruments.

2.10   WHAT'S SO OUTSIDE THE BOX ABOUT BOND INVESTING: HOW TO BETTER BUY BONDS, AND FURTHER READING

This chapter on bonds is the longest, and possibly most technical and boring, of all the chapters in this book, but the concepts of the time value of money and probability weighted scenario analysis are foundational to evaluating any investment in any asset class.

Some additional books I would recommend reading for more background on bonds and fixed income markets include:

- *A History of Interest Rates, Fourth Edition*, by Sidney Homer and Richard Sylla
- *How to Make Money with Junk Bonds*, by Robert Levine
- *The Handbook of Fixed Income Securities*, by Frank Fabozzi and Steven Mann
- *Fixed Income Analysis*, by Frank Fabozzi and Martin Leibowitz
- *Credit Risk: Pricing, Measurement, and Management (Princeton Series in Finance)*, by Darrell Duffie and Kenneth Singleton

The explanations and textbook references in this chapter may also beg the question "what's so out of the box about investing in bonds?" Some of the most important takeaways and lessons for better beating the bond market may include:

A. Rolling down the curve is one way to earn a higher total rate of return than the initial yield to maturity on a bond, especially when the curve is steep.
B. Low yields don't always mean low returns, and high yields don't always mean high returns. A and B were especially well illustrated by the performance of Japanese bonds in the first decade of the 2000s.
C. Run bootstrapping and forward curve calculations; computers make these easy to do, and the results can highlight the best opportunities on the curve.
D. The biggest buyers of long-term bonds tend to be portfolios with long-term liabilities. Watch what pension funds and life insurance companies are doing to better understand the dynamics of the long end of the curve.

E. Consider a wider range of issuers to the limits of acceptable liquidity and credit quality. Some bonds offer higher yields because they are not liquid enough or not rated highly enough for institutional investors to buy them.

Besides interest rate and credit risk, a major risk affecting most fixed rate bonds (a main exception being the inflation-indexed bonds described in Sect. 2.9) is inflation risk, or the risk that the value of the money paid back in the future won't have as much purchasing power as expected. The next chapter describes real estate as the next income-producing investment that many investors consider largely because physical property preserves purchasing power in ways fixed income typically does not.

CHAPTER 3

Real Estate and Property

Real estate is perhaps the most fundamental and tangible investment asset class most investors encounter one way or another. Humans need space to live, land to grow food on, and commit a fair percentage of their incomes to pay for office, storage, retail, and industrial square footage somewhere, whether directly or indirectly. Part of the American dream may be to own a home, but Asians have become known in many top cities around the world for their love of property investment. In some markets like London, Toronto, or Vancouver, Chinese buyers have a reputation of buying several homes at a time for cash, simply as a way of keeping money safely outside of China.

In terms of valuation and cash flow analysis, a real estate investment is similar to a fixed income investment with two key differences being tangibility and specificity.

A real estate investment like a building or piece of land, as opposed to a bond or loan, is said to be *tangible* because it is a physical asset made of matter that can be touched and identified with physical attributes, including location and area. Directly tangible assets are sometimes known as hard assets or real assets as opposed to financial or paper assets. This tangibility makes it simple to understand what the investor owns and feel secure about owning it. While accountants of course consider cash on a balance sheet to be a "tangible asset", cash and bonds are someone else's liability owed to an investor, rather than a piece of property the investor owns outright. As a physical, durable, usable asset, real estate also pre-

© The Author(s) 2018   55
T. Dennison, *Invest Outside the Box*,
https://Doi.org/10.1007/978-981-13-0372-2_3

serves purchasing power in a way fixed amounts of money may not. Real estate's preservation of purchasing power over long periods of time is why I consider this investment box to be the most ancient and easy to understand cornerstone of the "Four House Pension" introduced later in this chapter.

A real estate investment is also *specific* in that it is not exactly replaceable or fungible with other similar assets like treasury bonds or other securities. A $100,000 treasury bond with CUSIP 912810RX8 is identical to and completely interchangeable with any other treasury bond with the same face value and CUSIP. On the other hand, if Alice owns the 2,000-square-foot house at 123 Main Street and Betty owns another 2,000-square-foot house next door at 125 Main Street, the two properties may be very similar and comparable, but are neither identical nor interchangeable. Alice's house may have slightly better sun exposure, be slightly further away from a busy road, and may have improvements to it that may or may not affect the value of my house in the same way. On the risk side, there is also the possibility that a fire or lawsuit could affect the value of Alice's house and not Betty's. Each property could also be considered *exclusive* in that Alice's ownership of 123 Main Street means no one else can own the same unit at the same time, unlike the share ownership of a stock or bond issue.

3.1   ESSENTIALS OF A REAL ESTATE INVESTMENT

The many different types of real estate investments may be relatively easy to understand, not because they are as simple as bonds but because they underlie many of the most basic human needs and are assets most people often see and touch regularly. The terms "real" estate and "real assets" are not in contrast to estates that are "fake" or "unreal", but instead come from the same root as the Spanish word "real" meaning "royal". Owning landed estates and land rights was traditionally the domain of lords and kings, and in some countries, gold or other minerals found under your land still belong to the crown or state rather than to you as the landowner. Common law countries often contrast "realty" or "real property" with "personalty" or "personal property", while civil law jurisdictions like those on continental Europe contrast "immovable property" versus "movable property". The asset class of real estate and immovable property often includes land and all buildings and immovable fixtures built on that land, even though in modern times the land and the buildings on it often have different owners.

It is often said that the three main factors in real estate investing are location, location, and location, and it is true that a large part of the value in a property investment is not in the right to use a specific location and exclude others from using it. Urbanization has made specific locations especially desirable and valuable, especially those located near the intersection of two waterways, or a waterway and another form of transportation. The largest and most expensive cities in the world tend to be defined by the waterways which made them hubs for trading large volumes of valuable goods, from London's foundation at the widest bridgeable point on the Thames to New York's Manhattan island connecting Atlantic seaships with Hudson riverboats.

Some of the main boxes real estate investments get categorized in include:

1. Residential—These include apartments or houses that an individual or family lives in, and either owns or rent from the owner.
2. Commercial—A large percentage of square footage of buildings in cities and suburbs don't have anyone sleeping in them at night, but instead may be used as:

   a. Retail shops and restaurants
   b. Offices
   c. Parking spaces

3. Industrial—There may be some overlap between what defines industrial and commercial real estate, but this box often includes factories, warehouses, shipping and rail yards, airports, and other big properties found outside of city centers.
4. Agricultural—Agricultural land may be one of the oldest forms of real property, but takes up a good percentage of the earth's land area to grow crops and livestock to feed over seven billion people.

One of the more speculative forms of real estate investing is buying an undeveloped piece of agricultural land just outside a city, and waiting until the city planners decide to re-zone that land as commercial or residential land. This re-zoning brings roads, electricity, water, sewage, and other improvements which make the land many times more valuable per acre than the agriculturally zoned land, even before any developments have actually been made on this land. This strategy is often called "land banking", and the two biggest disadvantages are: (1) the raw land typically will not yield any income before it is re-zoned or developed, and (2) there is often very little liquidity or price transparency on these plots before they are re-zoned or developed, and almost no certainty on if or when such steps might happen.

Many real estate investors prefer buying properties that both (a) generate income and (b) have immediate understandable uses. Residential real estate is popular with individual investors, since many are familiar with the process of buying a home to live in, and often have experience with both sides of paying rent as a tenant and receiving rent as a landlord. The 2008 global financial crisis was triggered by the popping of a bubble in US house prices fueled by residential mortgages, as home price speculators were far less price sensitive and subject to far looser lending standards than most commercial or industrial property investors. As the global economy recovered in the 2010s, many cities saw new property bubbles brewing, this time levered not by US mortgage lenders, but by cash buyers from China, Russia, and other emerging markets seeking a safe place to store money outside the financial system, and at times not even bothering to rent out their properties for rental income. The effect of these buyers in pushing up home prices to levels unaffordable to many urban workers led governments in many of these cities, including Hong Kong and Vancouver, to impose transaction taxes and other "speed bump" measures intended to curb investment into apartments, especially by foreign investors. These measures have so far been mostly applied to residential property investments, not commercial, or industrial ones.

Commercial and industrial real estate is a mature asset class in many urban markets, and, while in many ways like investing in residential rental property, is a natural next step for those seeking diversification across a wider variety of income-producing hard assets. Some commercial properties, like individual parking spaces, may have much lower purchases prices (aka "ticket size") than a house or apartment, while an investment in an entire office building or shopping mall will often be well above the price range of even many wealthy individual investors. Some notable differences between commercial and residential real estate include:

- Commercial leases are often longer than residential leases, and may include a pre-agreed schedule of rent increases.
- Commercial mortgages often require more cash up front (i.e. a larger "down payment") than loans for owner-occupied home purchases.
- Commercial leases sometimes charge a percentage of the tenant's profits or revenues as opposed to a fully fixed rental rate. This feature

provides some risk management for the tenant as well as exposure to inflation and economic growth in ways many fixed income investments do not.

Agricultural real estate has made up much of the world's wealth throughout human history, but may be one of the less sought-after classes of property by urban investors in the twenty-first century. Real estate investors tend to prefer to invest in what they know, and while the idea of land growing an annually harvestable cash crop is easy enough to understand, the drivers of yields and resale values of farms, plantations, and timber fields are far removed from the factors in the neighborhoods where urban dwellers live and work. Location is mostly important to agricultural land as far as what can grow there, how far it is to the market for its crop, and the laws and market forces governing farm work on it, and it is far easier for two farms 1,000 miles apart to compete as sources of wheat, wood, or wool than it would be for two buildings even 100 miles apart to compete as a place a family or firm would consider moving to. Rather than location, location, and location, the primary factors for agricultural real estate might include commodity prices, climate, soil, and labor.

3.2   WHY INVEST IN REAL ESTATE?

The primary reasons investors buy real estate include:

- Use value—The first real estate investment many individuals make is buying the home they live in.
- Easy to understand value—Unlike bonds, whose value depends on interest rates or the risk of credit default events, or stocks, whose value is based on unknown future business performance, property values are more closely related to the need to use spaces which do not change or disappear quickly.
- Income—Most types of real estate not being used by the investor can be rented to a tenant to generate current income. This rental yield can often be higher than bond yields.
- Less risk of losing 100%—Companies regularly go out of business, and even currencies can significantly devalue over time, but it usually takes an extreme event (war, uninsured natural disaster, uncompensated eminent domain, etc.) for a property to become completely worthless to its owner.

- Inflation protection—Since real estate provides physical use value to its owner or tenant (a place to live, space to work, or land to grow food on), a general rise in the cost of those goods and services lifts real estate prices as well.
- Real appreciation—Over the past century, property prices in many cities have appreciated faster than the rate of inflation. This is due to increases in real wages for both the construction workers and real estate professionals who supply urban properties and for the tenants demanding these properties closer to city centers where they compete to live and work. This real appreciation is related to the final primary motivation to invest in real estate:
- Scarcity—While new stocks, bonds, and even dollar bills are regularly printed and increasing in supply, it is often said that "they aren't making any more land". Although one might argue that the reclamation of prime land in Victoria Harbour or the replacement of low-rise with high-rise buildings are examples of how even new real estate can be "issued", there remain greater costs and constraints to increasing the supply of real estate assets (Fig. 3.1).

In addition to these primary motives, there are also a few secondary advantages to investing in real estate vs stocks, bonds, or alternatives:

- Financing—Mortgage loans are generally easier for many investors, especially individual investors, to access than the repo market for bonds. Banks generally prefer to lend money against real estate collateral, and often do so at competitive interest rates on over 50% (sometimes even over 80%) of the assessed value of the property.
- No mark-to-market—Mortgage loans, unlike repos or margin financing, do not have "margin calls", and will not require the borrower to prepay or post additional collateral as long as timely payments continue, regardless of what happens to property prices. Some investors view this lack of liquidity an advantage or indicator that real estate is somehow less risky, but in Sect. 3.5, this liquidity risk is put in perspective.
- Tax deductions—Robert Kiyosaki is one of the many advocates of real estate investing who list tax advantages as one of the main reasons to prefer real estate over other asset classes. An example of how real estate can produce tax-sheltered cash flow is illustrated in Sect. 3.4.

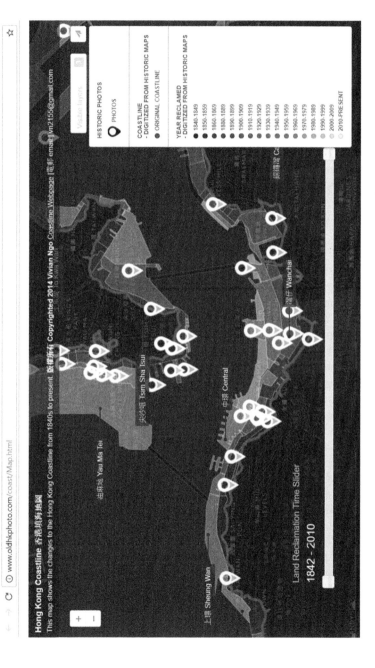

Fig. 3.1 A map of the new land created in Victoria Harbour, Hong Kong, from 1840 to 1910

While the ability to finance without margin calls and defer taxes is a real advantage, it is important not to let the "tax tail wag the investment dog" but instead keep a complete picture of overall net economic returns and risk.

Continuing the example of the Super Simple Bank illustrated in Sects. 1.3 and 2.8, the relative security and stability of real estate asset values and cash flows are why real estate assets often make up a large share of the assets of banks, primarily in the form of loans and mortgages secured by real estate collateral but also in the form of some real estate investments owned directly by banks.

3.3   The "Four House Pension": The Simplest Inflation-Indexed Pension Plan and Reason to Own Real Estate

One of the simplest usable answers to the question "how much money is needed to retire comfortably or to be idly rich?" is "four times the value of one's house". Setting a retirement goal of "the value of four houses" may not be as satisfying as a number like "$2,345,678.90", but has the advantages of naturally scaling to both the general cost of living and the specific retiree's lifestyle.

Four is not a magic number, but the Four House Pension works like this: owning four houses allows the owner to live in one of the houses and generate rental income from the other three houses. This rental income should generally be enough to comfortably cover the owner's living expenses, including property taxes and emergency reserves, for someone whose housing expenses are about one-quarter of their total expenses. Not only does owning the first house ensure that the owner's family should always have a place to live, but the rental income from the other three houses generally tracks the overall ups and downs of the cost of living, providing one of the most direct, ancient, and understandable forms of inflation-indexed income there is.

Throughout pre-industrial times, many affluent aristocrats and gentry might have lived off of a "two house pension": one castle or country house large enough for a family (plus perhaps some tenants or clients) and land on which tenants, serfs, or other farm laborers would work to feed and clothe the family. The medieval and early modern "middle class" label might be applied to the yeoman farmer, who like the gentry might have owned a house and land, but often had to work the farm himself, and rely on having enough children to take over the workload when he became too old or disabled to sow and reap.

The Industrial Revolution and expanding roles of government in the nineteenth and twentieth centuries expanded the supply and demand for a third and fourth house for an idly rich portfolio. On the supply side, industrialization and urbanization substantially increased the quantity, quality, and variety of buildings within cities, including taller apartment blocks with elevators to office blocks and factories for expanding ranks of workers commuting to jobs away from home. On the demand side, increasingly wealthy and numerous investors over these centuries have come to expect a far greater quantity, quality, and variety of goods and services to spend money on, from modern electronics to air travel and medical care, all of which required more income in excess of that spent on food and shelter. In addition, governments became far more centralized and organized in the collection of income taxes, which can typically consume between one-sixth and one-third of a modern affluent consumer's income and ranks alongside food and shelter as an essential and substantial budget item. Within this range, it seems like a prudent rule of thumb to consider roughly one-quarter of one's income should go to housing, perhaps one-quarter to taxes, and the other half to cover all other spending, saving, and giving.

As an idealized example of the Four House Pension assume Holly Houser is 35 years old, earning a salary of $100,000 per year, and has accumulated $100,000 cash in bank accounts or treasury bills. She uses the $100,000 in savings as a 20% down payment to buy a $500,000 home, borrowing the remaining $400,000 using a 20-year 4% fixed rate mortgage with a payment of about $2,500 per month, or 30% of her gross income. Then assume that her salary increases by 4% per year, while real estate prices appreciate by 2% per year.

Five years later, when Holly is 40 years old, her house is worth over $550,000, while her mortgage has been paid down to below $330,000, leaving her with over $220,000 in equity. She refinances her mortgage into a new $440,000 20-year 4% fixed rate mortgage, cashing out $110,000 of her equity while raising the loan-to-value ratio on her home back up to 80%, and her mortgage payments up to around $2,750/month ($33,000 per year, now about 27% of her $121,000/year income). She uses this $110,000 as a 20% down payment to invest in another $550,000 property, which she finances with a mortgage nearly identical to the one on her primary home. The monthly mortgage payment on this investment property is assumed to be just about covered by its rental income, net of expenses and vacancy, and hopefully rental increases will allow some surplus cash after a few years.

In another five years, at age 45, Holly's home and investment property are each worth around $600,000 with mortgage balances less than $360,000 each. Again, Holly refinances these properties up an 80% loan-to-value ratio with two $480,000, 20-year, 4% fixed rate mortgages, cashing out $120,000 ($600,000 – $480,000) from each of the two properties. This $240,000 is used as a 20% down payment for two more $600,000 properties, each also financed with a nearly identical mortgage whose $3,000/month payment is now just over 20% of Holly's now $148,000/year salary, and assumed to be roughly covered by net rental income on the other three properties.

By the time Holly reaches age 65 after another 20 years, the mortgages on all four properties would have been paid off, and Holly would now own full equity in her Four House Pension with no debt. Her house would now be hers to live in with no additional mortgage payments, and assuming a similar rental rate and yield, the other three houses (now worth a total of over $2.7 million) would generate a net rental income of about $110,000 per year, which would replace a large percentage of her income from working, especially considering she no longer needs to deduct expenses for a place to live, and in many countries will be taxed less on this rental income than on her salary. This rental income could be increased in an inflationary or high-growing economy, while decreases would probably be offset by falling expenses elsewhere in Holly's budget. If needed, Holly could increase her liquidity and cash flow by reversing her past 30 years of savings with a reverse mortgage (Fig. 3.2).

Holly's example is of course idealized, and in many ways unrealistic, but can still be used as a yardstick not only for saving for retirement but as an asset allocation template where some or all of the other three houses are replaced by investments in other asset classes. This idealized "30-year retirement plan" also has built into it relatively high levels of investment risk in the form of leverage, which also correspond to the traditional financial advice that younger workers should have riskier investment portfolios and reduce this risk as they get older.

Age	Real Estate Assets	Mortgage Debt	Net Equity	Action
35	$ 500	$ 400	$ 100	Buy 1st house, $100k down
40	$ 1,100	$ 880	$ 220	Buy 2nd house, using $110k equity from 1st house
45	$ 2,400	$ 1,920	$ 480	Buy 3rd & 4th houses, using $240k equity from 1st & 2nd houses
50	$ 2,680	$ 1,360	$ 1,320	No new investments, cash flows assumed to pay off debts
55	$ 2,960	$ 880	$ 2,080	Rental increases might allow net positive cash flows
60	$ 3,280	$ 280	$ 3,000	
65	$ 3,600	$ -	$ 3,600	Debt fully paid, rental income now provides the pension

Fig. 3.2 Holly's steps to build this Four House Pension

3.4 Accounting for Profits and Losses, Appreciation, and Depreciation in a Typical Real Estate Investment

Although it may not sound attractive, depreciation is a defining feature of investing in most forms of "improved" real estate. "Improved" refers to buildings and other built "improvements" which make land more useful and valuable, but which, by their nature, depreciate over time. Land itself, by contrast, does not depreciate like the improvements on the land, but building investments are sometimes made on land that is leased (often in the form of a "leasehold" in the United Kingdom and many former British colonies) rather than owned outright (known as a "freehold"), and land leases can sometimes be accounted for in a way similar to depreciation.

While investors may hope that a purchased building may appreciate in value by the time they sell it, any such appreciation faces the depreciation headwinds of buildings getting older, wearing down, going out of style, needing repair, and in almost all cases eventually getting torn down and replaced with a new building. The following scatterplot chart plots the price per square foot of apartments in 14 different buildings in Hong Kong's Sai Ying Pun district ranging in age from 3 to 48 years. Although anyone who bought one of the older apartments in 2004 would have almost certainly been able to sell it at a much higher price in 2014, this chart clearly shows that these apartments, on a cross-sectional analysis, are HK$300 per square foot less valuable on average for each year the building ages (Fig. 3.3).

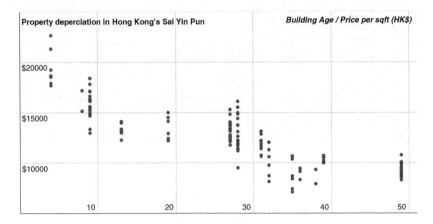

Fig. 3.3 Plotting price per square foot vs apartment age for apartments in Hong Kong's Sai Ying Pun district. (Source: Centadata)

Some investors actually see depreciation as a net positive feature of investing in real estate, as it can often provide tax advantages by allowing cash income to be offset by the non-cash depreciation expenses, and so effectively allow the cash flow income to be received tax deferred.

As an example, assume an investor buys a $1,000,000 investment property using $500,000 cash and the other $500,000 from a 15-year interest-only loan at 4%. Assume the property:

a. Appreciates in market value by 2% per year
b. Has $750,000 of its value in building improvements (vs $250,000 in land) that will be depreciated "straight line" over 30 years for tax purposes ($25,000 per year)
c. Generates a gross rental yield of 5% of market value
d. Incurs cash expenses equal to 20% of gross rental receipts
e. Is allowed to carry forward tax losses indefinitely
f. Is subject to 25% income tax net of expense and losses carried forward

Figure 3.4 shows how the following numbers would add up over several years of the investment:

- The property market value, gross rental income, and cash expenses rise by 2% per year

- The interest expense is 4% of the $500,000 borrowed, reducing both the net cash flow and taxable income, but levering up the total return
- The depreciation is a constant non-cash expense, so initially reduces the taxable income below zero while leaving the investment cash flow positive.
- The pre-tax losses accumulate over the first six years, and the accumulated losses carried forward continue to keep the taxable income at zero for another six years.
- By year 13, the pre-tax income overcomes the accumulated losses, and the investor must start paying income taxes on this investment.
- After 14 years, the property has accumulated depreciation of $350,000, which would be deducted from the cost basis when calculating capital gains taxes. As far removed as it may seem to be from the accounting, a large share of the profits from investing in real estate comes from the tendency of buildings to hold their value or rise in value, rather than depreciate as accounting rules imply. For example, if the property is sold at the end of year 14 for $1,300,000, the capital gains for tax purposes would be ($1,300,000 − ($1,000,000 − $350,000)) = $650,000. Accounting for depreciation vs capital gains this way is how it is often considered simple tax deferral (Fig. 3.4).

Year	Property Market Value	Gross Rental Income	Cash Exp	Interest Exp	Deprec Exp	Pretax Inc	Cumul Pretax	Tax (25%)	Net Cash Flow
0	$ 1,000,000								
1	$ 1,020,000	$ 50,000	$ 10,000	$ 20,000	$ 25,000	$ (5,000)	$ (5,000)	$ -	$ 15,000
2	$ 1,040,400	$ 51,000	$ 10,200	$ 20,000	$ 25,000	$ (4,200)	$ (9,200)	$ -	$ 15,800
3	$ 1,061,208	$ 52,020	$ 10,404	$ 20,000	$ 25,000	$ (3,384)	$(12,584)	$ -	$ 16,616
4	$ 1,082,432	$ 53,060	$ 10,612	$ 20,000	$ 25,000	$ (2,552)	$(15,136)	$ -	$ 17,448
5	$ 1,104,081	$ 54,122	$ 10,824	$ 20,000	$ 25,000	$ (1,703)	$(16,838)	$ -	$ 18,297
6	$ 1,126,162	$ 55,204	$ 11,041	$ 20,000	$ 25,000	$ (837)	$(17,675)	$ -	$ 19,163
7	$ 1,148,686	$ 56,308	$ 11,262	$ 20,000	$ 25,000	$ 46	$(17,629)	$ -	$ 20,046
8	$ 1,171,659	$ 57,434	$ 11,487	$ 20,000	$ 25,000	$ 947	$(16,681)	$ -	$ 20,947
9	$ 1,195,093	$ 58,583	$ 11,717	$ 20,000	$ 25,000	$ 1,866	$(14,815)	$ -	$ 21,866
10	$ 1,218,994	$ 59,755	$ 11,951	$ 20,000	$ 25,000	$ 2,804	$(12,011)	$ -	$ 22,804
11	$ 1,243,374	$ 60,950	$ 12,190	$ 20,000	$ 25,000	$ 3,760	$ (8,251)	$ -	$ 23,760
12	$ 1,268,242	$ 62,169	$ 12,434	$ 20,000	$ 25,000	$ 4,735	$ (3,516)	$ -	$ 24,735
13	$ 1,293,607	$ 63,412	$ 12,682	$ 20,000	$ 25,000	$ 5,730	$ 2,213	$ 553	$ 25,176
14	$ 1,319,479	$ 64,680	$ 12,936	$ 20,000	$ 25,000	$ 6,744		$ 1,686	$ 25,058

Fig. 3.4   Income, depreciation, cash flows, and deferred tax accounting in a real estate investment

Accounting standards and tax laws for depreciation, income taxes, and capital gains taxes of course vary from country to country, and may even depend on how the investment is made (personal vs corporate, etc.), but these guidelines should be a useful starting point for many cases.

3.5   RISKS IN REAL ESTATE INVESTING

Unlike with stocks and bonds, where the most obvious risks are market risk, and similarly interest rate risk, credit risk, and the risk of corporate fraud, liquidity risk tends to be the greater risk facing real estate investors.

On the way in, the great risk is paying too much, as an investor wanting the buy a specific property may have some date to estimate a fair price from some comparable offers or recent transactions, but these will often be distanced by time, location, and/or other factors that would not be different between two of the same bonds or shares of stock. One valuable guideline to remember in investing is that "the best investments are found; the worst investments are sold" and that many of the most obvious and available real estate investments tend to be the ones that are the most heavily marketed and commanding the highest premiums to cover new build costs and agents' commissions.

In other words, *price discovery* is one of the greatest challenges in real estate investing, providing both the risk of paying too much, but also the opportunity to get substantial discounts on assets no one else may be paying attention to at the time.

While owning rental real estate, a landlord also faces the risk that their property may go vacant without being able to find a tenant, or that the tenant may be unable or unwilling to pay the full amount contracted in the lease. The second risk is similar to the default risk when buying a bond, and laws vary from city to city on when and how a tenant can be evicted and how much can be recovered, but eventually the owner should get the property back in some condition and so is not likely to experience as total a loss of principal as a bondholder might. The first risk is more similar to the risk many businesses face in finding and maintain customers at a certain price point. Together, these two risks highlight how real estate is often considered a halfway between stocks and bonds.

On the way out, many investors don't face as much risk in charging too little, as they already know how much they paid and often have an idea of how similar properties have since risen (or fallen) in value since, but bear the full liquidity risk of having to wait a long time before a buyer comes along willing to pay their desired price, and so not being able to convert their property into cash as quickly as with a stock or bond.

Some investors, oddly enough, view this illiquidity as an advantage, saying that not having regularly quoted fluctuating prices makes property investments look far steadier and less volatile. While confusing high liquidity risk with a lack of volatility or market risk is faulty, it has helped real estate investors hold for the long term and avoid many of the behavioral mistakes with cost emotional, ticker-watching traders dearly.

The next section introduces real estate investment trusts (REITs), which wrap an investment in physical real estate in an instrument divisible and tradable as shares of stock.

3.6   REAL ESTATE INVESTMENT TRUSTS (REITS)

A real estate investment trust (REIT) is simply a real estate investment wrapped as stock investors can buy shares in. Modern REITs were initially developed in the United States in the 1960s through rules allowing such companies to pass rental income to their shareholders without having to pay taxes at the corporate level (i.e. no double taxation) provided that certain rules are met. Like stocks of other companies, REITs can either be private or public, and public REITs have an advantage when listed on a stock exchange of providing daily price quotes, liquidity, and ability to invest or divest in increments smaller than $1,000 in a market mostly known for requiring $100,000+ investments with far less liquidity and price transparency. REITs also provide the advantage of institutional financing and management with economies of scale that can end up being far more cost effective than an investment many smaller individual investors would be able to mortgage and manage on their own.

The requirements for a REIT to be a "pass-through" entity exempt from tax on a corporate level often require that a large percentage (say over 90%) of net income or cash flows are passed through in the form of (often fully taxable) dividends, that the REIT primarily own and operate real estate assets, and not be involved in other businesses (including, for example, managing an operating a hotel business in a building it owns).

The United States remains by far the largest listed REIT market in the world, in large part because of the mature tax legislation supporting it, which has also led to a mature institutional investor base owning much of the US commercial real estate. Some numbers on the number and total

Market	Total Market Cap (US$ billion)	Number of Listed REITs
United States	$1,107	230
Japan	$ 100	50
Australia	$ 100	39
Eurozone	$ 90	39
United Kingdom	$ 63	26
Singapore	$ 56	37
Canada	$ 44	31
Hong Kong	$ 31	9

Fig. 3.5   Eight major listed REIT markets by market cap and number of listings

market cap of listed REITs across eight major markets around the world are shown in Fig. 3.5:

As will be discussed in part 4, Japan is understandably a large and increasingly important REIT market, as the advanced, cash-rich, and aging economy has an enormous need for inflation-protected assets yielding 3–4% in rental income after decades of ultra-low interest rates. Hong Kong, on the other hand, should surprise some investors with how few REITs are listed in the world's sixth largest stock exchange and gateway to and from China, especially given how much Chinese investors are known to like investing in property.

These other markets lag the United States not only in size and number of listed REIT issues, but also in variety. US-listed REITs include not only the expected apartment buildings, office blocks, and shopping malls, but also timber farms, self-storage facilities, and hospitals. As mentioned earlier, REITs can finance their ownership in these properties through institutional sized and priced mortgage loans or bond borrowings, and these REITs which own equity stakes in properties are called "equity REITs". There are also a separate class of REITs called mortgage REITs or mREITs, which, instead of owning and renting out buildings, own and collect payments from a pool of mortgage loans, often purchased from and serviced by banks. Mortgage REITs may also be leveraged to multiply the difference between lower, often floating, interest rates at which they can borrow versus the higher yields on the mortgages they invest in, so mREITs often show very high dividend yields compared with equity REITs.

A relatively simple example of a REIT is Champion REIT, listed on the Hong Kong Exchange under symbol "02778". Champion REIT owns three properties: Champion Tower (a prime office building in Central Hong Kong), Langham Place Office Tower, and Langham Place Mall (the latter two in Hong Kong's high-density residential and commercial transport neighborhood of Mong Kok). According to Champion REIT's 2016 annual report, these three properties had a total book value of about HK$67 billion, were partly financed with an HK$11 billion bank loan, and generated about HK$2.5 billion that year in gross rental and management fee income, of which about HK$1.3 billion of which was paid out as dividends to shareholders. As of this writing, Champion REIT is currently trading on the stock exchange at around 60% of its book value (a discount commonly seen across many Asian REITs recently), resulting in a dividend yield to REIT holders significantly higher than rental yields on many physical properties in Hong Kong.

One common misconception about REITs is that they only provide investors with rental income in the form of dividends, and do not provide upside appreciation exposure to rising property prices, but in the case of equity REITs this is usually not true. Shareholders in a REIT that owns a building will participate in their proportionate share of a rising (or falling) market value of that building in the same way as if they owned the building directly. The one additional variable shareholders of listed REITs are exposed to, which may be what causes this confusion, is that listed REITs can be traded on the stock exchange at multiples or fractions of the actual market value of the underlying building, due to factors like overall sentiment and institutional fund flows on the broader stock exchange, and the movement of this multiple may be unrelated (or weakly correlated) to the physical property market.

3.7   WHAT DRIVES RETURNS FROM INVESTING IN PROPERTY

As one of the drivers of inflation is often described as a time when "too many dollars are chasing too few goods", a primary driver in rising rents and property prices is "too many dollars chasing too little land or building space". Like many other prices, rents and property values are, perhaps all too obviously, driven by the economic forces of supply and demand.

On the demand side, some of the factors that tend to drive higher returns to real estate investors include:

- Natural population growth: Through babies being born and growing to an age where they need their own homes, offices, and other spaces.
- Migration into the area: Over the past century, this has mostly been seen in the form of "urbanization", or movement of people from the countryside to cities.
- Accessibility: Related to the effect of migration is how the market for a property is affected by a new road or transit rail line that makes it substantially faster and easier to travel from that property to other highly valuable properties, like the central business district of the nearby city.
- Rising incomes: As consumers and businesses have more money to spend on residential and commercial space, whether through inflation or real income growth, that money will compete to bid up prices.
- Availability and terms of financing: This may be the most powerful and often underestimated factors driving real estate markets. Even assuming all else remains the same, someone who can afford a $1,000/month mortgage payment would get a $209,000 30-year fixed rate mortgage at 4%, but a $237,000 mortgage if the fixed rate falls to 3%, or a 13% higher buying power due simply to lower interest rates.

On the supply side, factors affecting property prices include:

- Government zoning: In many areas, the government may either own or restrict development on undeveloped land, which can limit supply and keep prices high.
- Infrastructure development: Related to government zoning, previously undeveloped or agricultural land may be used to increase the supply of residential or agricultural real estate if roads, water, and electrical infrastructure are built out to it.
- New development/redevelopment: A classic example of increased supply is when a single-family or low-rise building is demolished and

replaced with a high-rise building, allowing many more units to occupy the airspace over the same land area. Subdivision is another form of this, where no new area is created, but one unit is turned into two smaller units that can now serve more consumers.

CHAPTER 4

Equities and Stock Markets

Ask 100 laypeople what first comes to mind when they think of investing, and chances are "stocks" and a "stock market" will be in a plurality of answers. Stocks occupy many of the headlines of financial newspapers and much of the airtime of financial radio and TV shows, and the ups and downs of "the market" seem to get more popular attention than daily moves in interest rates or the price per square foot of office space. Part of this is simply due to the availability of information: stock prices, like interest rates but unlike real estate, are quoted and traded on many times every second during business hours, and unlike most bond trades, stocks provide at least the widespread expectation of being able to double one's investment relatively quickly. Beyond their "excitement" and volatility, stock do play an important role as one of the key asset classes both individual and institutional investors allocate money to for long-term real returns, alongside stocks and real estate.

Investing money into a "box" called "stocks" can be thought of from the outside as somewhat similar to the bond or real estate investments described already: a stock is a piece of a business generating payments of money back to the investor over time that will (hopefully) add up to substantially more than if the same amount of money were invested elsewhere. Businesses have a wide variety of ways and models of how they make money and return it to shareholders, perhaps even more varied than all the different types of real estate, but the basics can be summarized and compared with a few simple steps. This chapter looks at how buying a

© The Author(s) 2018
T. Dennison, *Invest Outside the Box*,
https://doi.org/10.1007/978-981-13-0372-2_4

business differs from buying a bond or a building by looking at different angles and examples of stock investing.

4.1   What Are Stocks, Equity, and the Different Types of Stock Markets?

A simple definition of a stock is that it is simply a share in the ownership of a corporation, partnership, or other legally defined company business structure. Stock investors in a company differ from bond investors in priority (bondholders and other creditors must be paid back before any stockholders) but also in upside (stock investors get to participate in all the profits left over after the creditors are paid back, while the latter only gets back their principal plus interest as promised). Shares of stock of the same type and class are entitled to an equal share of the profits, dividends, and voting rights as other shares of the same class, and these equal ownership rights may be one reason shares of stock are called "equities", but the primary root of the term "equity" refers to how questions of ultimate property ownership were settled in English courts of equity, in contrast to courts of law which handled criminal and other legal categories. The terms, "stocks", "shares", and "equities" are often used interchangeably.

As with bonds or real estate, there are two types of stock markets: the primary market and the secondary market. The primary market is where new shares are issued and sold for the first time to investors, and the money from these investors goes to the company's balance sheet to be invested in the company's business. Primary market equity investment for a start-up private company is about raising money, perhaps initially from friends and family, and then from venture capital investors (more on venture capital in Chap. 6), with the expectation that these investors will eventually enjoy profits many times the amount of their investment. The first time shares of a company are offered to "the public", beyond a limited group of private investors, is called an "initial public offering" or "IPO". One main reason a company goes from being a private investment of a few equity shareholders to a public company, where millions of individual and institutional investors can invest in the company, is to provide its investors the ability to sell their shares in the secondary market described in the next paragraph. Another primary market for shares, not to be confused with a secondary market, are secondary offerings of shares, where a company that has already publicly offered shares through an IPO offers additional shares to raise additional money from investors. Tesla, Inc. has been a high-profile issuer of secondary offerings in the mid-2010s, as the electric car maker has needed extra capital to continue expanding despite losing money on its existing business. Although issuing additional shares increases the size of a company's balance sheet, it also results in dilution as any profits made from the increased total capital base must now be split over a larger number of shares.

A secondary market, unlike a primary market, is where shareholders trade shares with each other, and no money from these trades goes into or out of the company, but rather from the buyer of the shares to the seller of the shares. Secondary markets are valuable in that they provide liquidity to investors who would like to cash out some or all of their investment in a company, while allowing the company to continue its business without liquidating any assets. Just the existence of a secondary market providing this exit option makes it more attractive for many investors to consider investing in businesses where they might not otherwise lock up long-term capital. Secondary markets often, but not always, take place on public stock exchanges, which provide a central meeting point where buyers and sellers can competitively bid on prices for shares, and where these prices can be widely and quickly disseminated to large numbers of current and potential investors. Stock exchanges include traditional trading floors, like those of the New York Stock Exchange ("NYSE"), and electronic inter-dealer quoting systems, like the National Association of Securities Dealers Automated Quotation ("NASDAQ") system. Exchange around the world have mostly shifted to electronic-only trading systems (most recently with the Hong Kong Exchange closing floor trading in late 2017), but exchanges still provide the significant advantage of centralizing buyers and sellers into the competitive market for finding the best bid and offer on any share, without the expensive counterparty-by-counterparty *price discovery* process seen in bonds and real estate.

Shares that publicly trade on stock exchanges have many advantages over the stocks of privately held companies, but in many jurisdictions, opening a company's shares beyond a small, limited group of investors comes with many additional and expensive requirements to publicly file and disclose financial and other information in a timely manner.

4.2   Why Invest in Stocks?

One of the most obvious answers of why someone would buy a stock is because "they expect the stock price will go higher", and so they will be able to sell it for a profit. Long-term investors may point to plenty of long-term data showing that investing in stocks produces a higher absolute rate of return over long periods of time than investing in bonds (though a strategy to outperform stock returns by adding bonds is described at the end of Chap. 7), while short-term stock traders may point to opportunities where they have been able to double the amount invested in a short amount of time. Critical investors should then ask why they would expect a stock to go higher, and factors driving stock prices higher or lower are described in more detail in Sect. 4.4.

Some investors also buy stocks in order to receive dividends at a higher rate than paid on bank deposits or bonds, although finding such higher-yielding stocks has become more difficult in the twenty-first century than in the early twentieth century. As with REITs but unlike with bonds, dividends can rise over time due to inflation or real increases in a business's profitability, making companies with rising dividends a core holding of many "growth and income" funds.

A comprehensive, though perhaps somewhat unconventional, statement of why someone should own stocks is that stocks are a form of insurance against falling behind financially, or insurance against the rest of the world's capital growing at a faster rate than the capital invested in stocks. This is an attractive "asset liability management" or "needs matching" answer in that it justifies the amount invested in stocks as what should double if the world gets twice as wealthy, but also as money they investor shouldn't mind losing half of if the rest of the world suddenly becomes half as wealthy (presumably with prices of real estate and other needs also falling by half or more).

4.3   Share Classes, Preferred Stock, and an Example of Higher Returns on a Bank's Stock

Some companies have more complex equity capital structures with different share classes having different voting, dividend, and other rights. Share classes with different voting rights are often issued to raise capital from new shareholders while allowing the original or other smaller groups of shareholders to own less than 50% of the total equity but over 50% of the voting shares. A blue chip US example is Warren Buffett's Berkshire Hathaway, which in 1996 created a class B share with 1/30th of the ownership stake but 1/200th of the voting power of a class A share, while on the other extreme, Snap Inc. issued only the non-voting class of shares to the public in its 2017 IPO.

In addition to different voting rights, different share classes can also differ in seniority or preference in receiving dividends or offers to buy out the company. These "preferred stocks" or "preference shares" resemble a halfway point between investing in the bonds or common stock of a company, in that preferred equity holders must be paid before common stockholders but after any bond or other debtholders. For example, a 5% preference share with $25 par value is expected to pay a dividend of $1.25 (5% of the face value) per year, but if the company is unable or uninterested in making this dividend payment one year, it can simply cancel or defer the dividend payment without triggering any default, bankruptcy, or other credit events (which would occur if the $25 were true debt), but by not paying the preferred dividend, it means the common stockholders cannot receive any dividends until the preferred stockholders are paid first. Preferred stock can be either "cumulative" (meaning all previously missed dividends must be paid up before any other dividends can continue) or "non-cumulative" (meaning a missed dividend need not be made up). These preference shares can then, like a bond, trade at a premium or discount to their face value, but generally trade at higher yields than the bonds of the same issuer to compensate for the risk of being junior to bondholders (and possibly having to miss dividends even when bondholders get their payments). Preferred stockholders also do not benefit in the same level of upside in the company's growth as do common stockholders, but preferred shares are sometimes convertible into common shares.

Note that the terms "A shares" and "B shares" of companies to denote share classes with different voting and seniority rights are different from what defines "A shares" and "B shares" of Mainland Chinese companies, as will be described in Sect. 10.4 on the Greater China markets.

Continuing the example of the Simple Sample Bank from Sects. 1.3 and 2.8, suppose that in its third year, Simple Sample Bank expands its capital structure by issuing two additional classes of stock: class B shares with limited voting rights and class P 5% non-cumulative, non-convertible preferred shares (Fig. 4.1).

The increased equity capital allowed the bank to substantially increase its deposit base and to invest somewhat more aggressively given the wider buffer the extra equity provides bondholders and depositors against losses on the asset side. In banking terms, the common and preferred equities are considered "Tier 1 capital", and the important "Tier 1 capital ratio", calculated as Tier 1 capital divided by the value of its "risk-weighted assets". For Simple Sample Bank, the risk-weighted assets might, for

Balance sheet at the start of the bank's third year, with three equity share classes

Assets		Liabilities & Equity	
Short Term Loans	$1,000	Deposits from Customers	$3,500
Long-term Loans	$4,000	2% Senior Note	$900
		Equity Capital (5% P)	$200
		Equity Capital (B shares)	$200
		Equity Capital (A shares)	$200
Total Assets:	$5,000	Total Liabilities & Equity:	$5,000

Income Statement for the bank's third year

Interest income on $4,000 of LT loans @5%	$200	(+)
Interest income on $1,000 of ST loans @4%	$40	(+)
Interest expense on $3,500 of deposits @1%	$35	(-)
Interest expense on $900 senior debt @2%	$18	(-)
Provision for loan losses @1%	$50	(-)
Salaries and other expenses	$37	(-)
Tax on $100 pre-tax profit @30%	$30	(-)
Net Income	**$70**	

Return on Equity = $70 Net Income / $600 Equity Capital = 11.6%

Fig. 4.1 Balance sheet and income statement for Simple Sample Bank with three classes of equity

example, weigh the long-term loans at 100% and the short-term loans at 50%, resulting in a risk-weighted assets value of ($4,000 × 100% + $1,000 × 50%) = $4,500, and a Tier 1 capital ratio of $600/$4,500 = 13.3%. This contrasts with the 10.5% ratio for the bank in its first year (when it had no debt or preferred equity), and the 5.7% Tier 1 capital ratio in the second year (when the bank expanded using only debt), and the 6% minimum Tier 1 capital ratio required by Basel III. The use of preferred equity enabled this bank to increase its Tier 1 capital ratio above even its pre-debt level, while retaining a return on equity rate almost as high as in year two.

Although issuing the preferred equity did result in a lower return on equity rate, $200 of the $600 equity capital is in the form of preferred shares that pay out only 5%, or $10, leaving the remaining $60 of net income entirely to the shareholders of the $400 in common equity, raising the return on common equity up to 15%.

So far, it was assumed that all of the net income in the first and second years of the Simple Sample Bank were all paid out as dividends, but shareholders often choose not to pay out some or even all of the profits and instead keep these inside the company as retained earnings. Retained earnings are another form of equity capital that comes not from capital injection investments from shareholders, but by keeping and reinvesting the profits from prior years, and ultimately adds to value to common shareholders above the amount they invested into the company.

When valuing shares of a company, many of the numbers on financial statements are divided out on a per share basis, so that the net income divided by the number of common shares is the "earnings per share" or "EPS", and there is also the net book value of equity per share, cash flow per share, dividend per share, and so on. The per share numbers may be divided by the current number of shares outstanding, or by the total number of shares that would be outstanding assuming all potentially issued shares from warrants, convertible bonds and convertible preferred shares, stock options, and so on to get "fully diluted" per share numbers often reported in annual reports.

The next section describes how dividends, retained earnings, and other per share numbers relate to the value and price of a stock traded on a stock exchange.

4.4   How to Value a Stock, and Understand Why Stock Prices Go Up and Down

Because stock prices are quoted so regularly and their prices so easily available, it is easy to forget that stocks are shares of actual businesses with intrinsic values that may differ significantly from the prices quoted on stock exchanges. A company with rising earnings per share or book value per share may see its shares rise, fall, or trade sideways on the stock exchange, based more on what the highest bidder for those shares on a stock exchange is willing to pay than how any underlying fundamentals of the company may have actually changed.

In theory, the intrinsic value of a stock can be calculated as either:

a. The liquidation value of the assets minus liabilities on the balance sheet, or
b. The certainty equivalent present value of all expected cash flows paid to holders of the stock, first introduced in Sect. 2.8, and illustrated by an example later in this section. This present value approach is also related to the expected return "edge" described in Chap. 7.

In practice, stock prices are often broken down into one or more fundamental per share factors driving their value (e.g. earnings per share, dividend per share, sales or revenue per share) and the multiple the market applies to those factors to get to the stock price. For example, there may be two stocks both reporting $1 in earnings per share over the past year, but one stock may be trading at $10 per share while the other trades at $50 per share. The ratio of the price per share divided by the earnings per share of a stock is known as the price to earnings or P/E ratio, giving these two stocks P/E ratios of 10 and 50, respectively. The P/E ratio is one of the most used (and mis-used) ratios to assess which stocks may be overvalued or undervalued. The P/E ratio is examined in more detail and contrasted with other valuation ratios in Chap. 10 on value investing.

As an example, now that Simple Sample Bank has had three years' track record and reported financials, the numbers from these financial statements can be applied to calculate some values for shares of the bank and come up with prices at which an investor might want to buy or sell these shares.

Approach 1: Liquidation Value As mentioned, one approach to valuing a company is to calculate how much cash all the shareholders would get if they were to liquidate all the assets; pay off all the liabilities, debts, and preferred shareholders; and keep whatever was left over. In the case of a bank or REIT, this may be relatively straightforward, as the loan assets may get relatively competitive bid prices from other banks that will likely be close to book value, while on the other extreme, the intangible assets of a pharmaceutical or software company may get sold at an enormous premium or discount to book value depending on how much a competitor may want the asset or see the motivation of the selling company as an opportunity to get a knockdown price.

Based on the above example, if at the end of year 3 Simple Sample Bank paid out the preferred dividend but retained the remaining $60 in net income as retained earnings, and estimated the loan book could all be sold off at 95% of book value after all expenses, the liquidation value of Simple Sample Bank would be:

Assets
Short Term Loans: $1,000 sold at 95%	$950
Long-term Loans: $4,000 sold at 95%	$3,800
Liquidation Value of Assets:	$4,750

Minus: Liabilities
Deposits from Customers: redeemed at 100%	$3,500
2% Senior Note: Bought back at par	$900
5% Preferred, Redeemed at par	$200
Cost of Redeeming Liabilities:	$4,600

Plus: Retained Earnings at the end of year 3	$60
Net liquidation value to common equity shareholders:	$210

Given that the 5% assumed cost of liquidating the loan portfolio would wipe out almost half the book value of the equity owned by common shareholders, it is unlikely that the shareholders would choose to voluntarily liquidate and realize this loss as long as they had a reasonable expectation that the bank's business would continue profitably, which in this case of this bank would mean the loans being repaid at a rate greater than 95%.

One notable exception for B shareholders and other minority/non-controlling shareholders to watch out for is the risk that the A shareholders (with a controlling majority of voting power) may own another bank (call it "Sweet Deal Bank") to which they would want to fix the sale of Simple Sample Bank's loans at 95% and vote to liquidate in order to sell these assets to Sweet Deal Bank at this lower price. In doing so, they are effectively losing only half as much on the liquidation of Super Simple Bank as they are taking as a below-market discount through Sweet Deal Bank. This is a sinister form of what is called a related party transaction, and effectively transfers value from the pockets of non-controlling shareholders to other pockets of controlling shareholders. Related party transactions are not always bad or detrimental to minority shareholders, but are an important keyword to watch out for on audited financial statements, especially in emerging market countries.

Approach 2: Discounted Cash Flow A second, more general approach to valuing a stock (and arguably most other financial assets) is to add up the present value of all expected future cash flows from the stock. These future cash flows may include regular dividends as well as special one-time cash flows, such as the expected cash acquisition or liquidation price of the business at some future date.

The only real variable in a discounted cash flow analysis is what the certainty equivalent of a stock's future cash flows should be, since the rate at which those future cash flows is already determined by the bootstrapped PV curve calculated in Sect. 2.6. Many analysts may disagree with the idea of using a risk-free rate of interest to value a risky asset like a stock, but alternatives like discounting with a higher, arbitrary IRR means that fudge factors must exist in two variables (the discount rate and what the future cash flows are) rather than in the single variable of certainty equivalent future cash flows. Estimating future cash flows of a stock is certainly neither easy nor unambiguous, but what should be clear is how the market price of a stock implies how high future cash flows must be to justify today's price, and then let each investor decide how much higher than the certainty equivalent value they actually have to be in order to generate a satisfactory rate of return for taking the risk.

As an example, consider the two American car markers: the established incumbent General Motors Company ("GM") and the "new economy" electric car maker Tesla, Inc. These two companies made news in 2017 when the shares of 13-year-old Tesla, which has never made a profit and sold less than 100,000 cars in 2016, surpassed the roughly $60 billion total market value of the 109-year-old GM which sold about 10,000,000 cars the same year, booking over $8 billion in net profits. Below is an example of how the prices of the two stocks, and the certainty equivalent future cash flows they imply, compare for the two companies (Fig. 4.2).

First, General Motors was, at the time of this writing, trading at around $43 per share with a dividend yield of around 3.5% at a time the 30-year US Treasury bond is yielding 2.9%. A dividend yield higher than the yield on "risk-free" government bonds means that the market is already pricing in a risk premium into the stock price and that earnings and dividends do not even need to grow in order to produce bond-beating returns. In this

	Initial Dividend	$	1.50	$	-
	Annual Increase	$	(0.01)	$	1.00
	Residual Value	$	43.00	$	500.00
	CE Present Value:		43.44		359.66

Year	DF	GM	TSLA
1	97.0000%	1.500	0.000
2	94.0900%	1.490	0.000
3	91.2673%	1.480	0.000
4	88.5293%	1.470	0.000
5	85.8734%	1.460	0.000
6	83.2972%	1.450	1.000
7	80.7983%	1.440	2.000
8	78.3743%	1.430	3.000
9	76.0231%	1.420	4.000
10	73.7424%	1.410	5.000
11	71.5301%	1.400	6.000
12	69.3842%	1.390	7.000
13	67.3027%	1.380	8.000
14	65.2836%	1.370	9.000
15	63.3251%	1.360	10.000
16	61.4254%	1.350	11.000
17	59.5826%	1.340	12.000
18	57.7951%	1.330	13.000
19	56.0613%	1.320	14.000
20	54.3794%	1.310	15.000
21	52.7481%	1.300	16.000
22	51.1656%	1.290	17.000
23	49.6306%	1.280	18.000
24	48.1417%	1.270	19.000
25	46.6975%	1.260	20.000
26	45.2965%	1.250	21.000
27	43.9377%	1.240	22.000
28	42.6195%	1.230	23.000
29	41.3409%	1.220	24.000
30	40.1007%	43.000	500.000

Fig. 4.2   DCF valuation of General Motors vs Tesla shares

case, the model shows that GM's "certainty equivalent" dividends could decline by a penny per year over each of the following 30 years, and leave a residual value of the company at about what it trades for today (not even adjusting for inflation), and the shares would still not underperform bonds.

By contrast, Tesla, as of this writing, has yet to book a profit and yet to pay out a dividend, and trades at around $360 per share. Assuming it still takes another several years for Tesla to become profitable enough to pay a dividend, this model assumes the dividend would have to start out at $1 per share in year 6, and then increase by another $1 per share per year without pause over the next 24 years, and leave a company with a residual value of $500 per share by year 30, just for the shares to earn a rate of return equal to that on government bonds. Given the high level of uncertainty about whether Tesla might become the world's dominant auto, battery, or mobility data company, or whether it will go bankrupt before it ever makes a profit, it is worth breaking out Tesla's future into at least three different scenarios for a better idea of what its current stock valuation implies, as shown in the below table (Fig. 4.3).

In the above example, Tesla's future is expanded into three possible scenarios:

a. The company never makes a profit and the stock goes to 0, without even any of the recovery value some of the bondholders might get. This scenario has a present value of 0 and is assigned a probability of 25%.

b. The second scenario is the same baseline scenario used in the certainty equivalent valuation comparison with GM, with the same PV of $359.66 and here assigned a probability of 70%.

c. The final scenario, sometimes called the "lottery ticket", assumes that dividends grow at double the rate of the baseline scenario and that the value of each share in 30 years grows to $4,400 per share.

It is worth highlighting that these are all per share numbers and that Tesla has been raising money by issuing new shares of stock each year in the mid-2010s, while GM has been using its profits to buy back stock at the same time. This means that Tesla's certainty equivalent aggregate numbers would have to be higher while GM's could be lower to produce the same per share returns.

Unlike the liquidation approach, the discounted cash flow makes far more assumptions about what will happen far into the future and, like any model, is more a tool for testing which numbers and assumptions are compatible with today's price rather than a definite calculator of what that price should be.

Total PV:		$355.90		
Scenario PV:		0.000	359.66	2082.74
Probability:		25%	70%	5%
Year	**DF**			
1	97.0000%	0.000	0.000	0.000
2	94.0900%	0.000	0.000	0.000
3	91.2673%	0.000	0.000	0.000
4	88.5293%	0.000	0.000	0.000
5	85.8734%	0.000	0.000	0.000
6	83.2972%	0.000	1.000	2.000
7	80.7983%	0.000	2.000	4.000
8	78.3743%	0.000	3.000	6.000
9	76.0231%	0.000	4.000	8.000
10	73.7424%	0.000	5.000	10.000
11	71.5301%	0.000	6.000	12.000
12	69.3842%	0.000	7.000	14.000
13	67.3027%	0.000	8.000	16.000
14	65.2836%	0.000	9.000	18.000
15	63.3251%	0.000	10.000	20.000
16	61.4254%	0.000	11.000	22.000
17	59.5826%	0.000	12.000	24.000
18	57.7951%	0.000	13.000	26.000
19	56.0613%	0.000	14.000	28.000
20	54.3794%	0.000	15.000	30.000
21	52.7481%	0.000	16.000	32.000
22	51.1656%	0.000	17.000	34.000
23	49.6306%	0.000	18.000	36.000
24	48.1417%	0.000	19.000	38.000
25	46.6975%	0.000	20.000	40.000
26	45.2965%	0.000	21.000	42.000
27	43.9377%	0.000	22.000	44.000
28	42.6195%	0.000	23.000	46.000
29	41.3409%	0.000	24.000	48.000
30	40.1007%	0.000	500.000	4400.000

Fig. 4.3   Tesla certainty equivalent share valuation based on three scenarios

4.5   Stock Investing Outside the Box

Arguably, investing in stocks is one of the most "inside the box" investments most individuals might make. While it is true many individuals do not yet own individual stocks directly, most citizens of developed countries are exposed to stock investments indirectly through mutual funds or variable annuities they may have voluntarily purchased, or through pension plans, options, and stock grants with their employer.

Chapter 8 will describe the many different instruments and vehicles through which investors may indirectly own stocks, while Chap. 7 describe several different strategies and styles that mostly apply to equity investing. To complete this chapter, here is a list of a few ways outside the box thinkers might invest in stocks differently than many of their colleagues:

- By running a full certainty equivalent discounted cash flow model on a stock before buying it. Even many professional fund managers (especially indexers, as described in Chap. 8) do not do this on many stocks they buy.
- By selling a stock short when it appears to be significantly overvalued compared to the likely future cash flows (shorting stocks is one of the strategies covered in Sect. 6.5 on hedge funds).
- By buying a stock that is not a component in a major stock market index (investing in smaller companies is described in Sect. 8.4).
- By buying a stock listed in a foreign country, many of which are described in Chap. 10. The geographic box may still be the one with the strongest walls as of 2018, as investors in many countries have still severely underweight stocks listed outside their home country.

The last listed approach of buying a foreign stock will often require converting one's money into a foreign currency. Foreign currencies and FX markets are the subject of the next chapter.

CHAPTER 5

Currencies and Foreign Exchange Markets

Currencies are not really an asset class of their own but rather the medium through which almost all other current consumption and capital asset investments are denominated. Just as many individuals are familiar with the Australian dollars in their wallet or bank account they use for day-to-day purchases or investments in Australia, they understand that they will need British pounds in their wallet or bank accounts to buy groceries, properties, or stocks in Britain. In Sect. 1.3, cash and currency was described as the liability of a bank, ultimately the central bank or monetary authority in many countries or monetary unions. Cryptocurrencies like Bitcoin and Ethereum, which have been increasingly developed and used in the mid-2010s, are covered separately in Chap. 9, though some of the mechanics described here will also apply to digital currencies.

Modern cash money, as a liabilities of a central bank, often backed by government debt and legal tender for purchases of goods, services, and capital assets, is money simply because governments say it is. This is the root of the term "fiat money" or "fiat currency", from the Latin word "fiat" meaning "let it be done". As artificial as it may seem, this fiat money has provided modern economies a degree of flexibility, lubricant of growth, and safety valve of monetary stimulus that was not possible over the centuries when money was in the form of metal coins whose supply might be entirely unrelated to a country's economy.

For most of human history, there were no central banks buying and selling the bonds of its government to drive the unit value of a national currency. Wealth was generally held in land, sometimes generated through

89
T. Dennison, *Invest Outside the Box*,
https://doi.org/10.1007/978-981-13-0372-2_5

trades and crafts (which sometimes, but rarely, sold investment stakes resembling stocks), and could be traded through coins made of metals like gold, silver, or copper. While merchant banks in Renaissance Italy did use "exchange rates" as a way of financing trade while skirting church prohibitions on lending money and charging an interest rate, these exchange rates more closely resembled interest rates and service fees than the rate between the dollar and the euro today. The US dollar bills were redeemable into gold or silver in some form or another until as recently as 1971, when the United States unilaterally terminated the conversion of the US dollar into gold and broke pegs to other major currencies in place under the Bretton Woods system since 1944. This chapter looks at the risks and opportunities of moving money into the different major currencies issued by the major central banks around the world as of the early twenty-first century.

5.1   MAJOR CURRENCIES AND CATEGORIES OF CURRENCIES

Some currencies, like the US dollar, may need almost no introduction to many readers of this book. Traders identify currencies with three-letter codes, for example, "USD" for the US dollar. In addition to the US dollar, the Australian dollar ("AUD"), British pound sterling ("GBP"), Canadian dollar ("CAD"), euro ("EUR"), Japanese yen ("JPY"), New Zealand dollar ("NZD"), Norwegian krone ("NOK"), Swedish krona ("SEK"), and Swiss franc ("CHF") make up what are often referred to as the "G10 currencies" by many banks and currency traders. "Group of Ten" G10 countries (actually made up of 11 countries, many of which share the euro as a currency) which support the International Monetary Fund (IMF) and which separately count many countries that use the euro, but does include Norway, New Zealand not Australia. These G10 currencies are not only among the most internationally used and heavily traded currencies of the world's currencies but are also free floating currencies, meaning that their exchange rates with other currencies are largely set by market forces with minimal restrictions or direct influence by any government or central bank.

Of the G10 currencies, the euro is unique in not being a national currency but rather the latest and largest monetary union of European countries who have agreed to join their national currencies into a common single currency as their legal tender. Originally, 11 European countries joined this arrangement and locked their exchange rates for conversion to the euro in 1998 at the rates shown in the below figure (Fig. 5.1). As of 2018, the number of official "Eurozone" countries is 19 with the addition of Greece in 2001, followed by Slovenia, Cyprus, Malta, Slovakia, Estonia, Latvia, and Lithuania between 2007 and 2015.

The euro has provided several advantages to its member states, from removing the currency cost and risk component of trade and investment between, say, France and Germany, to making the currency of smaller countries, like Belgium and Slovenia, less of a factor to non-European investors. One trade-off is that by locking in their exchange rates with each other, member countries no longer have the safety valve of devaluation as an option in cases where their real economies are less productive than other parts of the Eurozone. One consequence was highlighted in the Eurozone debt crisis of 2011–2012, when Greece and other Eurozone countries with relatively high interest rates and a history of devaluation of their national currencies had difficulty making payments in euros (which they could not unilaterally devalue) even at the lower interest rates at which they were able to borrow in the common currency. Another noticeable

Fig. 5.1 Conversion rates of the 11 original currencies forming the euro. (Source: ECB https://www.ecb.europa.eu/press/pr/date/1998/html/pr981231_2.en.html)

Currency	Units of national currency for € 1
Belgian franc	40.3399
Deutsche Mark	1.95583
Spanish peseta	166.386
French franc	6.55957
Irish pound	0.787564
Italian lira	1936.27
Luxembourg franc	40.3399
Dutch guilder	2.20371
Austrian schilling	13.7603
Portuguese escudo	200.482
Finnish markka	5.94573

impact of being part of a common currency it could not devalue has been the increased difficulty of, for example, Greek feta cheese to compete with products from Denmark. One statistic highlighting this is the following chart, showing productivity (measured by GDP divided by hours worked) increased by 6% in Denmark between 2006 and 2016 while declining by about 7% in Greece over the same decade (Fig. 5.2).

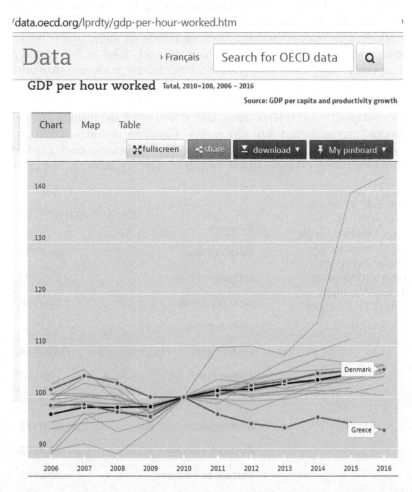

Fig. 5.2   Productivity (GDP per hour worked) in Denmark vs Greece, 2006–2016

Although Denmark is not in the Eurozone and continues to use its own currency, the Danish krone is an example of a *pegged currency*. A pegged currency is one where the exchange rate does not float freely but has been artificially fixed by its central bank at a rate of around 7.4 Danish krone to the euro since the creation of the euro. Pegging a currency around a single exchange rate for long periods of time is an extreme form of managed exchange rates, which many countries prefer to freely floating exchange rates to provide predictability to foreign importers, exporters, and investors and as a way of running monetary policy.

The most widely used managed currency as of 2017 is the Chinese yuan ("CNY") also known as the renminbi ("RMB", Chinese for "People's Money"), which was pegged at around 8.28 yuan to the US dollar from 1997 to 2005 and then managed against a basket of currencies.

To maintain a currency peg, a central bank must maintain reserves of the foreign currency or currencies against which it wishes to manage its currency. For example, if the People's Bank of China ("PBOC", Mainland China's central bank) wanted to maintain the renminbi exchange rate at 6.68 yuan to the US dollar, but high demand for renminbi from the market would put pressure for the currency to strengthen, the PBOC can simply issue and sell an unlimited quantity of renminbi at the 6.68 exchange rate (in other words, the PBOC is buying dollars at a floor price of 6.68 while it is the highest bidder). Conversely, if the rest of the market wants to sell renminbi against the dollar (which would ordinarily weaken China's currency if it were freely floating), the PBOC could buy yuan / sell dollars at the 6.68 exchange rate. The difference between the two sides of this peg is that while the PBOC can create an unlimited quantity of yuan to buy dollars, the PBOC cannot create dollars, and so must have a reserve of dollars to buy back its currency at the desired price. China built these foreign exchange reserves from around US$10 billion in 1990 to almost US$4 trillion in 2014 by running massive current account surpluses (i.e. China has been exporting far more than it imports and earns this difference in foreign currency). Some economists attribute these trade surpluses to China maintaining its currency exchange rate below where the market would otherwise set it, effectively holding down costs of exporters and their products while keeping imports artificially expensive to the Mainland Chinese. In 2015 and 2016, China used some of its foreign exchange reserves to slow the decline in the yuan during those years as the dollar generally strengthened against other currencies (Fig. 5.3).

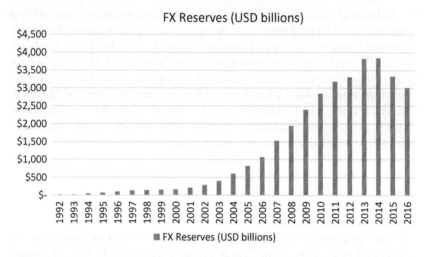

Fig. 5.3   China's foreign exchange reserves, 1992–2016, according to the State Administration of Foreign Exchange (SAFE)

In a mechanism simpler than how the PBOC manages the RMB exchange rate, the Hong Kong Monetary Authority ("HKMA") has maintained a pegged exchange rate of around 7.77 Hong Kong dollars to the US dollar since 1983 by simply holding 100% of the equivalent value of US dollars in reserve for all Hong Kong dollars outstanding. Effectively, the Hong Kong dollar has simply been the US dollar in disguise over the decades surrounding the former British colony's handover back to China, with the option retained by the HKMA to revalue the currency if it were ever deemed necessary or desirable.

If a managed currency is not fully backed by foreign exchange reserves, there is ultimately the risk that speculators may "attack" the currency and break the peg beyond a central bank's ability to support it. One high-profile example of a speculative attack on a currency was that on the Thai baht, which the Bank of Thailand had pegged at around 20 baht to the dollar in the 1960s and 1970s, and at around 25 baht to the dollar through the early to mid-1990s. As he did with the British pound against the German deutsche mark when he "broke the Bank of England" in 1992, billionaire hedge fund manager George Soros estimated the foreign exchange reserves of the Bank of Thailand, and then borrowed enough baht to sell to the Bank of Thailand to deplete those reserves. Without

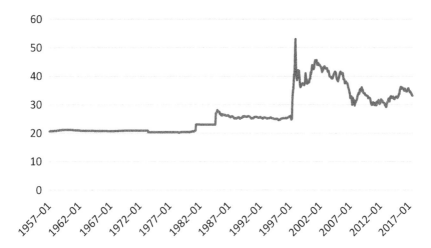

Fig. 5.4   US dollar-Thai baht exchange rate, 1957–2017, according to the Bank for International Settlements (BIS)

reserves, the Bank of Thailand was unable to maintain the peg, and the Thai baht collapsed from 25 until the market settled in the range of 40–50 baht to the dollar, where Soros was able to pack back his borrowed baht at an enormous profit (Fig. 5.4).

Although few foreign exchange trades are as profitable as the most famous ones of George Soros, currency trading remains one of the largest and most profitable markets in the world. The next section explains more generally how foreign exchange markets and currency trading work.

5.2   How Foreign Exchange Markets Work

Like most bonds, but unlike listed stocks, most currency trades are "over the counter", and often direct with a bank. The most basic type of institutional foreign exchange trade is called a *spot FX* transaction, where an exchange rate is executed over the telephone or an electronic trading system, and the two parties settle the currencies into each other's accounts generally two business days after the trade (T+2). One notable exception to T+2 settlement is the US dollar versus the Canadian dollar, where trades have long been settled T+1 due to the proximity of the two countries.

As an example, suppose a customer wanted to trade one million euros (€1,000,000) and saw the prices on the below screen. The bid and offer prices could be read on the screen as "1.077250 bid, 1.077300 offer", or for short "72½ at 73" where the "big figure" (in small print on the screen) of 1.07 is understood by both parties following the market while the "pips" (in large print, representing the last two significant digits of the exchange rate). At this market price, the customer would either pay US$1,077,300 to buy €1,000,000, or sell €1,000,000 to receive US$1,077,250. As with other liquid markets like bonds and stocks, the difference between the bid price and offer price is called "the spread" and is one way banks make money offering currency trading to their customers. Spot FX markets typically trade in sizes on the order of at least US$1 million and are liquid enough to scale up to trades in the billions of dollars with some of the lowest percentage transaction costs of any asset class (Fig. 5.5).

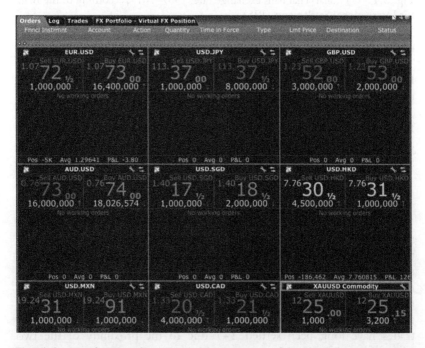

Fig. 5.5 Sample FX trading screen showing prices of the US dollar against eight currencies and gold. (Source of quote screen: Interactive Brokers)

Although currencies trade OTC between banks like bonds, *price discovery* is usually less of an issue, since it is more likely that hundreds of banks will have positions in euros than in a specific treasury bond. That said, without a centralized exchange and equivalent securities regulation covering banks, there is arguably less customer protection against being given a bad rate by their bank.

Note that the convention for quoting currency pairs in FX markets is with the "round number" currency on the left, so that a USD/CAD rate of 1.3321 should be read as "US$1 buys C$1.3321" or "US$1 costs C$1.3321". Another way of looking at this currency pair notation is to think of the currency on the left as being the asset priced in terms of the currency on the right, so that if any USD/XXX exchange rate number goes up, it means the USD is going up and vice versa.

Spot FX trades should not be confused with cash trades, which refer to currency trades which settle sooner than the T+2 or T+1 conventions. Cash trades would include exchanges of dollar bills at the airport (where the spread between bid and offer is far wider than the 0.005% euro vs dollar spread above) but also include larger currency conversions many banks do for customers in their bank accounts.

Given that currencies are used daily by billions of people around the world and that globalization has made international trade and investment an increasingly important share in world trade over the past several decades, it is understandable that the global foreign exchange markets for currencies would be enormous. According to the below charts from the Bank for International Settlements ("BIS"), global foreign exchange markets averaged a daily volume of over US$5 *trillion per day* between 2013 and 2016, of which US$1.5–2 trillion per day was in spot FX trades and the remainder in forwards, swaps, and other types of trades. Given that global economic activity totaled less than US$80 trillion per year (less than about 1/7th the volume of all spot trades or 1/20th the volume of all FX trades), the majority of this measured FX volume is not immediately related to daily commercial or investment transactions but rather includes a large volume of hedging, rebalancing, and speculative trading by both banks and investors (Fig. 5.6).

As of 2016, USD was on one side of about 87% of recorded currency trades globally, and much of the global foreign exchange volume is between USD and EUR, JPY, and GBP. CNY is notably as the most traded emerging market and managed currencies, as well as the major currency with the most significant increase in trading volume between 2013 and

Foreign exchange market turnover by instrument

Net-net basis,[1] daily averages in April

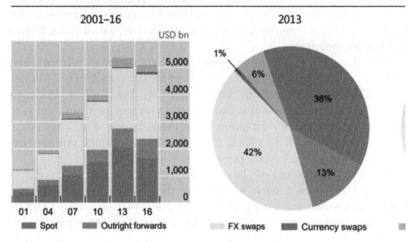

[1] Adjusted for local and cross-border inter-dealer double-counting.

Source: BIS Triennial Central Bank Survey. For additional data by instrument, see Table 1 on page 9.

Fig. 5.6 Average daily volume of foreign exchange spot and derivative markets, 2001–2016, according to the BIS

2016. Note that since there are two currencies in every FX trade, the total percentages of currency trades by currency will add up to 200%, while the shares of currency pair volumes will add up to 100% (Fig. 5.7).

Although spot FX trades are the most basic and foundational of the interbank currency market, it is important to explain the FX forward and currency swap transactions that have also been totaling over US$3 trillion in average daily volume in 2013–2016. The first of these are outright forward trades, which are practically the same as spot trades but with extended settlement dates.

For example, suppose Ellen Exporter has just invoiced a customer in Mexico almost 20 million pesos for an order on which she expects to get paid about one month later. Ellen wants to convert those 20 million pesos into dollars immediately, and is worried about the risk that the peso will decline in value over the one-month period, but does not have the peso yet to be able to settle a spot transaction. Ellen instead calls her bank and

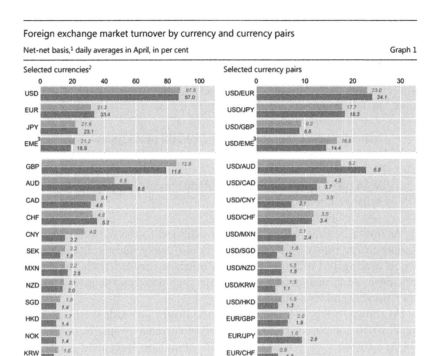

Fig. 5.7 Top 15 most traded currencies and currency pairs in 2013 and 2016, according to BIS

agrees to buy US$1 million at an outright forward price of 19.345 versus the current spot price of 19.2491. She has locked in the price today, and then one month later when her invoice has been paid, she delivers 19,345,000 pesos to the bank in exchange for 1,000,000 dollars.

In the above example, the one-month forward exchange rate is higher than the spot exchange rate, which one would read as saying the US dollar was at a forward premium to the Mexican peso. A forward premium or discount has nothing to do with whether the market thinks a currency will rise or fall over that one-month period (if a trader was confident enough the dollar would rise, she would bid it up now in the spot market rather than pricing it only in the forward), but mostly on the interest rate differential between the two currencies. As of this example, one-month US dollar interest rates were around 1%, while one-month Mexican peso interest rates were around 7%. In other words, from the bank's point of view, the following two are equivalent:

- Exchange US$1,000,000 for 19,249,100 pesos today
- Let the dollars earn 1% interest for one month and let the pesos earn 7% interest for one month, and exchange the ~US$1,000,833 for 19,361,386 pesos at the end of that month, equal to a forward exchange rate of 19.345

As might be expected of a bank, in addition to the bid-offer spread it would charge on spot FX trades, banks also apply slightly different rates when making bid-offer prices for an outright forward trade, effectively pricing in additional profit on the difference between the rates at which they borrow and lend money.

As shown in Fig. 5.4, the volume of outright forwards is still relatively small when compared with the volume of currency swaps. In its simplest form, a currency swap is like a sale and repurchase agreement (or "repo" for short, introduced in Sect. 2.4) on a currency. Continuing with the Mexican peso as an example, suppose Felix Financier is a US-based investor who has a business lending money in Mexico at net interest rates of 12% (500 basis points above the 7% one-month bank rate), while he would only be able to earn about 3% net interest rates in the United States (200bps above the 1% rate). Felix uses the currency swap to hedge his currency risk in his investment as follows:

- Felix sells US$1 million for Mexican pesos at a spot rate of 19.25, and simultaneously buys the $1 million back one month forward, locking in a forward rate of 19.34.
- Felix settles the spot trade, converting US$1,000,000 into 19,250,000 pesos
- Felix invests the pesos in his lending business at 12% for one month, turning the 19,250,000 pesos into 19,442,500 pesos
- Felix settles the forward trade, converting back 19,340,000 of his proceeds back into US$1,000,000, leaving his 102,500 peso profit in pesos for now.

Note that in the above example, Felix's US$1,000,000 principal was 100% hedged back into dollars, and would not be exposed to any rise or fall in the dollar-peso exchange rate over the course of the month, but in this case the 102,500 peso interest profit was not hedged. If the peso were to fall 10% against the dollar over the course of this month (an extreme move in major currency markets), his peso profit would be about US$500 less valuable in dollar terms, compared with the risk that Felix would have lost over US$100,000 in this case if he had not hedged.

Currency swaps can be far longer in tenor and structured to more closely match the cash flows of individual bonds, loans, or portfolios, but in general should be seen as a standard way of hedging currency risk for longer-dated assets. Strategies for deciding whether or not to hedge currency risk for riskier assets, like stocks or real estate, will be covered in Sect. 5.4, after the next section addresses some of the drivers of why currencies go up and down in the markets.

5.3 What Drives Currency Exchange Rates Up and Down

Like other prices, currency exchange rates are set by supply and demand. Unlike many other prices, foreign exchange markets, even those of freely floating currencies, are heavily influenced by their issuing central banks, whose policy goals are often to keep the prices of goods and services denominated in their currency relatively stable and attractive for consumers to keep the economy going. In other words, central banks are some of the biggest players in currency markets, but their goals in trading in the interest rate and currency markets are policies other than to maximize their own profits. This can drive returns in carry and momentum trades, to be described in more detail in the next sub-section.

Back to the basics of supply and demand, if the supply of a currency rises faster than the supply of worthwhile goods, services, and assets to spend that currency on, the currency should be expected to decline in value. This is known by American economists as "too many dollars chasing too few goods", and results in inflation domestically and currency devaluation internationally. Conversely, if an economy is especially productive and can supply more goods and services than there is currency to buy them "too many goods chased by not enough dollars", the prices of those goods and services will decline against the currency, which is seen as price deflation domestically and as currency appreciation internationally. Although there are many more economic details one can dive into, the long-term "purchasing power parity" value of a currency is as simple as the balance between supply and demand of a currency and what it can buy.

One indicator of the relative productivity of two economies is their relative real interest rates, that is, the currency's interest rates minus the rate of inflation. In an economy where there are so many productive investments producing high real rates of return, businesses will have high levels of demand to borrow money, even a few percentage points above inflation. Lenders, domestic and foreign, will be attracted by these high real interest rates, and the latter will tend to bid up the currency when making unhedged investments (hedging, as seen in the previous section, can wipe out the interest rate differential, so investors attracted to the higher real interest rate may choose not to hedge). Unhedged flows into higher-yielding currencies are called "carry trades" (described in more detail in the next sub-section), and have the effect of strengthening higher-yielding currencies in the short run. On the other hand, a weak economy with a dearth of productive investments will see little demand from borrowers. In such an environment, the central bank may see the need to push interest rates well below the rate of inflation to both encourage more borrowing and to make it less attractive to keep money in low-yield deposits rather than riskier investments that might at least keep pace with or outpace inflation.

An extreme example that may illustrate the point of dollars vs goods and productivity is to look not at overall inflation and price levels but to take the specific example of US dollars versus television sets. When RCA introduced a 15-inch color television set to the US market in 1954, it was the size of a small refrigerator and cost $1,000. As the below ad shows, by 1960, a 21-inch color television that could sit on a table cost only $495. As of this writing in 2017, the price of a 40-inch 1080p high-definition flat-screen smart LED TV that can access literally millions of videos the 1960s viewer could only dream of costs less than $270 on Amazon.com. Note that these prices have **not** been adjusted for inflation but rather show, in nominal terms, how tremendous productivity and technological advancements in televisions have made the dollar appreciate against the price of televisions. By contrast, the dollar has declined in value against the price of services like healthcare and higher education, especially in the United States (Fig. 5.8).

Now twice the picture at half the cost! Six years ago, a Color TV set with a 9 x12-inch picture cost $1,000. Today, 260-sq. in. big-screen RCA Victor Color TV's start as low as $495. Ask your dealer for a demonstration and see the wonderful difference that today's Color TV makes.

Full-year warranty on all parts and tubes! When you buy your RCA Victor Color TV, you get a one-year warranty on all parts, excluding only labor. Everything in the set, from picture tube on down, is warranted for 12 months . . . proof that RCA Victor Color TV is dependable!

Service is no problem. See your local dealer, serviceman, or nearest RCA Service Co. office. Nationally advertised list price shown, optional with dealer —UHF optional, extra. Price, specifications subject to change without notice.

Fig. 5.8   RCA ad from 1960 showing rising quality and falling prices of color television sets. (Ad source: http://www.tvhistory.tv/tv-prices.htm)

For some historical perspective on the difference exchange rates can make over the long term, it can be worth looking at three different sets of long-term currency charts: those of currencies that have appreciated, those that have depreciated, and those that have remained roughly range bound since 1971. 1971 marks the beginning of the modern currency era, after the 1944–1971 period where major currencies around the world were effectively locked into fixed exchange rates with the US dollar, which in turn was pegged to gold (discussed in the next chapter) at a price of $35 per ounce through the "Bretton Woods" system, signed by the allies near the end of World War II at the Mount Washington Hotel in Bretton

Woods, New Hampshire, in the United States. Some notable exchange rates during the Bretton Woods era include the Japanese yen at 360 to the dollar (a post-war exchange rate supposedly set in reference to the circular sun on the Japanese flag), the Swiss franc at 4 to the dollar, and one British pound costing around US$2.40.

As the first long-term chart shows, the Japanese yen, the Singapore dollar, and the Swiss franc are three currencies that have significantly appreciated against the US dollar since 1971. As with the television example, this appreciation of the first two should not be surprising given how dramatically the economies of Japan and Singapore have developed since the early 1970s, but Swiss appreciation arguably was driven more by the supply side and the constraint of the Swiss National Bank over its monetary policy. By contrast, the Australian dollar, the British pound, and the Canadian dollar have traded relatively sideways against the US dollar in the same 46-year period with a slight depreciation trend that would have averaged less than 2% per year, which is less than the month-to-month volatility of many of these currencies. Comparing the relative size of the trend drivers versus the noise and fluctuations in exchange rates can be done with the same mean-variance technique explained for other assets in Chap. 7 (Fig. 5.9).

Another view focused on a smaller and more interconnected region is to look at the relative appreciation/depreciation of the European curren-

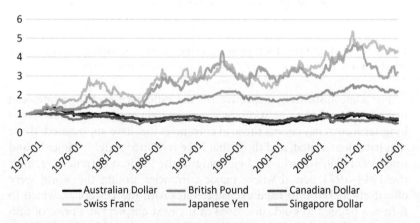

Fig. 5.9 Appreciation and depreciation of six major currencies vs USD, 1971–2017

cies that joined the euro in 1998. Since 1998, currency traders have had to focus more on how the euro itself moves against other currencies, but the trends showing the relative productivity of, say, Germany and France versus Spain and Italy in the exchange rates of the mark and franc versus peseta and lira before the euro have persisted in the relative credit spreads of these same four countries' debt denominated in euros. When combined into the single currency (where sometimes the euro is considered the "deutsche mark in disguise"), the euro itself looks more like one of the range-bound currencies described at the end of the previous paragraph.

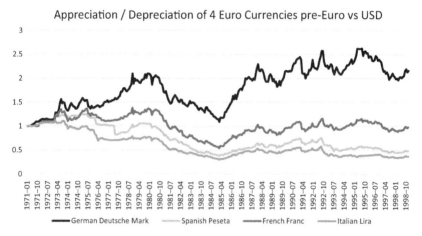

Appreciation / Depreciation of 4 Euro Currencies pre-Euro vs USD

Last but not least, it is important to look at the effect of long-term depreciation in the currencies of emerging markets whose monetary policy has not been as constrained as Singapore's (when it was still considered an emerging market). Showing the different orders of magnitude of long-term depreciation across major emerging market currencies is most dramatic on a logarithmic chart like the one below which shows:

- The Chinese yuan (renminbi) fell to about ¼ of its 1971 value by 1994, but since has been pegged and managed to moderately appreciate, as described earlier.
- The Indian rupee and Philippine peso have declined to about 1/16th of their 1957 value and 1/8th of their 1971 value. Not being fully locked into the Bretton Woods system, the Philippines

faced a currency shock which cut the value of its currency in half between 1960 and 1962, while India faced a similar shock in 1966.

- The South African rand has fallen to about 1/16th of its 1971 value and in the twenty-first century has been largely driven by booms and busts in commodity prices.
- The Mexican peso faced far more severe devaluation in the 1980s and 1990s, after defaulting on its bonds in 1982. The devaluation led to the redenomination of the peso in 1993 where one "new peso" ("MXN") replaced 1,000 "old pesos" ("MXP").

Redenomination of severely devalued currencies, like the Mexican peso did in 1993, has been seen across many emerging market currencies. Two redenominations which may seem more "in the past" include Taiwan (whose current currency is called the "New Taiwan Dollar" or "NT$" since 1949, with symbol "TWD") and Israel (the "new Israeli shekel" replaced the old shekel 1,000:1 in 1986 after a period of hyperinflation, known as "NIS" domestically but as "ILS" internationally). As a more extreme example, Turkey redenominated the Turkish lira at a rate of 1,000,000 old lira equal to 1 new Turkish lira (the new symbol "TRY" ending with the first letter of "yeni", the Turkish word for "new"), reflecting a post-1971 devaluation of over 1,000,0000:1, which would have been off this next chart. Even further off the chart, Brazil's successive currencies would have totaled a cumulative devaluation of about 1,000,000,000,000: 1 (i.e. one trillion to one) since 1971, closer to the order of magnitude of hyper-devaluation that Weimar Germany or early twenty-first-century Zimbabwe experienced in shorter periods of time (Fig. 5.10).

While the above examples may seem like extreme, and even almost comic, examples of hyperinflation and devaluation, the loss of value in these currencies was very real to wealthy and middle-class residents of these countries. Living with this kind of currency devaluation encourages habits of not saving money in the home currency, of spending money as soon as you get it, and to keep as much wealth as possible in hard assets or outside the country. As an Argentine once said: "the smart money is either hidden in the mattress, or in Miami".

At a slower pace, one might also point out that in overall inflation-adjusted terms, the US dollar has lost about 99% of its purchasing power in the first 100 years following the founding of the Federal Reserve and the 1971 severing of any linkage between the dollar and gold prices.

Depreciation of 5 Emerging Market Currencies, 1971–2017

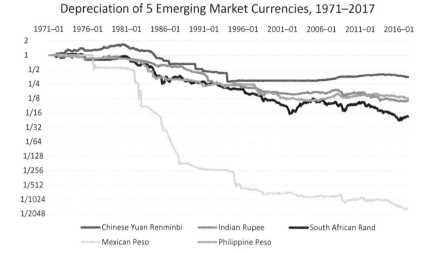

Fig. 5.10   Long-term depreciation of five emerging market currencies

Losing 99% of one's purchasing power over a century is indeed less dramatic than losing the same over a decade, but should be a reminder that whatever currency an investor is based in, the greatest long-term risk is not day-to-day fluctuations, but ensuring whatever money is returned is worth enough to buy real goods, services, and assets.

The next section describes a few strategies investors can use to approach currency markets, from hedging to carry and momentum trades.

5.4   How Investors Use Currency Markets and Currency Futures: Hedging, Carry and Momentum Trades

As mentioned at the beginning of this chapter, currencies are not really an asset class of their own, so one does not really "invest in a currency" but rather in assets denominated in a foreign currency that have currency exposure. As a simplest example, a Belgian trader who converts €125,000 into US$146,325 with the view that the dollar will rise (and equally, the euro will fall) over the next one month will have to keep the dollars in some form of dollar-denominated asset, whether treasury bills or even a USD bank account. In this case, the trader is earning interest in dollars, and either forgoing or paying interest in euros, also described as being "long dollar" and "short euro".

There is a sizeable industry of retail FX brokers promoting the ease and scalability of trading in a liquid 24/7 market where the brokers can offer leverage of 100× or more the amount invested, but statistics **consistently show that the majority of this category of retail FX traders lost money**. One feature some find attractive about FX markets is that they are international and relatively lightly regulated, with no prospectuses, corporate actions, or other company filings to file or follow, and many securities regulations do not apply. For example, in Hong Kong, non-leveraged currency trading can be offered by any banks or holders of simple money changer licenses, while leveraged foreign exchange is regulated as "Type 3" activity by the Securities and Futures Commission ("SFC").

This chapter is not focused on speculative retail FX trading, but rather on ways more moderate and long-term investors might use currency markets to improve returns and manage risk. Two widely known strategies for choosing which currencies to allocate long and short positions to are "carry trades" and "momentum trades".

An FX carry trade is when a relatively low interest rate currency is borrowed or sold to buy a higher interest rate currency, similar to the bond carry trade of borrowing at low short-term interest rates to lend at higher long-term rates. For example, the above investor may have chosen to convert euros into dollars because short-term euro-denominated deposits and treasury bills at the time paid 0% interest, while US dollar deposits and T-bills at least pay around 1%. For an even wider spread, the investor could instead choose to convert the money into Mexican pesos and earn Mexico's even higher 7% interest rates, though higher-yielding currencies are widely expected to have a higher risk of depreciation. While retail or small company traders may not be able to borrow euros at close to 0%, or get similarly good pricing on an FX forward contract from a bank, the currency futures markets offer institutional pricing on the interest rate differentials of currencies for trades on the order of US$50,000–$150,000. For example, below is a sample screenshot of quotes for the Chicago Mercantile Exchange ("CME") euro currency futures, traded electronically on the system "Globex". The above Belgian investor, instead of converting the €125,000 cash into US dollars today, could instead sell one December 2017 futures contract to lock in an exchange rate 39 pips higher (1.1782 in December vs 1.1743 for October), effectively earning the higher US dollar interest rate through a higher futures exchange rate, as with the forward contract.

← → ○ ⌂   cmegroup.com/trading/fx/g10/euro-fx.html

⊕ CME Group   Trading   Clearing   Regulation   Data   Technology   Education

Month	Options	Charts	Last	Change	Prior Settle	Open	High	Low	Volume	Hi / Low Limit	Updated
OCT 2017	OPT	ⅲ	1.1743	+0.0005	1.1738	1.1742	1.1745	1.1742	7	1.2138 / 1.1338	17:40:34 CT 08 Oct 2017
NOV 2017	OPT	ⅲ	-	-	1.17555	-	-	-	0	1.21555 / 1.13555	17:15:49 CT 08 Oct 2017
DEC 2017	OPT	ⅲ	1.17825	+0.0005	1.17775	1.1779	1.1785	1.17765	2,118	1.21775 / 1.13775	17:51:51 CT 08 Oct 2017
JAN 2018	OPT	ⅲ	1.18065	+0.00055	1.1801	1.18065	1.18065	1.18065	30	1.2201 / 1.1401	17:25:42 CT 08 Oct 2017

Carry trades are profitable if the exchange rate does not move, or strengthens in favor of the higher-yielding currency (in the above case, the dollar versus the euro), and only lose money if the higher-yielding currency weakens by more than the interest rate differential. There are three historical currency carry trades worth reflecting on as examples: the Thai baht carry rate of the 1990s, the yen carry trade of the first decade of the 2000s, and the Swiss franc mortgages popular in Hungary over the same decade.

Before the Asian Financial Crisis of 1997, a widely performed carry trade was to borrow US dollars at relatively low interest rates and then convert and invest in higher-yielding Southeast Asian currencies like the Thai baht. These carry trades were seen as being safely supported by the official currency pegs at the time, but as with many financial crises, complacency led to unsustainable debt levels, leading to a crash when the debt burden became excessive.

In the first decade of the 2000s, another popular carry trade started in Asia when Japanese yen interest rates fell to around 0% while short-term rates in the United States, the United Kingdom, and Australia averaged around 4–6%, and as high as around 12–19% in currencies like the Brazilian real. This became known as the "yen carry trade", and was profitable as long as the yen remained weak, but resulted in huge losses when the global financial crisis of 2008–2009 drove many Japanese investors to sell foreign assets and repatriate yen, driving the yen higher and forcing more unwinds of the carry trade, one example of a momentum trade described later in this chapter.

Borrowing money at a lower interest rate to finance an asset denominated in a higher interest rate currency, such as a foreign currency mortgage loan on a house, is also a form of FX carry trade. In the same 2000–2008 period as the yen carry trade, it was popular for Hungarian home buyers to take out mortgages denominated in Swiss francs rather than at much higher Hungarian forint ("HUF") interest rates. These saved Hungarian homeowners thousands of francs, or hundreds of thousands of forint per year in interest costs as long as the CHF/HUF exchange rate remained stable, but proved disastrous when CHF/HUF appreciated from 143 forint to the franc to 203 forint to the franc during the 2008–2009 GFC. A Hungarian buying a HUF 17,000,000 house with a CHF 100,000 mortgage (initially providing HUF 14.3 million in financing toward the house) in early 2009 would have had a mortgage debt costing 20% more than the value of the house, in many cases resulting in default or increased financial distress.

On average, carry trades have historically provided a little bit of a profitable edge, but this edge is relatively small compared to the volatility of most currency pairs. For example, the following chart is a scatterplot of the monthly interest rate differential (x-axis) versus the monthly price return (y-axis) of a long JPY/short USD position (Fig. 5.11).

The above chart shows that there is a large amount of month-to-month noise in many FX carry trades, but carry trades are generally of interest to investors willing to hold them over longer periods of time to ride out the noise and earn the interest rate differential. The following chart shows what the cumulative total return would have been from borrowing JPY at short-term interest rates and investing in USD at short-term rates (Fig. 5.12).

As with many financial charts, the above chart of the carry trade shows a tantalizing pattern of trends where the trade seems to consistently make or lose money over periods often exceeding a year or more. This leads to a second popular FX strategy known as a momentum trade. Momentum trades basically buy what is going up and sell what is going down, with maxims like "the trend is your friend". Momentum trades arguably work better in markets like foreign exchange, where major price setters include central banks that are not profit maximizing and may implement policy rate pressure in one direction over months or years, than in securities markets.

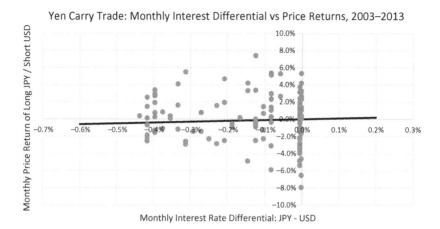

Fig. 5.11   Scatterplot of monthly interest rate differential vs price return of the yen carry trade, 2003–2013. (Data from BIS)

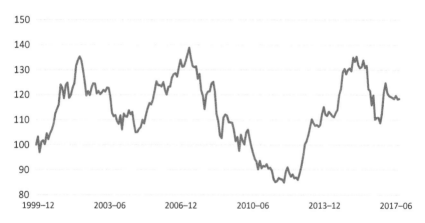

Fig. 5.12   Cumulative return of the USD/JPY carry trade, 2000–2017. (Data from BIS)

There are many different ways of designing a momentum trading strategy, but the following chart shows one of the simplest based on a simple momentum modification of the yen carry trade shown above. The below chart plots the total return of a momentum strategy based on a simple "moving average" rule: if USD/JPY is higher than its average value over the preceding three or six months, go long USD/short JPY, otherwise go short USD/long JPY (Fig. 5.13).

The above charts would seem to show that a momentum strategy can complement a carry trade, but also depends highly on how the momentum signal is defined.

One big advantage of currencies being a "meta-asset" in which other investment assets are denominated is that any currency trading strategy can be done as an "overlay" on top of any investment made in that foreign currency. For example, a US-based investor wanting to buy Japanese stocks has several different choices on how to do this:

A. Buy a USD-denominated Japan stock fund or ETF, most of which are unhedged.
B. Convert USD into JPY and buy stocks directly on the Tokyo Stock Exchange ("TSE").
C. Convert and buy stocks as in (B), then sell JPY/USD currency futures.
D. Borrow JPY on margin to buy stocks on the TSE without converting any currency.
E. Buy Nikkei futures, maintaining minimal margin requirements and converting futures P&L promptly into dollars.

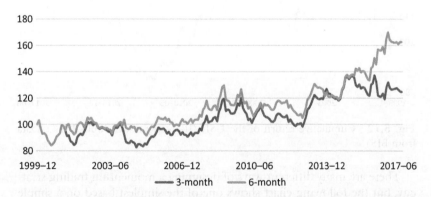

Fig. 5.13   Total return of USD/JPY momentum strategies based on three- and six-month moving averages. (Data from BIS)

Choices (A) and (B) remain 100% exposed to the ups and downs of the Japanese yen against the US dollar. Strategy (C) is the most direct hedge of this currency risk, since it locks in the rate at which at least a notional amount of US dollars will be bought back for yen.

Approach (D) may be a less obvious way to invest in Japanese stocks with minimal currency exposure but is just as simple if not simpler than the convert-and-hedge technique. Buy financing JPY-denominated stock with a JPY-denominated margin loan, the notional amount and currency of an asset with its liability are initially 100% matched, and the investor is mostly exposed to whether the stock is profitable in JPY rather than to whether USD/JPY goes up or down. Unless the margin loan is continuously refinanced, any profits or losses will remain yen denominated and exposed to whatever exchange rate those yen will eventually be converted back into dollars, but as in the case of Felix's financing business earlier in this chapter, the residual risk is a tiny fraction of the overall FX risk if left unhedged.

Buying Nikkei futures, as in choice (E), is just as simple a way to trade the Japanese equity index with minimal currency exposure. As with approach (D), an investor wanting exposure to 1 Nikkei futures contract (with a notional value of ¥500 × ~20,000 index points = ¥10,000,000 or around US$100,000) could keep most of their US$100,000 in US dollars, and only convert/maintain yen margin as needed. These futures contracts make or lose money as the Nikkei 225 stock index (described in both Sect. 8.1 and 10.3) goes up or down, and only the yen margin or P&L is directly exposed to FX risk in dollar terms.

For many investors, simply making an investment in a foreign currency is already a step outside the box, and this chapter has shown how overlay and hedging strategies make currencies a more strategic part of an investor's overall allocation. In addition, there are macro-oriented hedge fund strategies, like those mentioned earlier of billionaire George Soros, and it is likely that currency strategies ranging from simple to Soros may soon become available in a portable overlay form on top of other stock and bond portfolios.

CHAPTER 6

Alternative Assets from Gold, Commodities, Art, Fine Wine, and Other Collectibles to Private Equity and Hedge Funds

"Alternative investments" generally refer to the "everything else" boxes of investments that are left out of one of the traditional boxes of stocks, bonds, and real estate purchased by "mainstream" mutual funds. Perhaps contrary to the name, many of the investments twenty-first-century advisors commonly consider "alternatives" are actually far older than the modern form of listed stocks or traded bonds. Consider the ancient history of investing in gold coins or art, private investments in shipping ventures, or Lloyd's early insurance contracts.

There is no universally agreed-upon definition of what investments go into the "traditional" box and which should go into the "alternatives" box, but as a rough rule of thumb, alternative assets are generally more difficult to purchase, more difficult to sell, and often limited to wealthier investors (giving them a degree of "prestige value"). In general, alternative assets are those that cannot be purchased by mainstream retail mutual and are traded "by appointment" rather than traded "on screens" like stocks and bonds. Gold and other commodities have somewhat straddled this line with the launch of ETFs holding physical gold or rules-based commodity futures trading strategies since 2004, but those that directly buy gold coins or artwork do not. Many advisors classify private equity and hedge funds as "alternatives", even those that invest in traditional stock and bond assets, more because of how they are bought, sold, and regulated and by their ability to invest in assets and strategies traditional mutual funds cannot. This chapter also introduces listed investment vehicles including MLPs and BDCs that are publicly accessible and tradable like

© The Author(s) 2018   115
T. Dennison, *Invest Outside the Box*,
https://doi.org/10.1007/978-981-13-0372-2_6

stocks, though sometimes considered "alternatives" as they are rarely included in mainstream indices and mutual funds.

Gold and silver, despite being traditional forms of money and coinage and trusted as a store of value largely due to their continuous use as such for centuries, are widely considered "alternative assets" because holding money in them is seen as an alternative keeping money in mainstream banking and brokerage institutions. Committing capital to natural gas, nickel, corn, or lean hogs, purely to get paid to take price risk rather than for any need of the actual commodity, would need even less argument to be classified as "alternative". Similarly, investing in contemporary Chinese paintings, rare whiskeys, or antique cars with the goal of earning higher returns uncorrelated to stock markets is well outside the box of most investors.

Many of the alternative assets listed in this chapter will have similar *price discovery* challenges and opportunities like physical real estate (described in Chap. 3), with the notable exception of exchange-traded commodity futures and the listed MLPs, BDCs, and SPACs in Sect. 6.6.

After introducing these asset classes, this chapter concludes with the diversification value of alternative assets, introducing the need for the risk-return analysis techniques of the next chapter.

6.1   GOLD, SILVER, AND PRECIOUS METALS

Gold has historically been used as a currency, and, like a currency, may seem like a place to keep money, but is not really an investment in itself. Unlike a stock, bond, farm, or rental property, a gold coin pays no dividend or interest, and you can't grow food on it or live in it. Rather, gold imposes regular costs for storage and security, as do investments in art, wine, and other collectibles described later in this chapter, costs cash to store and secure. $1,000 invested in General Electric stock in 1900 (eight years after its founding) would have generated a century's worth of growing dividends and stock splits, and now be a share in a much larger company expanded across many more business lines and geographic regions. $1,000 used to buy a New York City apartment in 1900 would have incurred maintenance and rebuilding costs a fraction of what it would have generated in rental income, and would now be a multi-million-dollar unit in a far wealthier and dynamic neighborhood. $1,000 invested in about 48 ounces of gold in 1900 (at the gold standard price of $20.67/ounce, at which price it was confiscated from US citizens by Franklin Delano Roosevelt's government in 1934) would have incurred a century's worth of storage and security costs, but produced no income, and still be the same 48 ounces of gold over a century later. Gold may roughly preserve purchasing power over long periods of time (the 60-fold rise in gold prices over the past century would have covered most of the 50–100× rise in consumer prices over the same period), but it does so with significant volatility in the short term.

Gold's effectiveness as an inflation hedge varies significantly from country to country. Asia seems to especially like gold, as can be seen by the percentage of Hong Kong high street shops that are jewelers or Indian advertising billboards for gold retailers, and have long used it as one of the main alternatives to real estate as a place to store, preserve, and transfer wealth. The below chart compares the "real gold price" in the United States, India, Japan, Malaysia, and Singapore, adjusting gold prices in dollars, rupees, yen, ringgit, and Singapore dollars against the IMF-reported inflation statistics (Fig. 6.1).

Gold's main attraction is that, like land, but unlike fiat currencies printed by central banks, its supply is relatively fixed. Gold is a metal that does not react chemically, is easy to sub-divide, and large amounts of value can be transported in a relatively compact space. As element 79 on the periodic table, the only way to "make" more gold from other cheaper elements would be through a nuclear reaction which was impossible for alchemists and still not economical with early twenty-first-century technology. Gold continues to be discovered and extracted from mines, but

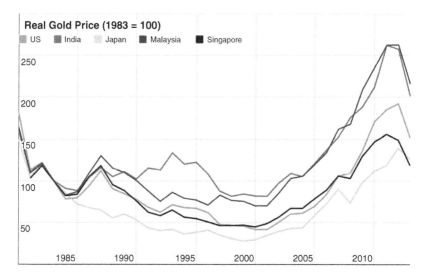

Fig. 6.1 Real gold prices in US dollars vs four Asian currencies

the cost of finding and extracting new gold has also kept up with gold prices, allowing miners a modest profit margin.

"Investment grade" gold or "fine gold" is usually 99.9% ("three nines" or "999") or 99.99% ("four nines" or "999.9") pure gold, with the remaining 0.01–0.1% in other impurities. Many investors purchase gold as bars or coins certified by a government or other gold authority to their weight and purity, and then store these in bank safety deposit boxes or with other vault and security providers. Some of the most internationally known gold coins include the American gold eagle, the Canadian maple leaf, and the South African Krugerrand.

Jewelry is another, often cost-ineffective, way to buy and hold value in gold. As the below two figures show, over half of global gold demand is for jewelry production, and over half of global demand is from two countries: China and India. Chinese jewelry is generally made with 999 gold and sold by weight plus a design charge. Indian jewelers prefer gold that is only 91.6% pure ("916") to increase the metal's hardness and enable designs more intricate than can be done with soft 999 gold. A large percentage of western gold jewelry is made of metal that is less than 75% gold (known as "18 karat" on the 24-karat system), and, despite what late night television commercials might imply, would have most of their value lost to

Table 3: Gold supply and demand World Gold Council presentation

	2014	2015	Q3'14	Q4'14	Q1'15	Q2'15	Q3'15	Q4'15	Q1'16	Q2'16	Q2'16 vs Q2'15 % change
Supply											
Mine production	3,152.6	3,221.4	831.0	845.2	730.0	789.6	850.5	851.2	750.7	786.9	→ 0
Net producer hedging	104.5	13.5	-8.3	50.6	-2.4	-15.2	14.4	16.7	52.7	30.0	-
Total mine supply	3,257.0	3,234.9	822.7	895.8	727.6	774.4	864.9	868.0	803.3	816.9	↑ 5
Recycled gold	1,202.1	1,123.2	274.4	270.0	358.6	267.4	260.7	236.5	369.0	327.7	↑ 23
Total supply	4,459.2	4,358.0	1,097.1	1,165.7	1,086.1	1,041.7	1,125.7	1,104.5	1,162.3	1,144.6	↑ 10
Demand											
Fabrication – Jewellery[1]	2,502.7	2,438.7	639.5	648.6	606.1	542.5	662.6	625.4	476.4	448.3	↓ -17
Fabrication – Technology	347.9	332.9	89.3	89.3	83.1	83.3	82.7	83.8	80.3	80.9	↓ -3
Sub-total above fabrication	2,850.6	2,771.6	728.8	737.8	691.2	625.9	745.3	709.2	555.8	529.2	↓ -15
Total bar and coin demand	1,037.7	1,049.8	233.0	275.4	257.3	209.1	294.9	288.5	273.1	211.6	↑ 1
ETFs and similar products[2]	-183.8	-128.3	-40.9	-92.1	25.6	-23.0	-63.4	-87.6	342.5	236.8	- -
Central banks and other inst.[3]	583.9	566.7	174.9	133.9	112.4	127.3	168.0	159.0	108.2	76.9	↓ -40
Gold demand	4,288.3	4,259.8	1,095.8	1,055.1	1,086.6	939.2	1,144.7	1,069.2	1,279.5	1,054.5	↑ 12
Surplus/Deficit[4]	170.8	98.2	1.3	110.6	-0.5	102.5	-19.1	15.3	-117.2	90.1	↓ -12
Total demand	4,459.2	4,358.0	1,097.1	1,165.7	1,086.1	1,041.7	1,125.7	1,104.5	1,162.3	1,144.6	↑ 10
LBMA Gold Price, US$/oz	1,266.4	1,160.06	1,281.94	1,201.4	1,218.45	1,192.35	1,124.31	1,106.45	1,182.56	1,259.62	↑ 6

1 For an explanation of jewellery fabrication, please see the *Notes and definitions*.
2 For a listing of the Exchange Traded Funds and similar products, please see the *Notes and definitions*.
3 Excluding any delta hedging of central bank options.
4 For an explanation of Surplus/Deficit, please see *Notes and definitions*.

Fig. 6.2   Global supply and demand for gold by type

Table 7: Consumer demand in selected countries (tonnes)

	2015	Q2'15	Q3'15	Q4'15	Q1'16	Q2'16	Q2'16 vs Q2'15 % change
India	864.3	159.8	272.1	240.6	116.5	131.0	↓ -18
Pakistan	37.6	9.2	9.6	10.5	9.7	10.7	↑ 17
Sri Lanka	6.8	2.0	1.3	1.7	1.5	2.3	↑ 14
Greater China	1,047.8	227.9	251.2	271.0	274.2	195.9	↓ -14
China	981.5	214.1	233.8	253.4	260.3	183.7	↓ -14
Hong Kong	52.8	10.8	14.2	13.9	10.6	9.0	↓ -17
Taiwan	13.4	2.9	3.2	3.7	3.4	3.3	↑ 11
Japan	32.7	3.6	15.2	13.9	7.1	9.5	↑ 163
Indonesia	59.0	13.0	14.0	14.3	16.1	15.4	↑ 19
Malaysia	15.2	2.7	3.7	3.5	3.7	3.1	↑ 16
Singapore	18.1	3.9	4.5	4.7	4.5	4.3	↑ 10
South Korea	21.8	4.2	5.9	6.2	5.2	3.6	↓ -15
Thailand	90.2	19.2	23.5	24.6	25.7	18.3	↓ -5
Vietnam	63.4	14.5	15.0	15.0	16.2	12.4	↓ -15
Middle East	292.7	72.2	69.1	64.5	77.7	57.4	↓ -20
Saudi Arabia	86.3	22.0	19.9	22.3	18.1	18.7	↓ -24
UAE	60.1	17.2	11.8	12.0	16.9	12.5	↓ -27
Kuwait	13.6	3.3	2.5	3.9	3.3	2.6	↓ -21
Egypt	43.1	10.1	13.3	9.4	7.8	6.1	↓ -39
Iran	87.3	14.3	17.2	12.6	24.5	15.1	↑ 6
Other Middle East	22.3	5.4	4.4	4.3	7.2	4.4	↓ -18
Turkey	72.1	16.1	21.2	19.2	13.4	12.8	↓ -20
Russia	45.9	10.3	13.7	11.4	8.3	8.5	↓ -17
Americas	248.1	52.6	70.8	78.5	52.3	65.6	↑ 25
United States	190.8	38.0	57.3	61.6	40.1	50.7	↑ 33
Canada	17.1	4.0	3.6	6.1	3.6	4.7	↑ 17
Mexico	18.8	4.5	5.0	4.7	4.7	4.7	↑ 3
Brazil	21.4	6.1	5.0	6.0	3.9	5.6	↓ -9
Europe ex CIS	298.0	59.8	72.6	94.7	72.0	59.3	↓ -1
France	15.2	2.3	2.3	6.8	3.6	2.1	↓ -8
Germany	126.1	25.2	31.4	36.9	32.9	24.0	↓ -5
Italy	18.0	3.6	2.8	9.0	2.4	3.6	↑ 0
Spain	8.2	2.1	1.9	2.5	1.8	2.1	↑ 3
United Kingdom	35.3	6.0	7.6	15.8	7.2	7.2	↑ 20
Switzerland	49.2	10.7	13.3	11.6	12.9	11.2	↑ 5
Austria	12.2	2.6	3.5	3.2	2.9	2.3	↓ -5
Other Europe	33.7	7.5	9.7	8.9	8.2	6.6	↓ -11
Total above	3,213.5	670.9	863.4	874.3	703.8	610.2	↓ -9
Other and stock change	233.2	51.9	55.0	76.8	50.4	45.5	↓ -12
World total	3,446.8	722.8	918.4	951.1	754.3	655.7	↓ -9

Fig. 6.3 Consumer demand for gold by country

marketing and manufacturing rather than in any recoverable metal (Figs. 6.2 and 6.3).

After gold, silver is the second most widely held precious metal, with platinum and palladium in distant third and fourth places (Fig. 6.4).

A sticky quote from the University of California at Berkeley professor Jonathan Berk says "Gold is the only commodity the world will never run out of." Gold is like other commodities that miners pull out of the ground,

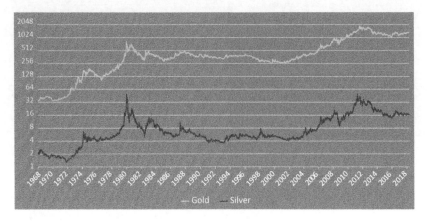

Fig. 6.4   Gold vs silver prices, 1968–2018, log scale

but unlike other metals that get used or burned, gold is mostly just cleaned up; shaped into bars, coins, or jewelry; and then put right back into the ground (often in a bank vault or basement safe). Of the commodities, this makes it most similar to land in having a "fixed supply". Nuclear engineering may one day make it economically feasible to fission off three protons from a mass of lead atoms, as alchemists have been trying to do for centuries before understanding the physics of element 79.

Unlike land, gold cannot be used to grow food nor to house commercial or residential tenants. At best, gold could be lent out at interest like any other currency, but these rates are typically at or near zero for secured or AAA-rated borrowers (the best indicator was the "gold forward" or "GOFO" rate, which was a USD interest rate vs gold collateral discontinued in January 2015, as shown in the below chart (source: Quandl, London Bullion Market Association). Since the 2004 launch of the first gold ETF (GLD, described later), GOFO (orange) has very closely tracked one-month USD LIBOR rates (red), reflecting interest rates as the dominant cost of holding gold (Fig. 6.5).

A more promising trend is the issuance of gold-denominated bonds. In the Republic of South Africa, five-year 0.5% bonds were issued by Randgold, and these bonds could be purchased and redeemed in physical Krugerrands. On an even bigger scale, India issued a series of gold-denominated bonds with a sovereign guarantee, eight-year term, 2.75% interest rate in gold, and, in later series, a capital gains tax exemption.

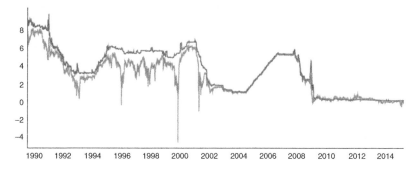

Fig. 6.5 One-month gold forward (GOFO) rate vs one-month USD LIBOR, 1990–2017

In some ways, these gold-denominated bonds in India are similar to the inflation-indexed units of account used in Latin America (e.g. the UDI in Mexico or the UF in Chile), which are basically inflation-indexed pesos which have historically had a real interest rate around +2%. Indians have traditionally entrusted a good share of their savings in gold, provided a tailwind for rising gold prices in the first decade of the 2000s.

For most investors outside of India, the main choices are to either hold physical gold (with all the associated costs and risks) or to invest in a gold ETF, the largest and best known of which is the SPDR Gold Shares (NYSEARCA: GLD). As of August 2016, GLD held about 960 tons of physical gold, about 0.5% of the ~186,700 ton global supply, but is unable to lend out this gold at interest, and so must sell off about 0.4% of the ETF's holdings annually to cover its costs. This may seem worth it for the security and physical administration of an ancient valuable, but paying for vaults, armored trucks, and security guards is easily less productive to the economy than paying farmers to harvest land, contractors to improve buildings, or almost any other kind of employee to operate a business that produces something. This may or may not be why US taxpayers are taxed 8 percentage points higher (28% vs 20%, plus 3.8% healthcare tax) on capital gains from gold held physically or in ETFs.

Gold is simply the most economically dense and durable of many commodities investors may trade as an alternative to stocks and bonds. The next section compares gold with other categories of commodities (oil and gas, base metals, grains, and livestock), and the difference between owning commodities (financially or physically) versus owning shares in companies that mine or produce those commodities.

6.2   OIL, COPPER, SUGAR, FEEDER CATTLE, AND OTHER COMMODITIES

A commodity can be defined as a physical good which can be measured, substituted, and traded, often by weight or volume. To say something is a commodity is a way of saying the thing is common, and can be purchased from many different companies in different places at competitive prices. Generic coffee beans are an example of a commodity traded in many markets, as opposed to Starbucks® coffee as an example of a branded product consumers pay a premium price for and can only get from one company. One way to identify a commodity is to ask whether a consumer cares which company supplied it: in the case of the fuel in a taxicab, sugar in the pantry, metal to repair the escalator, or memory chips in a computer, the vast majority of consumers do not care who the supplier is. Gold, silver, platinum, and palladium are four examples of commodities described in the last chapter on precious metals, and this chapter will introduce other commodities, especially crude oil and natural gas. Commodities, including gold, tick the boxes described in Chap. 3 as being tangible and fungible, as opposed to being financial or specific.

In 2005, at the beginning of a commodities bull market, a group of brokers wearing wool suits and cotton shirts were brought into a conference room and served a breakfast including coffee (with sugar), orange juice, wheat toast, corn muffins, and bacon. These items were driven in on a truck made of nickel-hardened steel, fueled by refined crude oil, started by a lead-acid battery, and rolling on rubber tires. The bacon was cooked on a natural gas burning stove in an aluminum pan, and the coffee juice were dispensed by a machine plugged into the building's network of electrical copper wiring. The point of pointing all this out at that time was to show the brokers how, on an daily basis, they were wearing, eating, and being served through many of these different commodities that traded on futures exchanges and whose rising prices they were to sell to customers.

Commodities go through boom and bust cycles, both in their prices and then investors chasing these prices, but on a different period than credit-driven economic cycles. Commodity prices, like other prices, are driven by supply and demand but have physical limits on how quickly their supply can respond to demand and to prices. The commodities' boom and bust cycle of 2004–2014 was largely attributed to the growing demand from China in the decade it grew from being a US$2 trillion to US$10 trillion economy (according to the IMF) and needed to import record amounts of crude oil to fuel its growth and aluminum, nickel, zinc, copper, and lead to build and electrify new buildings and industrial machinery. As with many markets, commodities generally need time to respond to a surge in demand, as it can take months or years to find and develop new mines and oil wells to full production capacity. Meanwhile, prices increase as rising demand keeps for limited supply until these new sources come online to sell at these higher prices. By the mid-2010s, many of these sources, perhaps most notably the oil shales in the United States, produced a glut of supply in commodities just as China's growth rate and demand for commodities was slowing down, resulting in a crash in oil prices in late 2014. A chart of this crash appears later in this chapter in comparison with "commodity currencies".

Investors not interested in trading physical commodities generally get exposure to individual commodities or to the broader commodities market through futures contracts or in funds that trade managed futures portfolios. Futures contracts are simply an instrument traded on an exchange where the buyer makes money if the underlying commodity goes up in price and loses money where it goes down in price. For most commodities, what ensures the price of the futures contract closely tracks the price of the actual commodity is the regular expiration of these futures contracts (at least quarterly) at which point the seller of the futures contract is to make physical delivery of a specified quantity and quality of the commodity to the buyer at the settled price.

For example, the Intercontinental Exchange ("ICE") describes its coffee futures contract as "the world benchmark for Arabica coffee", and specifies "A Notice of Certification is issued based on testing the grade of the beans and by cup testing for flavor. The Exchange uses certain coffees to establish the 'basis'. Coffees judged better are at a premium; those judged inferior are at a discount." It also specifies delivery prices be adjusted based on the coffee beans' origins: "Mexico, Salvador, Guatemala, Costa Rica, Nicaragua, Kenya, Papua New Guinea, Panama, Tanzania, Uganda, Honduras, and Peru all at par, Colombia at 400 point premium, Burundi, Rwanda, Venezuela and India at 100 point discount, Dominican Republic and Ecuador at 400 point discount, and Brazil at 600 point discount", and further adjustments based on delivery point are standardized at " New York and Virginia delivery points are par; the Bremen/Hamburg, Antwerp and Barcelona delivery points are at a discount of 1.25 cents/lb; and the New Orleans, Miami and Houston delivery points are at a discount of 1.25 cents per pound up to and including the March 2019 expiry, and at a discount of 0.50 cents per pound for the May 2019 and later expiries" (Source: https://www.theice.com/products/15/Coffee-C-Futures).

It is also worth noting that similar-sounding commodities can have significantly different contracts with different prices. A prime example of this are the two main globally traded crude oil contracts: Brent crude oil is a European standard of light, sweet oil with delivery at points in the North Sea between Scotland and Norway, and the American standard is "West Texas Intermediate" or "WTI" light, sweet crude oil delivered at Cushing, Oklahoma, in the United States. "Light sweet" crude oil is in contrast to "heavy sour" and is an indicator of the percentage of sulfur and other impurities in the crude oil which are considered undesirable. As with oil, there are also differences between Kansas and Minnesota wheat, Arabica and Robusta coffee, and world #11 sugar vs London #5 sugar.

Futures contracts on the same commodity with subsequent expiry dates often trade at different prices at the same time. When later futures contracts trade at a lower price than nearer-term futures, the commodity is said to be in *backwardation*, while a commodity whose later futures trade at a higher price than the nearer-term futures are in *contango*. Figures 6.6, 6.7 and 6.8 show examples of three different commodity futures curves exhibiting, as of late 2017, contango (copper), backwardation (crude oil,

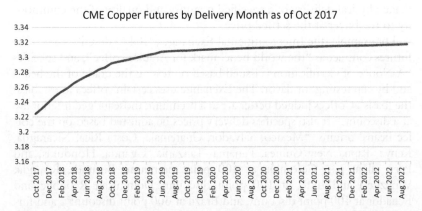

Fig. 6.6   Futures curve of copper as of October 2017, an example of contango

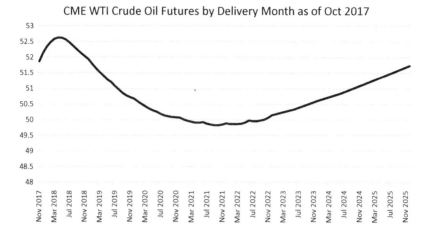

Fig. 6.7 Futures curve of WTI crude oil as of October 2017, an example of backwardation

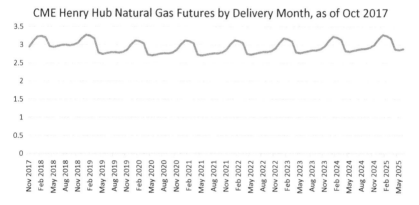

Fig. 6.8 Futures curve of CME natural gas as of October 2017, showing peaks in future winters where demand is already expected to pressure supply

between periods of contango), and cyclicality (natural gas). Data from the three charts below are from the Chicago Mercantile Exchange ("CME").

Investors looking to get long-term exposure to a commodity price without ever taking physical possession of a commodity generally have two choices: a. trade a long-term futures contract, locking in the spread between the "spot" and futures price of the commodity today, or b. roll the futures position every three months, earning a roll yield when there is backwardation or paying a roll premium when there is contango. Some investors learned this the hard way after the first exchange-traded fund ("ETF") to directly track oil prices, the United States Oil Fund LP (NYSE ticker "USO"), which would "underperform" oil prices during periods of contango and outperform in periods of backwardation. This makes sense considering every quarter a backwarded futures contract is rolled, a near-term contract is sold and replaced with the next contract at a lower price, and the difference between the old contract price and next contract price is called the "roll yield". Conversely, rolling a futures contract up a contango curve involves paying higher prices for the next contract, effectively earning a negative roll yield. As with bonds, it is important to remember that profit and loss depends entirely on how long-term futures or forward prices are realized by spot prices when that future comes.

As a more extreme example, the Chicago Board Options Exchange ("CBOE") began listing futures contracts on the S&P 500 volatility index, also known as the "VIX", in 2004, which has since allowed equity volatility to be traded like a commodity. Like natural gas, the volatility of the stock market is not something that can be "stored", so futures prices are set by market supply and demand for insurance against future volatility. In most calm market conditions, the VIX futures curve is in very steep con-

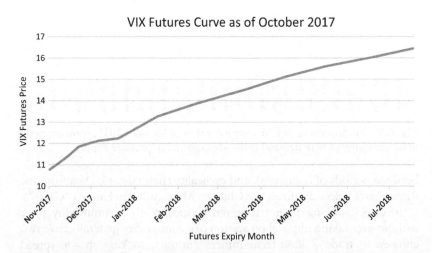

Fig. 6.9 Extreme contango in CBOE VIX futures curve as of October 2017, according to CBOE

tango, and the below example from October 2017 showing a 50% premium for VIX futures less than one year out is not unusual (Fig. 6.9).

An extreme example of the long-term cost of this contango is the iPath S&P 500 VIX Short-term futures exchange-traded note or "ETN" (NYSEArca: "VXX"). This security tracks a strategy of buying and rolling long positions in short-term VIX futures contracts, rolling up the curve and paying this contango premium each time. The result is a strategy that would have turned over $100,000 invested in 2009 into less than $35 by the end of 2017. The value in studying this strategy is understanding how a strategy of regularly selling and rolling short positions in VIX futures would have generated enormous positive returns, effectively as compensation for providing capital to insure the contract buyers against the risk that the VIX will rise above the futures-implied future levels (Fig. 6.10). As this book goes to press in early 2018, short volatility sellers experienced significant losses as the VIX soared from below 10 to over 30 in the first few days of February 2018 during a market correction, after which the VIX curve remained elevated and flat between 18 and 22 for many weeks.

Understanding the dynamics of contango and backwardation for a commodity involves knowing the production and storage possibilities within which a trader could arbitrage the difference between near-term and longer-term futures prices. This will be illustrated in the following paragraph with a relatively easy example (gold) and two somewhat more complicated examples (natural gas and crude oil).

Fig. 6.10 Chart of the "VXX" volatility exchange-traded note that turned $100,000 into less than $35 in eight years

Gold may be the simplest example, as it is one of the most inexpensive to store as a percentage of its value. The futures price of gold should simply equal: a. today's spot price of gold, plus b. the interest cost of financing the gold until the futures expiry date (or similarly, the interest that would have been earned if the money were kept in a bank deposit over the same period), plus c. the cost of storing and securing that gold. If the futures price were higher than this sum, traders would sell the futures contracts and buy, finance, store, and secure the equivalent amount of physical gold until the spread between these two prices converged to zero. Conversely, if the futures price fell below this sum, some physical gold holder would sell their physical positions (saving storage costs and freeing up cash to be invested elsewhere) and buy the futures contracts until this spread disappears.

Natural gas is a far more difficult and expensive commodity to store and arbitrage than gold. Gas cannot be kept in a simple bank safe deposit box or warehouse and will literally fly away or explode if not handled properly. Natural gas is generally piped from oil fields directly to large distribution centers, where it is either pumped into compressed natural gas ("CNG") cylinders for short-distance distribution or in large-scale liquefied natural gas ("LNG") tanker ships for long-distance delivery. Either way, the cost of storing and transporting natural gas is so high relative to its value (historically only a few dollars per million British thermal units or BTUs) that it makes no economic sense to try and store it for any period of time to arbitrage a difference between a spot and long-term futures price with any profit left over. Historically, many oil producers simply burned off their natural gas in the field rather than bear the cost of transporting or storing it at times when gas prices were so low, relative to the more valuable oil coming out of the same fields. This is why natural gas futures curves can be so cyclical, as there is predictable variation between summer and winter months for gas demand, while supply is relatively constant year-round and adjusts only slowly as gas fields come online or offline over longer time periods.

Oil is significantly easier to store and ship than gas, as it is a liquid at room temperature and atmospheric pressure. It sits nicely in barrels which are not cost prohibitive to store in a warehouse for a month or two, and can be shipped between most major shipping seaports in the world for a few dollars per barrel. The long-term futures curve tends to be driven by the imbalance of demand vs supply between long-term hedgers: oil producers selling future production that is not yet online, against oil consumers needed to hedge against future price increases (e.g. airlines).

In addition to trading commodities directly, there are stocks and bonds of companies whose whole business centers around certain commodities, and bonds and currencies of countries primarily considered "commodity economies". Using gold as an example, the first chart below compares the total return of gold mining stocks (represented by the Oppenheimer Gold & Special Minerals Fund; symbol, OPGSX), gold itself, and a broader portfolio of US stocks represented by the S&P 500 index (Fig. 6.11).

Similarly, the currencies of countries whose economies heavily depend on a single commodity tend to be highly correlated with changes in that commodity's price. One dramatic example of this is the crash in the Russian ruble coinciding with the crash in oil prices in late 2014. The below chart shows how the Russian ruble (red) traded against the oil ETF "USO" (black), from July 2014 to July 2015, and how the Norwegian krone was also affected (oil makes up about 22% of Norway's GDP and 67% of its exports, according to the European Commission) (Fig. 6.12).

As with currencies, commodities tend to be less of a "buy and hold" asset and rather one that traders may roll or replace long or short positions

Fig. 6.11 Total return of investing in gold vs gold mining stocks vs S&P 500 stocks, 1983–2016

Fig. 6.12 Crash in oil prices vs the Russian ruble and Norwegian krone, 2014–2015

in depending different rules and factors, two of the simplest being carry and momentum. The carry of a currency was described in the last chapter, while the carry of a commodity was described earlier in this chapter as rolling into contango vs backwardation. As with carry trades between low interest rate and high interest rate currencies, a commodity carry trade involves buying the currency or commodity with the higher yield, and hedging by selling the other that has the lower yield. This sort of carry trade may be considered somewhat safer than the currency carry trade in that the long and short sides of this trade are visible correlated with each other in a way two currencies generally are not. Momentum trades work similarly in commodities as with currencies. One category of hedge funds that specialize in actively trading commodities to produce absolute profits is called "commodity trading advisers" or "CTAs".

The next section contrasts commodities with other hard assets that are also considered "alternative investments" but in many ways are the opposite of commodities: art, gemstones, fine wine, and other collectibles.

6.3   Art, Gemstones, Fine Wine, and Other Collectibles

In Oliver Stone's 1987 film *Wall Street*, main character Gordon Gecko (played by Michael Douglas) points to a painting he bought for $60,000 ten years earlier and says, "I could sell it today for $600,000. The illusion has become real, and the more real it becomes, the more desperately they want it. Capitalism at its finest." Unlike with stocks, bonds, gold, or even most real estate, there would be no way to know how much a painting is actually worth without actually finding a ready buyer and negotiating or auctioning a price based on little else than the buyer's willingness to pay it. Reference points for what a painting might be worth could include: what the painting sold for before (which could have been years ago, or been done at a price far off where it might auction), what similar paintings have recently sold for, or based on some more advanced model that may be proprietary to auction houses or dealers that specialize in finding buyers.

Art, along with most other collectibles described in this section, has the opposite of the fungibility of commodities in that each piece of art is specific, limited, and irreplaceable with another asset, even of the same type. Unique pieces of art by old masters are obviously one of a kind, and their value is limited only by the supply of ultra-wealthy bidders who believe that specific piece is the best place to allocate tens of millions of dollars, partly for the "prestige yield" of being the only owner of that piece. As an example, in 2015, Pablo Picasso's 1955 painting *Les Femmes d'Alger* was sold for US$179,400,000 by an investor who purchased it in 1997 for $31,900,000 (https://qz.com/402938/this-179-million-picasso-is-now-the-most-expensive-painting-ever-sold-at-auction/). An earlier record was set by American painter Mark Rothko's *White Center (Yellow, Pink and Lavender on Rose)*, selling for US$72,840,000 in 2007.

Two points are worth noting about this extreme end of the art market:

A. Record prices for paintings, understandably, tend to be set when overall asset prices (stocks, real estate, etc.) are at cyclical highs, and
B. Highest bid prices of multi-million-dollar art correlate less with the broader "Consumer Price Index" of inflation, but rather with measures like *Forbes* magazine's "Cost of Living Extremely Well Index", which measures the cost of living a lifestyle representative of the 1% most wealthy.

Point A is understandable for two reasons: at the height of an asset price cycle, a wealthy investor would have more capital to allocate to alternative investments, as well as seeing more need to diversify away from other assets which may seem relatively overpriced.

Unlike many other movable physical assets and commodities, certain types of artwork can produce rental income when leased out to corporate offices or other lessees.

While original art pieces are unique, some art is also available as one of a series, such as in numbered prints. While #8 and #23 of a numbered series may be far easier to compare to each other for pricing and appraisal purposes, two differently numbered prints or copies of the same artwork are still not fully fungible and interchangeable with each other due to their possibly different conditions and ownership history, as well as some additional desirability for certain numbers in a series. Copies may seem to take away from the special uniqueness of a work of art, but is the most straightforward way to allow more people to own and enjoy each piece of work. As a prime example, many ancient Greek sculptures can only be seen today as Roman copies of the Greek originals.

Rare coins and postage stamps are another example of artwork where there are multiple but limited valuable copies, although historic coins and vintage stamps are often not numbered in a series. Two well-known examples are the 1840 British stamps "one penny black" and "two penny blue", with prices quoted in the range of $3,000 to over $1,000,000 (http:// www.2-clicks-stamps.com/article/rare-postage-stamps.html). Rare coins differ from the gold coins mentioned earlier in that their value is not in weight of the precious metal, but rather in the unique history printed on them. The unique and irreplaceable feature of a specific coin, for example the Aureus depicting Augustus Caesar that sold for £480,000 in 2014 (http:// www.dailymail.co.uk/news/article-2767275/Maximus-price-Roman-gold-coin-minted-reign-Emperor-Augustus-sells-auction-480-000.html),   makes these coins more similar to gemstones than gold bars.

Gemstones are a collectible asset sometimes compared with gold, but somewhat more similar to art and rare stamps in not being divisible, fungible, nor having the liquidity or transparency of gold prices. An individual stone has features and factors including those traditionally known as the "4 Cs" (color, clarity, cut, and carat, where "carat" with a "c" is a unit of weight) that allow many gemstones to be competitively priced according to a table of these factors, similar to how real estate in some neighborhoods or buildings might be priced per square foot depending on other factors like view and amenities. As with real estate and unlike gold, a gemstone twice the size of comparable one is often more than twice the price, as larger gemstones may be rarer or be a less efficient use of the volume of a given amount of raw stone. Diamonds are often not considered investible, as most people who have ever tried to sell a diamond quickly realize in a market long dominated by the De Beers Group of Companies. The three other types of precious stones are sapphires, emeralds, and rubies, where the cost of sourcing and room for negotiation make a significant difference to any return on the money invested in such stones. The one other advantage of gemstones over art or fine wine is that they are relatively small and inexpensive to store and secure, not requiring especially sensitive climate control. One extreme risk somewhat specific to gemstones are rapid developments in technology making it possible for gemstones physically identical, or even superior, to naturally mined gemstones to be synthesized in a laboratory, and for the market to accept natural and synthetic stones at comparable prices even as the costs of manufacturing the latter decline substantially. A large percentage of gemstones in the market are already "enhanced" by specialized treatments involving heat, and skilled gemologists can often identify evidence of this in a stone, but soon enhancement or synthesis may be impossible to detect in a physical stone, and rather require secure records on the source and supply chain of a stone, perhaps on a blockchain.

Fine wines and whiskeys are, like art and gemstones, another relatively luxurious form of collectible physical asset that may be bought for appreciation. All the wine dated 1997 was harvested in 1997, and no more genuine supply from that year can ever be made again. As the remaining 1997 wines that are still good to drink are opened and imbibed, the remaining supply shrinks and the demand for drinking rarer and older fine wines can push their prices higher. As with art, those buying a cellar of Burgundy for investment must be more interested in the price other buyers are likely to pay for the wine in a few years' time, rather than how much they may personally enjoy that wine now or in the future. Knowing which vintages from which wineries peak in which years and how to best store them is a specialized field with experts who spend years learning about one region. The increasing availability of information online is helpful for those that are interested.

Whiskey and other distilled spirits have the advantage of not "peaking" and going sour the same way wines do, and storing wealth in the form of whiskey is, by some historians, considered one of the triggers of the American Revolution. Besides being a luxury good, whiskey was one of the only ways eighteenth-century American farmers could convert and store the value of excess grain into a commodity that could be stored and sold over time. By taxing whiskey, the British crown was threatening one of the main forms of wealth preservation available to colonial settlers who routinely produced grain surpluses, unlike many of their European counterparts at the time.

The common features of investments in art, gemstones, and fine alcoholic beverages are that these assets are investments in scarcity versus future demand from buyers. By their very nature, investments in these assets are not scalable, and so might be wrapped in a closed-end fund but never in an open-ended fund or ETF. This might be seen as an advantage to those who value the prestige of being the only owner of something, but as with real estate, the lack of liquidity should not be confused with a lack of risk.

6.4   PRIVATE EQUITY

Private equity funds and hedge funds are often categorized as "alternative investments", although many have more similarities than differences to mainstream stock funds. The main difference between private equity funds, hedge funds, and public mutual funds is how they are regulated and distributed to investors and somewhat related to the strategies and assets they invest in. Both private equity and hedge funds tend to be limited to offering their shares to only a limited number of wealthy or institutional investors (often pension funds), may also impose lock-ups on withdrawals, and charge relatively high fees. For example, a PE fund may require an investor have at least $100 million in investible assets, invest at least $5,000,000 at a time into the fund, keep the money in the fund for at least one year and provide a one-year notice to any redemptions, and pay 2% per year of the amount invested plus 20% of any of the profits realized. The latter is commonly referred to as the "2-and-20" fee structure.

Private equity ("PE"), as the name suggests, consists of equity investments in private companies that are not yet or no longer listed or publicly traded, and broadly splits into two major categories: venture capital and buyout.

Venture capital ("VC") is often about investing in new and growing ventures, including "start-up" companies. The Internet booms that sent dotcom stocks soaring in 1999 and technology giants dominating the market capitalization of the US stock market by 2017 tempted many investors to want to find and invest in "the next big thing", hoping to replicate the explosive returns enjoyed by pre-IPO investors in Facebook, Amazon, Netflix, or Google (the group of stocks given the acronym "FANG" by Jim Cramer in 2012). VC investors in technology start-ups often seek one of the three "exit strategies": to take the company public in an IPO, to have the company bought out by a larger company, and to have the company become a self-sustaining cash cow in its own right. VC valuation is more art than science, as much of the value in many of the most promising start-ups may be based on astronomical growth projections or assumptions about future ecosystems which are far harder to predict than the likelihood of a public bond default or quarterly earnings miss. Almost by definition, companies VCs invest in are not publicly traded and have not actively observable secondary market, and private companies are not subject to the financial disclosure and reporting standards of public companies. Some stock exchanges, such as the London Stock Exchange's Alternative Investment Market ("AIM" board), Toronto's TSX Venture Exchange, Singapore's SGX "Catalist", and Hong Kong Exchange's Growth and Enterprise Market ("GEM" board), have different financial and reporting requirements intended for smaller companies not ready for each exchange's corresponding "main board" listing venue. Despite these halfway measures, the mid-2010s saw an increasing number of companies having grown to values in the billions of dollars while still choosing to remain private. These companies have been known as "unicorns", and include names like ride-hailing app Uber and homestay booking platform Airbnb, which are well known enough to have a private secondary market in some of their shares, with the challenges of not having the price transparency or information disclosure or dissemination standards of listed companies. Some unicorns have mentioned their motivations for staying private include retaining control within a limited group of investors, and not having to subject their long-term investments to Wall Street pressure to focus on quarterly earnings. One promising proposal for how to further bridge this gap is the Long-Term Stock Exchange, which aims to provide some of the benefits of a public stock exchange listing while allowing rights like voting control to vest only to shareholders who have held shares for a certain period of time.

Buyout PE can be considered a sort of flip side of venture PE, in that buyout funds buy the outstanding equity of a public company in order to take the company private. Large buyouts are often financed by borrowing a large amount of money from banks or bond markets using the assets of the target company as collateral, hence the term "leveraged buyout" or "LBO". In fact, LBOs are one of the major drivers of high-yield bond issuance and are often viewed as having different risks than "fallen angel" high-yield bonds. One of the most famous LBOs in history so far has been that of RJR Nabisco completed in 1988 by buyout firm Kohlberg Kravis Roberts (KKR) and described in the 1989 book *Barbarians at the Gate: The Fall of RJR Nabisco* by Bryan Burrough and John Helyar. KKR partner Henry Kravis once described buyout private equity like buying a distressed house, taking it off the market to repair and improve, and then putting it back on the market at a higher valuation after it has been fixed and renovated. As with VC, an investment in a company taken private can end in one of the three exits of a new public offering, a sale of the entire company to another buyer, or running the company as a cash cow. Unlike VC, buyout tends to focus more on undervalued or turnaround companies rather than new or growing companies, and buyout investments tend to be much larger, often in the hundreds of millions of dollars. *Liar's Poker, Moneyball,* and *Flash Boys* author Michael Lewis once described private equity as the "first class" or "private jet" of equity investing while public markets were the "coach" or "economy class" of equity investing, as much for their exclusivity as for their actual cost/benefit. It is widely understood that private equity managers would only take private a company whose shares they can buy from the public at a price significantly below what they believe is its intrinsic or potential value, and they would only sell these shares back to the public at or above this value at a significant profit. This has gotten more interesting as private equity firms themselves have gone public, with two landmark IPOs being that of Blackstone in 2007 and of KKR in 2010, listed on the NYSE as MLPs (described later in this chapter) with tickers "BX" and "KKR" respectively. This sector of publicly traded private equity manager firms is known as "listed private equity", and the shares are those of the management companies, whose revenue includes performance fees based on their investments, rather than being shares in a fund of private companies. As with other sectors, there

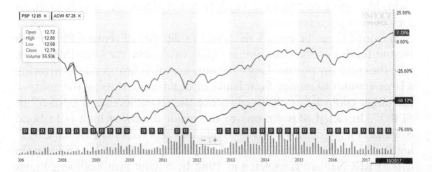

Fig. 6.13 Listed private equity ETF "PSP" has underperformed global public equities 2006–2017

are ETFs tracking listed private equity shares, one of the best known being the Powershares Global Listed Private Equity ETF, traded on the NYSE as "PSP". After its 2006 launch, this listed private equity benchmark has underperformed broader equities as measured by the iShares MSCI All Countries World Index ETF "ACWI" both during and after the 2008–2009 crash, as shown below (Fig. 6.13).

In addition to listed shares of private equity managers, there are also a few PE fund-like investment vehicles listed on stock exchanges called business development companies or "BDCs", which will be described later in this chapter after hedge funds.

6.5   Hedge Funds

Hedge funds, like private equity funds, differ from public mutual funds mostly in how they are distributed and regulated and in how their managers are compensated. Hedge funds also tend to be limited to a small number of wealthy and institutional investors, impose lock-ups on withdrawals, and have traditionally charged "2-and-20" fee structures, although many hedge funds have been facing increasing pressure to reduce their fees. Unlike PE, many hedge funds invest in the exact same publicly traded stocks, bonds, currencies, and commodities that are purchased by mutual funds, but do so with different strategies that include high amounts of leverage (borrowing money to multiply returns on positions) or short selling (borrowing securities to sell now in the hopes of profiting from buying them back later at a lower price—in other words, making money when a stock or bond falls in value). In the twentieth century, hedge funds were largely unregulated as long as they restricted themselves to a limited number of sophisticated and wealthy investors, but in 2004, the US Securities and Exchange Commission ("SEC") began requiring hedge funds to register and keep more formal counts of their investors and offerings for regulators, and many other regulators around the world followed suit. A bigger challenge for hedge funds may have started with the 2014 decision of the United States's largest public pension fund, the California Public Employees' Retirement System ("CalPERS"), to stop investing in hedge funds and instead look at more transparent, liquid, and low-cost alternatives.

In theory, a hedge fund is supposed to differ from mutual funds in their use of hedging strategies that are meant to generate "absolute return" whether the overall market goes up or down, as opposed to "relative

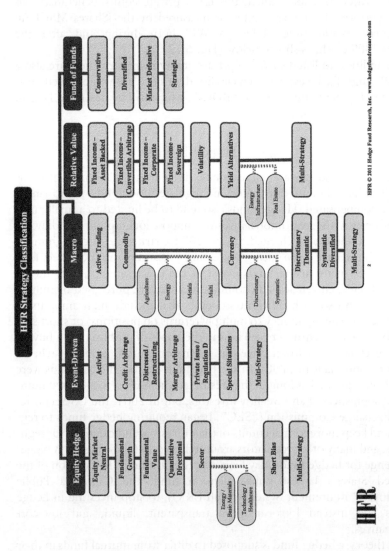

Fig. 6.14 HFR hedge fund strategy classifications

return" which drives most stock funds up and down with the broader market. In other words, hedge funds are theoretically supposed to be pure "alpha" funds with all the "beta" risk hedged out, though in practice, the charts later in this section show this does not describe most hedge fund assets. Chapter 8 describes alpha and beta in more detail.

The first diagram below shows a classification of hedge fund strategies according to Chicago-based firm Hedge Fund Research ("HFR") (Fig. 6.14).

The first column lists "equity hedge" and is probably the most widely known category of hedge fund strategies, which involves combining long and short positions in primarily equity and equity derivative securities. The idea is that the short positions should make money when the broader equity market goes down, offsetting losses or underperformance by the long positions that would get dragged down by the decline. The first category in this list covers "equity market neutral" funds, which buy long positions in some stocks and sell short positions in an equal value of different stocks with the expectation that the long positions will outperform the short positions, resulting in a positive return whether the overall market goes up or down. In doing so, the fund aims to capture a pure "alpha" return from the manager's skill in identifying the outperforming vs underperforming companies while neutralizing any "beta" exposure to the broader market. Equity market neutral funds tend to have a net cash position roughly equal to their AUM, as the proceeds from the short sales of stock cover funding of the long positions, leaving the AUM cash as collateral which can sometimes be invested for further yield enhancement.

Many equity long-short funds do not aim to be market neutral but rather choose to retain a long bias or short bias. Long bias funds are often motivated by clients who may not want to see substantial underperformance when markets are doing well, although such clients have started seeing more flexible and cost-effective options with the rise of "portable alpha" and "130/30" strategies. A "130/30" strategy invests 130% of assets into long positions and sells short other stocks worth 30% of assets, and so maintains roughly 100% beta exposure to the market, while having "light" exposure to the 30% long-short strategy that has even become available in some mainstream mutual funds and indices. "Portable alpha" refers to the ability to separate the long-short alpha strategy from the core beta exposure, which can be bought at a much lower cost in the form of an ETF, and requires only the 30% alpha exposure to be invested by the high-fee manager to generate the absolute return portion.

In the second column are "event-driven" strategies, defined by managers specializing in transformations such as mergers, restructurings, financial distress, tender offers, buybacks, debt exchanges, security issuance, or other capital structure adjustments. Investing in distressed or turnaround situations can be very specialized and require deep knowledge of bankruptcy law and boardroom politics. Some high-profile hedge fund managers that would fit in this category include "activist" investors including Carl Icahn, Bill Ackman, Nelson Peltz, and in some cases Warren Buffett, who take significant stakes in companies and publicly rally shareholders to support changes. Fans of Carl Icahn may be interested in the listed master limited partnership Icahn Enterprises LP (NYSE: IEP), which owns Icahn's diversified businesses. Less glamorous funds in this category include those that specialize in special capital situations of companies, including issues of private investments in public equity ("PIPEs") regulated in the United States under Regulation D.

The third column lists "macro" categories, which broadly describe strategies on the order of whole countries rather than individual countries. These managers execute an investment process predicated on movements in global or national economic variables and the impact these have on currencies, interest rates, commodities, and broad equity indices. Famous fund managers in this category would include George Soros and Ray Dalio.

"Relative value", in the fourth column of this chart, here refers mostly to fixed income strategies that take opposing positions in similar securities on different parts of the yield curve, capital structure, or issuance market. Perhaps the most high-profile example of this category focused on sovereign or government debt was Long-Term Capital Management ("LTCM"), which started by buying slightly higher-yielding off-the-run US Treasuries and hedging by selling slightly lower-yielding on-the-run bonds and earning a tiny spread which they could lever up (the leverage being the fuel for their 1997 collapse). Convertible arbitrage is another well-known strategy in this category that generally involves buying convertible bonds and hedging by selling short the underlying stock to capture mispricing between traditional bond vs stock investors. This category of strategies can also include specialists who may trade bonds issued by the same issuer in multiple different markets (say domestic Philippine bonds in the Philippines versus Philippine bonds in dollars and pesos issued overseas, hedged with credit default swaps).

Ideal "Absolute Return" 2-Sharpe return vs. S&P 500

Fig. 6.15   Returns of an ideal hedge fund with Sharpe ratio = 2 vs the S&P 500

Finally, there are funds that invest in diversified portfolios of hedge funds, called "Funds of Funds". These are often sold as safer ways to capture the average alpha from multiple hedge fund managers and strategies, with add-on services including due diligence and risk management, but of course funds of funds charge fees on top of the hedge funds' already high fees.

In theory, the ideal hedge fund should be a pure "alpha" instrument generating steady returns over time regardless of whether the rest of the market is going up or down, as shown in Fig. 6.15.

In practice, it is so rare to find a hedge fund without beta exposure that the above chart had to be generated using a random number generator simulating a volatility of half the target excess return and could not be based on any real fund data, but shows what sort of chart a pure alpha fund would aim for. Sharpe ratio is a measure of return divided by volatility and is explained in more detail in Sect. 7.2.

The below figure shows how hedge funds as a group, as measured by the Credit Suisse Hedge Fund Index, have actually performed when compared with a simple, low-cost rule-based strategy tracked by the CBOE S&P 500 Put Write Index. "Put writing" is a strategy that involves selling exchange-

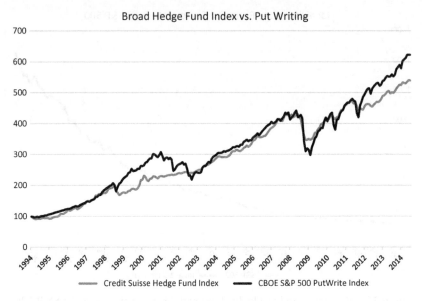

Fig. 6.16   Credit Suisse Hedge Fund Index vs CBOE S&P 500 Put Write Index

traded contracts to receive a fixed amount of money up front in exchange for having to pay out any declines in an index below a certain level on a certain future date. Put writing makes money when markets trade sideways or rise, underperform when markets rise significantly, and lose money when the index falls. This 20+-year chart plots a hedge fund index that seems broadly exposed to market losses and generally profiting from stable and rising markets, as would the simple put writing strategy (Fig. 6.16).

Legendary investor Warren Buffett famously challenged the ability of hedge funds to generate meaningful returns above market averages that in 2008 he bet hedge fund manager Ted Seides US$1,000,000 that a low-cost S&P 500 index fund would outperform Seides's choice of hedge funds over the following ten years (Source: https://www.cnbc.com/2017/09/18/warren-buffett-won-2-million-from-a-bet-that-he-made-ten-years-ago.html). As of this writing in November 2017, Seides has already conceded that Buffett won the bet after a nine-year period where the passive stock index would have returned over 80% while Seides's funds barely returned 20%.

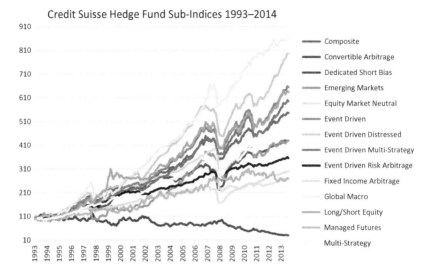

Fig. 6.17 Performance of different hedge fund strategies according to Credit Suisse indices, 1993–2014

Although hedge fund performance may seem unimpressive in the aggregate, returns do vary greatly from fund to fund and from strategy to strategy, as returns of individual stocks and sectors within an index vary. The below chart shows how different strategies, tracked by respective Credit Suisse sub-indices, have performed between 1993 and 2014. Some notable observations from this chart include (Fig. 6.17):

- Most strategies seem to have been broadly exposed to the ups and downs of the broader equity market, especially during the crash of 2008 which appears in most strategies' charts.
- The two strategies which seemed most unaffected by the crash of 2008 were managed futures and dedicated short equity strategies.
- Dedicated short equity was the only strategy that on average consistently lost money (as equity markets on average have been rising), and rose only slightly in 2008. Followers of this strategy will know that short sellers like Muddy Waters, Glaucus, and Citron have stood out in this sector.
- Of the many "event-driven" strategies, the distressed strategies did better on average, although risk arbitrage (which hedges long posi-

tions in acquisition targets against short positions in the stock of the acquiring company) fell less in 2008.

- Of all the strategies, global macro strategies seemed to have shown the best overall long-term performance, likely due to diversified factor exposure.

Although this chapter does not do justice to the depth and variety of the hedge fund industry and its strategies, the averages not surprisingly have drawn scrutiny from the institutions that traditionally formed the core of hedge fund investors, and along with increasing regulation and demands for transparency have come pressure to reduce fees to well below the traditional "2-and-20" model.

Hedge funds have also seen competition from products and strategies with names like "hedge fund replication", "smart beta", "alternative beta", and "liquid alternatives", where many of the principles and processes applied by hedge funds have been systematized and automated into a lower-cost investment vehicle (such as an ETF) less susceptible to human error. As artificial intelligence ("AI") technologies develop to replace and outperform the human skill and judgment that has traditionally been attributed to hedge fund returns, these strategies are likely to continue to get more regular, widely available, transparent, liquid, and cheaper.

So far, the largest hedge fund strategy ETF brand has been IQ Hedge, with over US$1 billion AUM in its Multi-Strategy Tracker ETF (NYSE: "QAI"), and just under US$300 million in a Mergers and Acquisition arbitrage focused ETF (NYSE: "MNA"). Both have expense ratios slightly over 0.75% per year, far less than most hedge funds, and not enough to explain these ETFs' significant underperformance relative to the S&P 500 index, as shown below. The third largest hedge fund strategy ETF as of this writing is the WisdomTree Managed Futures Strategy ETF (NYSE: "WDTI"), with about US$160 million in AUM and a 0.91% expense ratio, but WDTI has underperformed the other funds in this chart.(Fig. 6.18).

6.6   MLPs, BDCs, SPACs: Other Listed Alternatives

As mentioned, many private equity fund managers are themselves listed companies, forming a sector known as "listed private equity", and have been indexed and wrapped in ETF form. Similarly, some hedge fund strategies, though not the hedge funds themselves, have also been implemented

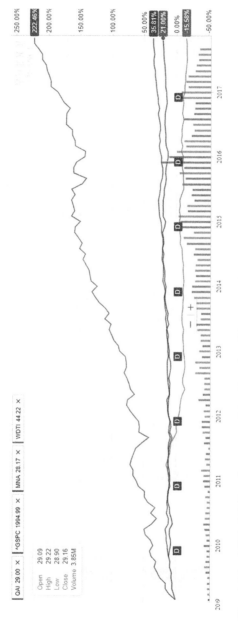

Fig. 6.18 2009–2017 performance of the S&P 500 (blue) vs hedge fund strategy ETFs "QAI", "MNA", and "WDTI"

as listed ETFs. In addition to these, there are also business development companies ("BDCs") which behave like closed-end private equity funds, master limited partnerships ("MLPs"), and special purpose acquisition companies ("SPACs") which in many ways look at trade like stocks, but

Ticker	Name	Market Cap US$mio
ARCC	Ares Capital Corporation	$6,876
MAIN	Main Street Capital Corporation	$2,297
PSEC	Prospect Capital Corporation	$2,169
FSIC	FS Investment Corporation	$1,954
AINV	Apollo Investment Corp.	$1,303
TSLX	TPG Specialty Lending Inc	$1,239
GBDC	Golub Capital BDC Inc	$1,134
NMFC	New Mountain Finance Corp.	$1,067
HTGC	Hercules Capital Inc	$1,044
TCPC	TCP Capital Corp	$956
SLRC	Solar Capital Ltd.	$901
GSBD	Goldman Sachs BDC Inc	$892
FSC	Fifth Street Finance Corp	$794
TCAP	Triangle Capital Corporation	$592
PNNT	PennantPark Investment Corp.	$532
BKCC	Blackrock Capital Investment Corp	$531
PFLT	Pennantpark Floating Rate Capital Ltd	$455
FDUS	Fidus Investment Corp	$410
TICC	TICC Capital Corp.	$335
GAIN	Gladstone Investment Corporation	$329

Fig. 6.19 20 largest BDCs as of November 2017, according to BDCInvestor. com

are structurally or operationally different than traditional companies whose stocks would be included in a mainstream stock index or mutual fund.

BDCs can basically be thought of as a REIT structure holding private equity or private debt investments instead of real estate and, like a REIT, often attract investors with their relatively high dividend yields. Their development is somewhat US-specific as their evolution has very much been driven by US tax law, making these entities tax exempt at the corporate level so long as they (a) pay out 90% of their income as dividends to shareholders and (b) limit leverage to a debt/equity ratio of 1.0 or less. Below is a table of 20 of the largest BDCs by market cap as of November 2017 (Fig. 6.19).

One notable name on the above list worth comparing with its namesake is the Goldman Sachs BDC Inc (NYSE: "GSBD"), which at just under US$900 million is not even 1% of the size of The Goldman Sachs Group Inc's (NYSE: "GS") US$93 billion market cap. As shown in the following chart, while the two names show some correlation on the exchange, GSBD has traded in a more stable range in the first two years since its 2015 launch. GS is very much an "inside the box" investment, being a large-cap blue chip stock belonging to benchmark indices including the Dow Jones Industrial Average and S&P 500, while GSBD is smaller than many stocks considered "micro caps" in the US market, and

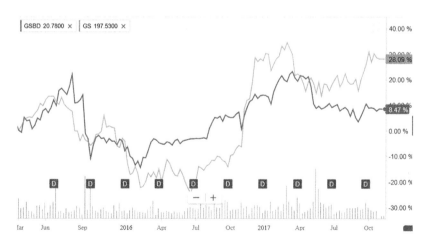

Fig. 6.20 Stock performance of Goldman Sachs ("GS") vs the Goldman Sachs BDC ("GSBD")

purchased more for its yield and specific portfolio management. While GS had a 1.25% dividend yield at the time of this writing, GSBD sported an 8% dividend yield, implying the total returns of the two listed issues were closer than the below chart would indicate (Fig. 6.20).

MLP stands for "master limited partnership" and represents another tax-advantaged structure treated as a pass-through entity for US tax purposes. The defining feature of an MLP is its legal structure as a partnership instead of as a corporation. A limited partnership ("LP") is a somewhat simpler legal structure than a corporation in that it is basically a contract dividing ownership between limited partners and general partners ("GP"). Limited partners are the investors who contribute capital, but are not allowed to participate in the management of the partnership, and so have their liability limited to their investment, while the general partners actively manage the investments of the partnership in exchange for a fee and/or share of the profits. In theory, the general partners have unlimited liability, but in practice this is limited by having the general partner incorporated as a separate limited liability management company which operates the investment management service without exposing the LP investors to its own profits or losses. Some securities categorized as "MLPs" are instead incorporated as limited liability companies ("LLC"), which is a legal structure technically different from the LP in that LLC shareholders are "members" instead of "partners", but few minority shareholders are likely to notice any practical differences. Legally, many hedge funds are set up as a GP/LP structure with the manager as the GP and the investors as the LPs. What makes a limited partnership a "master" limited partnership is the wrapping of the LP portion as a single master share class that is then listed on a stock exchange. Because of their light pass-through structure, US MLPs and LLCs are required by the Internal Revenue Service to issue form K-1 to their investors, which effectively pass through each investor's share of the profits and losses of the partnership. K-1 forms are not all bad, but they can make tax filing and calculation more complicated, as they can pass through income and losses from many different types of businesses and in many different US states that the investor must directly account for, as they are not consolidated at the partnership level.

Below are 30 of the largest US-listed MLPs as of November 2017 (Fig. 6.21).

Like BDCs, MLPs often attract investors with their high dividend yields. As can be seen from the list, currently the majority of MLPs own and operate oil and gas pipelines, and their dividends are largely pass-

Ticker	Name	Sector	Market Cap US$mio
EPD	Enterprise Products Partners L.P.	Natural Gas Midstream	$53,295
BX	Blackstone Group LP	Financial Services	$39,636
ETP	Energy Transfer Partners LP	Natural Gas Midstream	$19,989
ETE	Energy Transfer Equity LP	Natural Gas Midstream	$19,091
KKR	KKR & Co. L.P.	Financial	$16,370
MMP	Magellan Midstream Partners, L.P.	Crude & Refined Pipel	$15,681
BIP	Brookfield Infrastructure Partners L.P.	Utility/Energy/Timber	$15,635
OKS	Oneok Partners LP	Natural Gas Midstream	$14,689
PAA	Plains All American Pipeline, L.P.	Oil/Gas Pipelines	$14,335
MPLX	MPLX LP	Crude Oil Midstream	$13,995
CQP	Cheniere Energy Partners LP	Natural Gas Midstream	$13,605
SEP	Spectra Energy Partners, LP	Natural Gas Midstream	$13,550
IEP	Icahn Enterprises LP	Diversified	$9,086
WGP	Western Gas Equity Partners LP	Natural Gas Midstream	$8,541
WES	Western Gas Partners, LP	Natural Gas Midstream	$7,882
CG	The Carlyle Group LP	Diversified	$7,490
BPL	Buckeye Partners, L.P.	Refined Product Pipeline	$7,373
EQGP	EQT GP Holdings LP	Natural Gas Midstream	$7,365
OAK	Oaktree Capital Group LLC	Investments	$7,194
ENBL	Enable Midstream Partners LP	Midstream Gas and Oil	$6,497
EEP	Enbridge Energy Partners, L.P.	Oil/Gas Pipelines	$6,166
APO	Apollo Global Management LLC	Asset Management	$6,099
EQM	EQT Midstream Partners LP	Natural Gas Midstream	$5,937
CQH	Cheniere Energy Partners LP Holdings LLC	Natural Gas Midstream	$5,799
BEP	Brookfield Renewable Partners LP	Renewable Energy	$5,716
PSXP	Phillips 66 Partners LP	Oil/Refined Pipelines	$5,611
ENLK	EnLink Midstream Partners LP	Natural Gas Midstream	$5,508
AM	Antero Midstream Partners LP	Natural Gas Midstream	$5,428
ANDX	Andeavor Logistics LP	Oil Terminals	$5,058
DCP	DCP Midstream LP	Natural Gas Midstream	$4,762

Fig. 6.21   30 largest US MLPs by market cap as of November 2017, according to DividendInvestor.com

Fig. 6.22 Chart showing relative performance of the "AMJ" MLP ETN vs the "USO" ETF tracking oil prices

throughs of royalties for the fuel that passes through this pipe infrastructure, whether oil and gas prices rise or fall. Despite this, and the fact that a significant minority share of the market cap of MLPs includes asset management firms, timber farms, private equity managers, and diversified business conglomerates, portfolios of MLPs remain highly correlated with oil prices, as can be seen with the below chart comparing the JPMorgan MLP ETN (ETN stands for "exchange-traded note") traded on the NYSE as "AMJ" with the United States Oil Fund ("USO"). As some historic background, AMJ was originally structured as an ETN by investment bank Bear Stearns (the author's former employer) for tax reasons to consolidate all the K-1 forms at the bank level, and pass the high dividends to investors as simple interest payments, which was a feature of the note structure but not most fund structures (Fig. 6.22).

In addition to BDCs and MLPs, a third obscure category of listed securities that could be considered alternatives are special purpose acquisition companies ("SPACs"). A SPAC, as the name suggests, is a company incorporated and listed to raise money specifically for the purpose of acquiring private assets or businesses, which will then be owned and operated by the listed SPAC. This is somewhat similar to how a private company can be taken public through a "reverse merger" or "reverse takeover" ("RTO"), where a private company uses a listed shell company to acquire its assets and effectively take the private company public "through the back door", except that SPACs are brand new companies floated specifically for the

spacanalytics.com

Summary of SPACs

	#	Gross Proceeds (mn)	SPAC Annualized Return
SPACs looking for an acquisition	35	$8,548	0.0%
SPACs announced an acquisition target	10	$2,782	2.4%
SPACs completed an acquisition	150	$20,743	10.9%
SPACs liquidated	79	$10,395	0.0%
Total	274	$42,469	3.3%

Summary of Funds Raised

Year	# of SPAC IPOs	Average IPO Size (mn)	Gross Proceeds (mn)
2017	25	$311.5	$7,789
2016	13	$269.2	$3,499
2015	20	$195.1	$3,902
2014	12	$145.8	$1,750
2013	10	$144.7	$1,447
2012	9	$54.5	$491
2011	16	$69.4	$1,110
2010	7	$71.8	$503
2009	1	$36.0	$36
2008	17	$226.0	$3,842
2007	66	$183.2	$12,093
2006	37	$91.5	$3,384

Fig. 6.23 Statistics on the size, activity, and performance of SPACs from 2006 to 2017

acquisition rather than shells of older listed businesses and that the SPAC management is expected to run the target as opposed to the target management running the company after an RTO.

As with a BDC, PE fund, or hedge fund, investors choose SPACs based on their faith in the management team's ability to find and execute a profitable acquisition, but unlike a BDC, SPACs are not purchased for dividend yields, and investors should be prepared for delays between the IPO raising the money and the actual planned deal. Below are some statistics on SPACs from the site spacanalytics.com (Fig. 6.23):

6.7   WHY INVEST IN ALTERNATIVES?

A primary reason to consider investing in alternatives is to increase portfolio diversification, as described in the next two chapters. Some investors expect higher absolute rates of return from alternative investments, although this needs to be balanced against additional risks, including liquidity risk. In practice, many investors choose alternatives they are comfortable with, motivated by the peace of mind or prestige value that comes from owning a unique physical asset they can touch, or their relationship with a private equity or hedge fund manager that has closed to additional investors.

As highlighted in the section on hedge funds, alternative investments should ideally have little, none, or negative beta, but rather are expected to generate pure alpha returns unrelated to stock and bond markets, and do so with a high Sharpe ratio. In practice, alternatives do provide good diversification, and can enhance the risk-adjusted return metrics of an investment portfolio, as measured by these and other metrics which are described in more detail in the next chapter.

Part II

The "How" Boxes

The first six chapters compared some of the main boxes (asset classes) investments are often classified into. The following chapters step back from these categories and look at the different strategies, instruments, and frameworks an investor might consider when balancing objectives of risk and return. The first, and perhaps most obvious, way an investor can avoid losing 100% is by not investing everything in a single investment but rather diversifying across many different investments, preferably ones that are unlikely to collapse together.

CHAPTER 7

Diversification and Portfolio Construction: Maximizing Return and Minimizing Risk

Part 1 looked at different boxes of investment types individually, almost as though an investor would expect to find their one ideal investment in one of those boxes. This first chapter in Part 2 looks at how indices combine assets within a box to most efficiently earn returns from that box. Often, investors can expect better return and risk metrics by combining different assets with low or negative correlation with one another (i.e. ones that are at least as likely to move in opposite directions as they are to move up and down together). This chapter may be one of the most computationally intensive and technical in trying to provide one of the most accessible introductions to mean-variance analysis and optimization, but walks through the essential calculation in stock vs bond allocation that so many asset allocations get wrong. This chapter then finishes with the execution question by explaining the difference between implementing asset allocation through a top-down or bottom-up manner.

7.1   How Diversification Reduces Risk, Increases Returns, or Both

Imagine Casey lives in a village where the only available "investment" is to bet against a wealthy villager, Talia, who has an insatiable appetite for betting on coin flips. Talia will bet any amount against any other villager on any one coin flip, and Talia always bets the coin will come up "tails",

Talia will offer to do this again as many times as she can find villagers willing to bet against her. To entice villagers to "play", Talia now offers to pay $1.02 when the coin comes up "heads" versus every $1.00 she would win from her counterparty if the coin comes up "tails". Talia has offered to pay as much as $1.10 and as low as $0.98 versus every dollar bet on a coin flip, but for now, the rate is $1.02, and Casey is deciding if and how to "invest" in these bets with Talia. The $0.02 extra Talia is offering to pay can be thought of as an "edge" or "return premium", in this case as a form of incentive fee Talia is willing to pay to encourage villagers to play with her. This premium is similar to the premium investors should expect by providing the service of their capital, say, by investing in a high-yield bond, as will be described in later examples. Talia's coin is fair, but random, and has a known 50-50 chance of coming up "heads" versus "tails".

Intuitively, it seems obvious that Casey should take this bet at least once with at least some money, as the odds are in Casey's favor. The "expected value" from Casey's point of view is an average win of $1 per $100 bet on coin flip, calculated as:

$$\left(50\% \times \left(+\$100 \times 1.02\right)\right) + \left(50\% \times \left(-\$100 \times 1.00\right)\right) = +\$1.00$$

The problem with this "expected value" is that the win or loss on any one coin flip will obviously be very different than this expected value, and even likely to average a number far different from this expected value, even over many coin flips. Splitting $100 across two flips, there are four possible outcomes from Casey's point of view:

A. Flips two heads, winning $102 ($50 × 1.02 × 2)
B. Flip one head followed by one tail, winning $1 ($50 × 1.02 − $50 × 1.00)
C. Flip one tail followed by one head, winning $1 ($50 × 1.02 − $50 × 1.00)
D. Flip two tails, losing $100 (−$50 × 1.00 × 2)

These four scenarios can be notated as "HH", "HT", "TH", and "TT" as a way of keeping track of which coin flip came up heads or tails, which will be handy when tracking more flips.

Since the odds of heads or tails are known to be 50-50, and the outcome of the second flip is completely independent of the first flip, all four of these scenarios are equally likely. This reduces the chance of making $102 or losing $100 down to 25% each, and creates a 50% chance of earning a $1 profit from the two flips. In other words, diversifying from one flip to two flips cut the risk of losing money in half (from 50% to 25%), and made it more likely Casey would earn the edge while leaving a small, but still substantial, chance of a big win.

For even more diversification, the $100 can be split into four flips of $25 each, which could result in one of 16 possible combinations of flip outcomes:

1 way to get 0 tails, win $102: HHHH
4 ways to get 1 tail, win $51.50: HHHT, HHTH, HTHH, THHH
6 ways to get 2 tails, win $1: HHTT, HTHT, HTTH, THHT, THTH, TTHH
4 ways to get 3 tails, lose $49.50: HTTT, THTT, TTHT, TTTH, and
1 way to get 4 tails, lose $100: TTTT

In this model, splitting the same amount of money across more and more diverse investments makes it more and more likely that the realized return will be closer to the expected return premium, and less likely that the whole investment will be suddenly lost or multiplied.

Although this example of coin flipping may seem unrealistically simple, and has what some may consider an unsavory association with gambling, the math and motivation of looking for an edge or return premium and diversifying risk is perhaps the most important foundation for putting together an investment portfolio. Casey's bets with Talia in the above example are very similar to what insurance companies do every day when they write auto insurance policies: collect a certain amount of money in exchange for the risk of having to pay out more money to policyholders who crash their cars, but spread out among enough policies that total premiums cover claims, costs, and hopefully some profit. In fact, Casey's and Talia's example can also be compared to the businesses underlying Casino stocks like Sands or Wynn, whose "house edge" on the baccarat, blackjack, or craps table is known, even if their customer volume and expenses may not be. The advantage of using the coin flipping example to illustrate this concept is that it is very simply to understand and also has some obvious assumptions that cannot be assumed in insurance or investing:

A. Unlike with Talia's $0.02 edge, the real edge of an insurer or risk premium in a corporate bond is never known with certainty.
B. Unlike a coin, which always has a 50-50 chance of coming up heads or tails, real-world events driving insurance claims or investment returns may have actuarial or empirical estimated probabilities, but not exact, certain probabilities.
C. While any two coin flips are independent of each other, many real-world environmental and economic events are connected to each other, making insurance claims and investment returns more correlated with each other than coin flips.

That said, even though assumptions and estimates must be made, probability-based risk models are still a powerful tool for putting realistic numbers on how investments are likely to perform when put together in a portfolio.

7.2   Measures of Absolute Return and Risk

First an investor might consider is the *expected return* or *expected rate of return* of an investment, and when combined, of the portfolio.

Referring back to Chaps. 1 and 2, the expected return on a bank deposit or bond is known up front, and there is nearly a 100% probability that this will be the realized return if the deposit or bond is held to maturity and there are no defaults. Even in the case of credit risky or high-yield bonds, investors have access to good information on the probability of default and recovery in the event of default, so that a portfolio of 100 bonds with a weighted average yield to maturity of X% would be projected to have an expected return of (X-Y)% where Y is the expected allowance for defaults. As with the coin flips or insurance policy portfolio, a high-yield bond portfolio can be modeled as one where each asset has a relatively high chance of paying a small premium rate of return balanced by a small chance of a large loss. This asymmetry is known as skew and is explained below.

Estimating the expected return from a real estate, equity, or alternative investment is often far more difficult, requiring more variables and assumptions. As rough rules of thumb, real estate investors can often use net rental yields plus inflation plus a real return premium for many urban properties, equity investors often use earnings yields projected against economic growth forecasts, while alternative investors may use comparable models or a whole other art to projecting how much money to expect back in the future. As described in Chap. 2, expected return is often summed up as a total return, but can be broken down into income vs price return, or cash return vs excess return.

Second, but as important as expected return, is what risk must be assumed to earn that premium rate of return. Investors should not realistically expect a rate of return much above that of bank deposits or government bonds without assuming some level of risk, and this risk can come in many different forms, with some of the most common including:

- **Market Risk**: This may be the most obvious risk of buying any investment in "the market", namely, the risk that the investment can go up or down in value in the market after it is purchased.
- **Liquidity Risk**: This is a different kind of market risk than price risk, and refers to the risk that asset may not be quickly convertible into cash, or may require a substantial reduction in price to convert into cash quickly. This is especially true with illiquid real estate or alternative assets, but even bonds of similar credit quality can trade at a higher yield due to lower liquidity. Even stocks and other instruments traded on exchanges may occasionally be subject to "halts", making it impossible to exit a position at any price, and possibly resulting in a substantial change in price if and when trading resumes.
- **Interest Rate Risk**: Interest rates, whether short-term interest rates controlled by the US Federal Reserve or foreign central bank or longer-term interest rates determined by the bond market, move up and down. Changes in interest rates directly affect the market price of bonds, the rates earned on cash deposits, and the rates paid on borrowed funds, and indirectly tend to affect stock prices and currency exchange rates.
- **Foreign Exchange Rate/Currency Risk**: Foreign currency exchange rates move up and down. Declines in the value of a foreign currency means it is possible to lose money on a foreign asset that rises in value if the currency risk is not hedged or improperly hedged, and the loss in the currency position may exceed the gain in the foreign asset. Countries may also impose capital controls restricting the conversion or transfer of currency across borders, which could impact the value and/or liquidity of international portfolios.
- **Credit Risk**: Bonds and other debt instruments are subject to the risk that the borrower of the money/issuer of the bond may not pay back the promised interest and principal on time. Credit risk most

directly and obviously affects those that lend money that is not paid back, but can also impact those signing contracts that are not fully honored, or owners of businesses with unpaid receivables.

- **Dividend Risk**: Stocks that pay dividends may cut their dividends, making the cash flows from owning them different than expected.
- **Tax Risk**: Even if all the other values and cash flows of an investment remain the same, governments may change the tax rates they impose on dividends, capital gains, interest payments, transactions, and personal wealth; or they may invent and impose new taxes, or change how or where they apply them. Changes in tax law can directly affect the after-tax returns of an investment and indirectly affect the market value of investments. In extreme cases, changes in tax law may trigger bonds and other capital instruments to be redeemed, liquidated, or restructured.
- **Legal Risk**: Changes in law may affect the rights of foreign or domestic investors in owning or benefiting from certain investment products. An example of this in real estate is the risk of eminent domain, loss of title, or other legal seizures.
- **Risks Specific to Short Selling**: Accounts that borrow stock to sell short are exposed to risks including that of the lender raising the loan rate or calling back the stock loan altogether, which may force liquidation of the short position at an unfavorable price.
- **Operational Risk**: Despite best efforts, precautions, and safeguards in the best of processes, computers sometimes fail, planes sometimes fall out of the sky, key people become sick/injured/otherwise unavailable to perform functions, and service providers (including but not limited to brokers, custodians, banks, and government agencies) become temporarily or permanently unable to continue providing an expected level of service.

Although that may seem like a long and frightening list, it should not be considered complete, but rather an idea of some of the many risks and uncertainties that investors should be aware of but not paralyzed by. The first and most obvious of the risks listed was market risk, which is also the simplest to model numerically, and in many ways can be used as a proxy for other risks to the extent that they affect market prices.

One of the main, but not only, measures of market risk is volatility or standard deviation, specifically the standard deviation of returns over a standardized period of time, typically one year. Standard deviation is simply a way of measuring how widely dispersed the range of likely returns is over that period of time, and is based on probabilities, rather than an average like the expected return. Standard deviation can be calculated in Excel using the "STDEV()" function. A portfolio with an expected return of +$600 and an annual standard deviation of $1,000 should be expected to realize a one-year return between −$400 and +$1,600 68.3% of the time (1σ or "one sigma"), between −$1,400 and +$2,600 95.5% of the time (2σ or "two sigma"), and between −$2,400 and +$3,600 99.7% of the time (3σ or "three sigma"). Note that in each case, the ranges were calculated by taking the expected return plus or minus the standard deviation times the sigma multiplier. A "six sigma" event is theoretically one that should only happen once out of every 507 million observations if upside or downside extremes are counted (or once every billion observations if only downside extremes are counted), but events calculated as "six sigma" tend to happen far more frequently in financial markets due to skew and kurtosis, two additional measures to be described later.

Volatility and standard deviation work best when asset returns are distributed according to a "bell curve", as can be illustrated in the below chart of the likelihood of outcomes Casey flipping $1 each on 100 coin flips with Talia (Fig. 7.1).

Although difficult to see in the above chart, the expected value of splitting the $100 into 100 coin flips of $1 each is still $1.00, but there is less

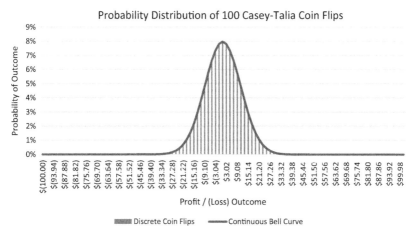

Fig. 7.1 Bell curve distribution of 100 coin flips

than 8% probability that Casey will flip exactly 50 heads and 50 tails and get exactly the $1.00 profit. The standard deviation of these outcomes is about $10, and as may be easier to see in the above chart, there is about a 95% probability Casey's net total will be between a loss of $19 and a profit of $21. Even diversification across this many independent coin flips does not completely eliminate the risk of loss, but does help make clearer samples of how likely losses of certain sizes are. This looks similar to how standard deviation of many stock and fund returns are measured, where monthly, weekly, or even daily price moves often exceed the average expected return of equities, making it very difficult to estimate the average or expected return for stocks, even when the large number of daily returns facilitates calculating and even trading of equity volatility. This is in contrast to many high-yield bonds, where the expected returns are relatively straightforward to estimate, but trading prices are not frequent enough to as easily estimate volatility.

Volatility is often standardized in investment reports as an annualized number, with a standard deviation of "15.3" meaning an expected range of ±15.3% around the expected return over annual (one-year) return periods. When fund reports say "3 year standard deviation", this often means that the number was calculated as a standard deviation of returns over a three-year period, though still scaled to an annual number. Unlike returns, volatility scales to different time periods with the square root of time, so calculating the monthly standard deviation of a fund from its annual standard deviation means dividing by the square root of 12. For example, the fund with the "15.3" standard deviation would have a monthly standard deviation of $15.3 / \sqrt{12} = 4.41$. This means that if the expected monthly rate of return of the fund is +0.5% (6% per year), monthly returns should be expected to fall between −3.91% and +4.91% 68.3% of months and so on. The reason for the square root scaling is because standard deviation is calculated as the square root of another measure called variance, which does scale linearly with time, but is calculated in such a way that it would measure variation in dollars squared, so the square root must be taken to return to a usable unit.

Beyond volatility is the measure of *skew*, which measures the balance between small, frequent returns in one direction versus rare, large returns in the other direction. Skew is independent of the average as measured by the mean, but skewed distributions can often be identified by having different mode (most likely individual outcome) and median (outcome at the point where half are better and half are worse). Investments with positively skewed return distributions are ones which most often return less than the expected return, but have a small chance of a big payoff. The classic example of positive skew is a lottery ticket, where the median and mode return is −100%, offset by a small chance of winning a jackpot, but many venture capital investments, technology stocks, and ICOs or initial coin offerings of cryptocurrencies (described in Chap. 9) could also be categorized as having positively skewed returns. The classic example of an investment with negatively skewed returns is a corporate or high-yield bond (Fig. 7.2).

After skew is kurtosis, a measure of "fat tails" in the return distribution. As mentioned earlier, a "six sigma" event, measured as a daily return six standard deviations away from the mean, should only be expected to occur about once every billion days (or once every 2.7 million years), but based on the daily standard deviations widely calculated in equity indices like the S&P 500, major stock indices seem to have six sigma events about once every ten years. Kurtosis as a number is a rather obscure measure, and in practice, tail risk is more often measured with metrics like "value at risk" ("VaR").

VaR statements are standardized measures of tail risk used widely by risk management departments. A proper VaR statement has three parameters: (a) a confidence level, (b) a loss level, and (c) a time horizon. The following two sentences are examples of a concise VaR measurement:

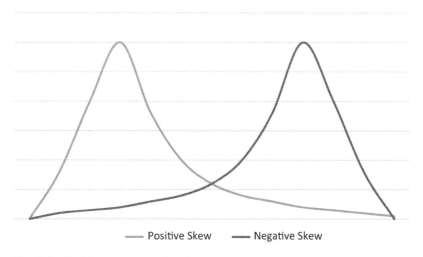

Fig. 7.2   Positive versus negative skew

- Fund A has a **99%** probability of losing less than **$10,000** over the next **24 hours.**
- Fund B has a **95%** probability of losing less than **$50,000** over the next **three months.**

Whole books have been written on the art and science of calculating VaR, starting with Philippe Jorion's 2000 book *Value at Risk*, but many investors can get a "good enough" idea of, say, a daily VaR exposure with 99% confidence simply by running a histogram of the past 500 daily returns and looking at the worst five (worst 1%) of daily returns as a sample. Past data is not meant to be an indication of future returns, but it does give an idea of how much different assets move around, and reminds us not to look for false precision in financial forecasts.

Next, when combining measures of risk and return to compare two different portfolios side by side, one of the most widely used metrics is the *Sharpe ratio*, named after 1990 Nobel Memorial Prize in Economics winner William F. Sharpe. The Sharpe ratio is calculated as excess return (i.e. total return minus bank interest over the same period) divided by volatility. For example, if one-year bank deposit/repo rates are 1%, and a fund returns 10% over the course of one year with 18% annualized volatility over that year, the Sharpe Ratio would be:

$$\text{Sharpe ratio} = (\text{Excess Return}) / \text{Volatility} = (10\% - 1\%) / 18\% = 0.5$$

The Sharpe ratio is a unitless ratio used for comparing two investments and does depend on time frame (so it would make no sense to compare one fund calculated based on a monthly volatility with another calculated based on annual volatility), but it does not depend on leverage. That means, as will be demonstrated in the next section on mean-variance optimization, that a fully invested fund will have the same Sharpe ratio as a half invested fund with the other half in cash or a levered fund borrowing money at the same rate.

The biggest criticisms of the Sharpe ratio often center around its use of volatility as the primary risk measure, which does not work well with assets like high-yield bonds or strategies that have low daily volatility but occasional large tail moves. One alternative to the Sharpe Ratio for some of these cases is the Calmar ratio, calculated similarly to the Sharpe ratio but using a measure of maximum drawdown (percentage that has been or is likely to be lost from peak to bottom over a period of time) instead of volatility.

Finally, all of the above measures of risk and return in this section applied to individual assets or portfolios, and did not provide any measure of how two different assets would move relative to one another or how they would affect risk metrics when combined into a portfolio. Here, the two main statistics are the correlation coefficient and the covariance between two assets or portfolios. The correlation coefficient is a unitless number between −1.0 and +1.0 where +1 indicates the two variables always move up and down together, −1 indicates they always move in opposite directions, and numbers in between indicate the degree to which their movements are tied. Covariance combines the correlation coefficient times the volatilities of the two assets for a combined measure of how much the assets move relative to one another. Correlation is often best visualized, as in the example charts below (Figs. 7.3, 7.4, 7.5, 7.6, and 7.7):

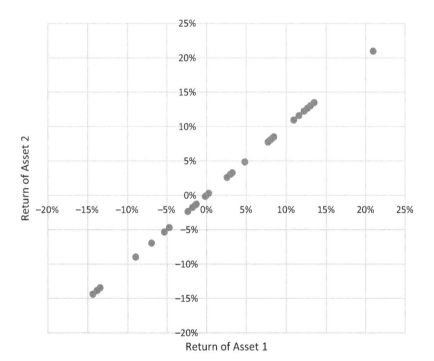

Fig. 7.3 Scatterplot of two assets with a correlation of +1.0, likely the same asset or two ETFs tracking the same index

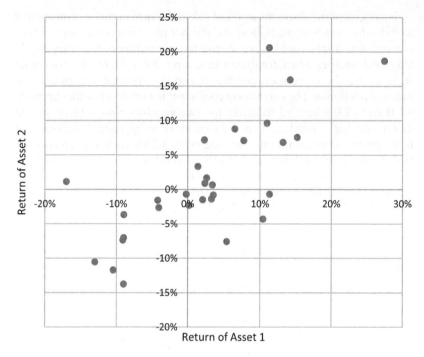

Fig. 7.4 Scatterplot of +0.8 correlation, in the range of many major stock indices with each other

Low or negative correlation, as will be repeated, is an important factor in reducing volatility in a diversified portfolio. As the chart below shows, a portfolio of stocks that each have 25% volatility can have its volatility reduced to below 5% if spread evenly across 30 uncorrelated names (which would probably be impossible to find in practice), while the portfolio volatility would level off around 13%, 18%, and 22%, respectively, for stock portfolios averaging correlations of 25%, 50%, and 75% after only ten stocks. One implication of this chart is that within the asset classes of a portfolio between which correlations are relatively high, only about ten assets are needed to get most of the diversification benefit (Fig. 7.8).

Next, these concepts of return and covariance are applied to putting together the combination of stocks and bonds with maximum return and minimal risk.

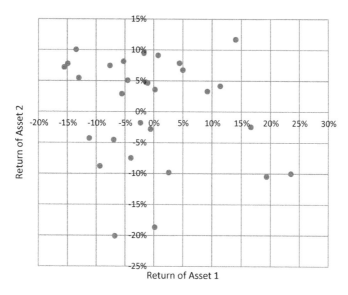

Fig. 7.5   Scatterplot of zero correlation

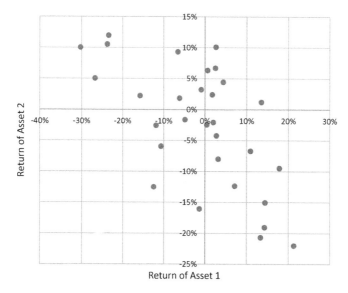

Fig. 7.6   Scatterplot of −0.5 correlation

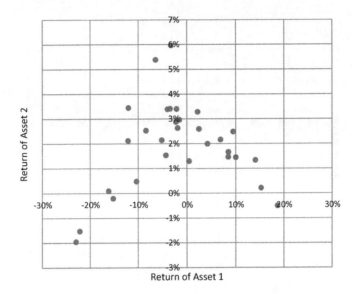

Fig. 7.7   Scatterplot with a statistical correlation of zero, but clearly a significant non-correlation relationship

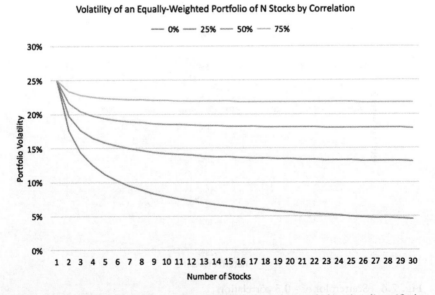

Fig. 7.8   Portfolio volatility versus number of stocks needed to be diversified, based on correlation

7.3 Mean-Variance Optimization and the Classic Maximum Return, Minimum Risk Portfolio

So far, this chapter has reviewed the essentials of measuring return, risk, and introduced how diversification can reduce risk. Now these will be applied to one of the most obvious goals in putting together an investment portfolio: to maximize returns and minimize risks. Using volatility as one simple measure of risk, this is classically done through the "textbook" technique of mean-variance optimization, which many practitioners do not put into practice when they suggest more aggressive investors should put less in bonds and more in stocks. The somewhat unconventional but practical implications of the mean-variance optimization examples calculated here show that even high-performing equity portfolios can be enhanced by adding bonds and that it is better to lever up a balanced bond-stock portfolio than to disrupt the balance by overweighting stocks.

The first step in a mean-variance optimization is to set up the calculation of the mean (meaning the average expected return) and the variance (square of the volatility) of the portfolio. Start with the following assumptions:

- The one-year bank interest rate is 1%—we can deposit money and earn this rate, or borrow money at this rate to invest in stocks and/ or bonds (more on this later).
- "Bonds" have an expected return of 3% and a volatility of 5%.
- "Stocks" have an expected return of 6% and a volatility of 15%.
- The correlation between the bond fund and the stock fund is −20%.

An investor with $1,000,000 has several choices on how to allocate investments. Of course the $1,000,000 could just be kept in the bank, where it would earn 1% interest with virtually no risk, but this $10,000 return is just not enough for the investor, even if it is certain. The below diagram plots the volatility (x-axis) of several possible portfolios against the expected return of those portfolios (y-axis). The investor would like to choose a portfolio as high (high return) and to the left (low risk) of this graph as possible. The points highlighted below are:

1. The portfolio marked (1) invests all $1,000,000 into bonds, where the expected return is 3% and the volatility 5%. This means a ~4–5% chance of having a net loss of $20,000 or more over the year.

2. The portfolio marked (2) invests all $1,000,000 into stocks, where the expected return is 6% and the volatility 15%. A 6% average return would double the investor's money roughly once every 12 years (as opposed to every 24 years at 3%), but there is a 4–5% the investor would have a net loss of **$240,000** in the first year.

3. The portfolio marked (3) is an 80-20 bond-stock portfolio that invests $800,000 into bonds and $200,000 into bonds. The expected return of this portfolio is 3.6%, simply calculated as the weighted average expected return of the bonds and stocks, but the volatility calculates out to a lower 4.2% due to the negative correlation indicating a loss in bonds is likely to be offset by a rise in stocks and vice versa. In this model, this portfolio has a higher return and lower risk than the bond portfolio and should always be preferred to the bond portfolio, based on these assumptions.

4. The portfolio marked (4) invests 80% in the 80-20 bond-stock portfolio and keeps 20% in cash earning 1%. This portfolio has the same 3% expected return of the bond portfolio, but significantly lower volatility. In other words, the risk of the bond portfolio has been reduced by "diluting" it with stocks and cash.

5. In the portfolio marked (5), the investor's capital is supplemented by borrowing an additional $1,000,000, and the $2,000,000 is invested in the 80-20 bond-stock portfolio. This portfolio has an expected return around 6% (net of the 1% interest that must be paid on the borrowed money) and a volatility of less than 9% (double that of the unlevered 80-20 portfolio). In other words, this levered balanced portfolio has the same expected return as investing 100% of the money in stocks, but with about half the volatility risk.

6. Portfolio (5) is an extreme version of portfolio (5), where the investor borrows about $2,500,000 and invests the $3,500,000 total in the 80-20 bond-stock portfolio. This multiplies the volatility of the portfolio to equal that of the 100% stock portfolio, but with a much higher expected return of 10% vs 6%. In other words, this levered balanced portfolio has a higher expected return than the all-stock portfolio with the same expected level of volatility risk.

7. Portfolio (7) is a more traditional example of a 40% bond +60% stock +0% cash portfolio, implemented as a typical "moderate" portfolio by many financial advisers. As illustrated above and in the chart below, this portfolio has a lower expected return and slightly higher volatility risk than portfolio (5) (Fig. 7.9).

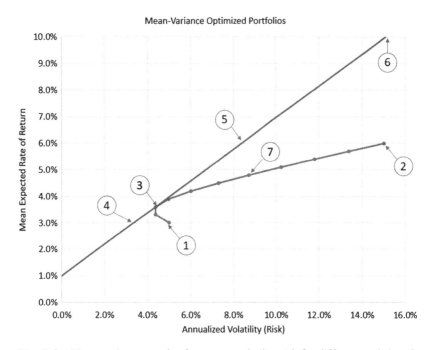

Fig. 7.9 Mean-variance graph of return vs volatility risk for different cash-bond-stock portfolios

This mean-variance optimization calculation and framework is widely taught in business schools and is a core part of curriculums like the CFA® exam, but its results are rarely put into mainstream practice. Many financial advisor models assume that aggressive accounts should allocate less to bonds and more to stocks, and rotate this to more bonds and less stocks as the client ages and becomes more conservative. According to this mean-variance model, such an approach leaves investors taking more risk or expecting lower rates of return than investing in the optimally balanced bond-stock allocation and using cash or leverage, rather than the allocation, to adjust the risk vs return target. In other words, the optimal balance between bonds and stocks is the same for everyone and based on the covariance between the two assets, and its relationship to the interest rates at which the investor can borrow or deposit money.

The negative correlation between stocks and bonds is a critical assumption in this framework and is how a portfolio of stocks and bonds can have lower volatility than either stocks or bonds. A correlation of +1.0 would mean portfolios of stocks and bonds would simply be a straight line between the two points, while a correlation of −1.0 would make it possible to create a perfectly hedged, risk-free portfolio, so most portfolio curves are between these two extremes showing some diversification benefit.

As a rule of thumb, the volatility of a portfolio of two negatively correlated assets will be minimized in a balanced portfolio when the weight of the asset is inversely proportional to its volatility, so that more is held of a less volatile asset and less invested in the more volatile asset. In the above example, the 5% volatility of bonds and 15% volatility of stocks would imply an optimal allocation with 3× as much invested in bonds as in stocks, or around 75% bonds +25% stocks. This rule of thumb is called "risk parity" and roughly involves matching the dollar volatility or VaR of two loosely or negatively correlated assets to maximize the diversification benefit. As can be seen in the above chart, the blue line of optimal portfolios runs closely through the 80-20, 75-25, and 70-30 portfolios on the red bond-stock allocation curve within the margin of error, and the best choice between these is based partly on error estimates and partly on the second important assumption: interest rates.

Interest rates are another core assumption in this model, as high risk-free rates will make it less attractive to buy risky assets with relatively low expected returns. Conversely, low rates steepen the incremental return impact of adding risky assets and multiply the benefit of borrowing at these low rates to invest in higher return assets. This also explains one factor of how low interest rates stimulate higher asset prices and greater complacency with risk, which on a macro level lowers forward-looking risk-adjusted returns.

One of the main excuses advisors use on why they change clients' asset allocation instead of levering up and down the same optimally balanced portfolio is the difficulty of borrowing money at the same interest rate as bank deposits, and there are two answers to this. First, many balanced funds are managed by large institutional investors who can and do borrow on a secured basis at interest rates within a few basis points of the rates their cash would earn on deposit, as illustrated in Sect. 2.4 on repurchase agreements ("repos"). Second, even moderately affluent investors can access leveraged exposure to stocks and bonds at these institutional rates by using listed futures contracts. Below are screenshots of futures quotes of CME-listed S&P 500 "e-mini" futures contracts and ten-year US Treasury futures (Figs. 7.10 and 7.11).

→ ○ ⌂   cmegroup.com/trading/equity-index/us-index/e-mini-sandp500.html

CME Group   Trading Clearing Regulation Data Technology Education

Month	Options	Charts	Last	Change	Prior Settle	Open	High	Low	Volume	Hi / Low Limit	Updated
DEC 2017	OPT	▪	2572.25	-0.50	2572.75	2572.75	2574.00	2571.00	9,626	2701.00 / 2444.00	18:40:30 CT 31 Oct 2017
MAR 2018	OPT	▪	2572.50	-0.50	2573.00	2573.25	2573.25	2572.50	20	2701.00 / 2444.00	18:34:12 CT 31 Oct 2017

Fig. 7.10 Quotes of CME S&P 500 "e-mini" futures

→ ○ ⌂   cmegroup.com/trading/interest-rates/us-treasury/10-year-us-treasury-note.html

CME Group   Trading Clearing Regulation Data Technology Education

Month	Options	Charts	Last	Change	Prior Settle	Open	High	Low	Volume	Updated
DEC 2017	OPT	▪	124'290	-0'010	124'300	124'280	124'295	124'275	9,460	18:40:48 CT 31 Oct 2017
MAR 2018	OPT	▪	-	-	124'195	-	-	-	0	18:34:26 CT 31 Oct 2017

Fig. 7.11 Quotes of CME ten-year US Treasury note futures

Futures contracts are sometimes considered "sophisticated" or "risky", but they are in fact very simple and only more risky than comparable securities strategies when traded with too much leverage or on too little margin. In the above two examples, the S&P 500 "e-mini" futures is electronically traded, and a buyer of one contract at, say, 2,573, will make US$50 profit for every point the S&P 500 index futures rises above this 2,573 and lose US$50 for every point the futures falls below 2,573, and these futures contracts expire quarterly to be cash settled against the official value of the index. A futures contract can also be sold short as easily as it is bought long, without the need to borrow or repo any securities, making them a very efficient tool for hedgers and short sellers. This $50 point multiplier means that as of 2017, one S&P 500 e-mini contract provides exposure to about US$125,000 of US stocks, but can be traded with only a few thousand dollars in a futures margin account. It is the accounts with only this minimum margin amount which are the first to get completely wiped out when an index moves a few points against them, but investors with $125,000 will see similar gains or losses as if the money were invested directly in stocks or an S&P 500 ETF.

As seen in the above quote screenshots, for the S&P 500 stock index futures, it is possible to trade contract expiring either in December 2017 or in March 2018, although most traders will focus on the nearer-term contract until it approaches expiry and is rolled into the next contract. In the above example, the March S&P contract is trading at a very slight premium to the December contract that is practically zero. This premium does not at all reflect any expectation on whether or how much the index will rise, but rather is a pure indicator of the cost paid and yield earned by an investor who would buy the S&P 500 stocks with cash (either borrowing the cash at 1% interest or forgoing 1% interest on investing the cash in a bank deposit) and in the meantime earn any dividends on those stocks. If the premium of the March contracts over the December contracts ever got too high, a well-funded arbitrageur would sell the March contract, and hedge by borrowing money to buy S&P 500 stocks until this premium disappeared. Conversely, if the March futures traded at a substantial discount, an arbitrageur could buy the March futures and hedge by selling short the S&P 500 stocks. Competition among arbitrageurs to keep these futures prices in line is what (as with ETF arbitrage explained in the next chapter) ensures that smaller individual investors who use these futures will get accurate and liquid pricing. Although the ten-year US Treasury futures March contract is not trading yet, it can be seen from the CME's official "prior settle" price that the March future is trading at a 10.5 32nds of a point (remember from Sect. 2.3 that US Treasuries are quoted in 1/32nds of a point) or 32.8 cent discount to the December future. This discount is due to the coupon accrual or "carry" rate from owning the bond being higher than the repo rate paid by a hedger to finance the bond. In other words, an arbitrageur can buy the ten-year US Treasury note at a yield of 2.25% and finance it by borrowing the money for three months at 1%, and the 1.25% per year "carry spread" translates to the 32.8 cent discount. In other words, an investor who buys and rolls long positions in bond futures will still earn the higher yield from owning the longer-term bonds, but these will show up as roll yield when a near-term contract is replaced with the next cheaper one rather than as accrued interest.

As an example, suppose an investor with $1,000,000 to invest wanted to implement portfolio (6) above and buy exposure to $3,500,000 total notional of an 80% bond + 20% stock portfolio, with extra $2.5 million effectively financed at 1%. This breaks down as $2,800,000 in bond exposure plus $700,000 in stock exposure. The investor could buy most of the required bond exposure by buying 22x December ten-year note futures at 124-30 (notional value = 22 × 124,937.50 = $2,748,625) and the required stock exposure by buying 5x S&P 500 e-mini futures at 2,573 (notional value = 5 × 50 × 2,573 = $643,250). About $50,000 of the $1,000,000 would be tied up as a margin requirement to maintain these futures positions, while the rest could be kept in safe and liquid treasury bills or ETFs in case losses require more margin, or more likely gains come back to increase the investor's account balance to buy more March contracts as these Decembers expire. As the contracts mature and roll, the number of new contracts may need to be modified to maintain the same notional multiples and 80-20 balance.

The chart below compares how a monthly rebalanced, 2x leveraged 80% bond + 20% stock portfolio would have performed relative to a 100% stock, 100% bond, and unlevered 80-20 portfolio since 1986.

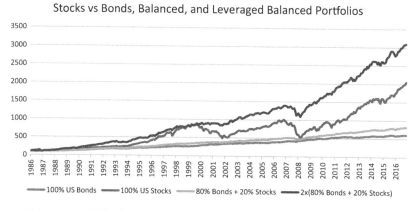

Stocks vs Bonds, Balanced, and Leveraged Balanced Portfolios

Advocates of the long-term superior returns of stocks only are likely to be surprised by the superior performance of the leveraged balanced portfolio. The leverage multiplies the blended bond-stock return to a level higher than that of stocks or bonds, while the negative correlation and risk-parity weighting of holding more bonds than stocks results in a portfolio with less volatility risk than an all-stock portfolio. The assumptions and implementation details can certainly be questioned, but investors should definitely ask why leveraged balanced asset allocations like this are not a standard part of financial planning frameworks, or why the increasing number of leveraged ETFs are predominately all-stock or all-bond and not balanced as would seem optimal. The opening chart in Jeremy Siegel's classic book *Stocks for the Long Run* highlights the superior long-term returns of stocks over bonds, but investors should not be too simplistic in thinking of stocks versus bonds as an either-or rather than two important ingredients that should be properly balanced and leveraged.

Legendary investor Warren Buffett is another high-profile advocate of owning stocks over bonds over any long period of time, and shareholders in his holding company Berkshire Hathaway (NYSE: BRK/A) have profited greatly from the Oracle's skill investing in companies. An investor with a little over $1,000 in 1980 could have purchased four class A shares of BRK/A which by October 2017 would be worth over $1,000,000. This is about a 20% annual compounded rate of return, compared with the 10% average annual return from an S&P 500 index fund that would have turned $1,000 into $43,500 over the same 37-year period. In the mean-variance optimization framework, BRK/A might be expected to be much higher on the chart, assumed to be 12% instead of 6% in the below diagram, but the negative correlation and low interest rates still show that a leveraged balanced portfolio of bonds and BRK/A would have a higher expected return and/or lower volatility risk than 100% BRK/A. With the below assumptions, the optimal portfolio seems to be 70% bonds and 30% stocks (Fig. 7.12).

The higher absolute return of BRK/A would mean that a portfolio of 70–80% bonds and only 20–30% BRK/A would need more leverage to generate a higher total return, and the below chart shows how this would have worked using a 3x levered, monthly rebalanced portfolio of 80% bonds and 20% BRK/A. Berkshire fans will note that even this 3x levered portfolio only allocated $60 per $100 invested into BRK/A and generates the higher return with lower risk from the bond diversification (Fig. 7.13).

Although mean-variance optimization is often considered a "textbook", "academic", or "theoretical" technique, hopefully this chapter has demonstrated, convincingly, how it can be practically used to generate better risk/return balances in real investment portfolios. The challenge for practitioners, as with any model, is in understanding the assumptions and

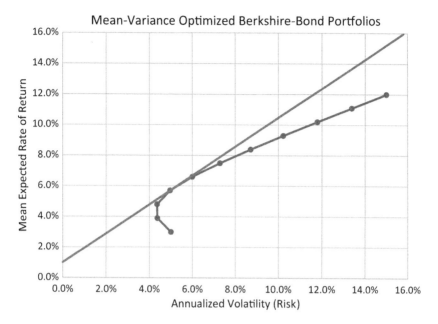

Fig. 7.12 Mean-variance optimization curves for Berkshire Hathaway vs ten-year US Treasuries

Fig. 7.13 Beating Berkshire by balancing Berkshire, bonds, and borrowing

the sensitivities the results have to them, as a model supplements rather than replaces experience and judgment. It is important to remember that a model is just a framework for translating a set of assumptions into the conclusions they are logically consistent with.

Some of the major reasons investors do not apply mean-variance optimization and other rational, quantitative techniques for maximizing risk-adjusted return have less to do with theory vs practice or the difficulty of estimating useful parameters but rather for behavioral and agency problem reasons described in Chap. 11. Meanwhile, the rise in indexing, ETFs, and robo-advisors has helped many investors have more rationally invested portfolios, as will be described in the next chapter.

CHAPTER 8

Indexes, Benchmarks, Mutual Funds, and ETFs

Stock market indices are widely known as benchmarks whose values are reported on TV, newspapers, and fund fact sheets, and whose returns most professional managers have not been able to consistently beat. In many asset classes, there is at least one index meant to track what an average investment would make or lose over time investing in that asset class. This chapter introduces some of the major types of investment benchmark indices, mostly focusing on stock indices, and describes their role in both passive and active portfolio management.

One of the oldest, simplest, and still most widely respected of such indices is the Dow Jones Industrial Average, which, along with Japan's Nikkei 225 index, is one of the very few price-weighted indices still widely used in the twenty-first century. Most stock indices used as benchmarks by fund managers are market capitalization weighted rather than price-weighted, which, as explained in Sect. 8.2, has the effect of representing the average performance of all stockholders and can be tracked at minimal cost. Other methods for weighting indices include equal weighting or filtering and weighting by growth, value, size, or other factors increasingly marketed as "smart beta" strategies. Benchmark indices have evolved from being a simple indicator of how the market is doing to guiding how trillions of dollars of assets are traded and invested, and this is measured through relative performance metrics including alpha, beta, and tracking error in the form of open-ended, closed-end, and exchange-traded funds (ETFs).

© The Author(s) 2018   179
T. Dennison, *Invest Outside the Box*,
https://doi.org/10.1007/978-981-13-0372-2_8

Investing in an ETF that tracks an index can be thought of as one of the most "inside the box" ways of investing, but the growth of this space into thousands of different indices and ETFs has made it easier than ever to diversify across more boxes, both in number and in variety.

Note that the plural of "index" is alternately written as "indices" or "indexes", and this book chooses to use "indices".

8.1   Price Weighting

The modern stock index is often said to have started with the calculation of the Dow Jones Industrial Average by Charles Dow in 1885, who, along with his partner Edward Jones, started the company that publishes *The Wall Street Journal*. Charles Dow began publishing an index that was a simple arithmetic average of the prices of [11] of the most widely followed and traded railroad stocks as a way to follow, in a single number, whether these stocks were broadly rising or falling on any given day. Railroads were the Internet giants of their day, and this index originally known as the Dow Railroad Average continues to be published as the Dow Jones Transportation Average (or "Dow Transports" for short). In 1896, Dow began calculating a more diverse index of large companies, the Dow Jones Industrial Average (now mostly known as the "DJIA", "the Dow", or "Dow 30" for short) meant to more broadly represent blue chip stocks and the US market as a whole. The Dow was originally an average of 12 stock prices, later expanded to 30 stocks, and remains the most widely broadcast stock price indicator in mainstream US media, although it has largely been surpassed by the market cap-weighted S&P 500, Russell 1000/3000, and MSCI indices as a benchmark for managed assets.

The Dow is also an example of a "blue chip" index, as its components only narrowly include 30 companies considered to be among the most respected on a particular stock market (blue chips are traditionally the highest denomination chip on a poker table). The opposite of a blue chip index is a "broad market" index like the Russell 1000 or 3000, which of course includes a far larger number of names, often covering over 90% of the total market capitalization of the respective market. The Russell 3000 is obviously broader than the Russell 1000, though the 1,000 stocks in the Russell 1000 already represent over 80% of the US market cap, and combined with the other 2000 cover about 98% of the value of the US market.

The Nasdaq also has a narrowed "Nasdaq 100", on which futures contracts and one of the most liquid ETFs are traded, and the "Nasdaq Composite" quoted on the news (meant to include all stocks quoted on Nasdaq). In Europe, there is a similar difference between the Euro STOXX 50 and the Europe STOXX 600, and in Asia there are two similar examples with the Hang Seng Index and the Hang Seng Composite Index (more on these in Chap. 10).

The beauty of the Dow, besides its long and continuous history, is in how simply its value can be calculated and tracked by an easily traded stock portfolio. The underlying portfolio of the Dow is simply one share in each of the 30 stocks, and initially the index simply divided the sum of the 30 stocks' prices by 30 to calculate the Dow Jones Industrial Average. Over time, as stocks "split", the divisor of 30 was revised to maintain the same index level before and after each split, while retaining the underlying weighting of holding one share in each of the 30 stocks. The below table shows how owning one share of each of the 30 stocks on April 26, 2017, would have added up to one of the simplest ways to invest $3,062.81. The table also shows how this portfolio gives a higher weight to smaller companies with higher per share stock prices. For example, this simple Dow portfolio would have over seven as much money invested in Goldman Sachs than in General Electric, even though GE (#11 in the S&P and Russell indices) is a much larger company than GS (#53 and #51 in the S&P and Russell, respectively). This effect of having the amount invested in a company based on the price of each share, rather than the size of the company or any other factor, is why this style of index is known as "price weighted" (Fig. 8.1).

The many stock splits are why the Dow divisor is no longer 30, but about 0.146 as of April 26, 2017, meaning the 20,975.09 value of the Dow that day was simply the $3,062.81 value of the portfolio divided by this divisor. The below table shows how the divisors are revised with each split, using the hypothetical example of a 5:1 stock split by Goldman Sachs that day. Note that in the below example, the index value remains the same even though the sum of the share prices changes, resulting in the change in divisor. The divisor can be interpreted as the need to take the value of the extra four shares of Goldman received in the stock split (worth $180.96) and spread this amount among all 30 stocks (Fig. 8.2).

Symbol	Company Name	Last Price	Rank in Russell 1000	Rank in S&P 500	Rank in Dow 30
CSCO	Cisco Systems, Inc.	33.40	26	27	29
JNJ	Johnson & Johnson	123.51	5	6	9
MMM	3M Company	195.00	36	35	2
MSFT	Microsoft Corporation	67.83	2	2	22
AXP	American Express Company	80.52	81	82	20
INTC	Intel Corporation	36.93	24	22	27
GS	The Goldman Sachs Group, Inc.	226.20	51	53	1
JPM	JPMorgan Chase & Co.	88.43	7	8	16
UNH	UnitedHealth Group Incorporated	174.38	30	26	4
IBM	International Business Machines Corporation	160.06	32	32	5
CAT	Caterpillar Inc.	104.66	84	81	14
PFE	Pfizer Inc.	33.85	16	17	28
KO	The Coca-Cola Company	43.24	27	29	26
V	Visa Inc.	91.82	22	23	15
DIS	The Walt Disney Company	115.58	20	25	12
XOM	Exxon Mobil Corporation	81.40	4	5	19
WMT	Wal-Mart Stores, Inc.	75.43	38	37	21
NKE	NIKE, Inc.	55.16	66	65	24
TRV	The Travelers Companies, Inc.	122.01	139	142	10
AAPL	Apple Inc.	143.68	1	1	7
MCD	McDonald's Corporation	140.84	35	36	8
CVX	Chevron Corporation	106.08	17	16	13
MRK	Merck & Co., Inc.	62.70	25	24	23
GE	General Electric Company	29.26	11	11	30
DD	E. I. du Pont de Nemours and Company	81.61	68	69	18
HD	The Home Depot, Inc.	154.22	19	19	6
BA	The Boeing Company	181.71	40	40	3
UTX	United Technologies Corporation	118.20	46	51	11
VZ	Verizon Communications Inc.	47.36	18	18	25
PG	The Procter & Gamble Company	87.74	15	15	17
	Sum of 1 of each share:	3,062.81			
	Index Value:	20,975.09			
	Divisor:	0.1460213			

Fig. 8.1   Stock portfolio that tracks the Dow Jones Industrial Average, and how its ranks compare with the S&P and Russell

In 1998, an ETF called the DIAMONDS (now the SPDR Dow Jones Industrial Average ETF) was launched to make it easier for investors to buy and sell the basket of Dow shares like a single stock. ETFs will be explained in more detail later in this chapter, but given the falling costs and greater automation in stock trading, it is likely that many investors will

Symbol	Company Name	Pre-split	Post-split
CSCO	Cisco Systems, Inc.	33.40	33.40
JNJ	Johnson & Johnson	123.51	123.51
MMM	3M Company	195.00	195.00
MSFT	Microsoft Corporation	67.83	67.83
AXP	American Express Company	80.52	80.52
INTC	Intel Corporation	36.93	36.93
GS	The Goldman Sachs Group, Inc.	226.20	45.24
JPM	JPMorgan Chase & Co.	88.43	88.43
UNH	UnitedHealth Group Incorporated	174.38	174.38
IBM	International Business Machines Corporation	160.06	160.06
CAT	Caterpillar Inc.	104.66	104.66
PFE	Pfizer Inc.	33.85	33.85
KO	The Coca-Cola Company	43.24	43.24
V	Visa Inc.	91.82	91.82
DIS	The Walt Disney Company	115.58	115.58
XOM	Exxon Mobil Corporation	81.40	81.40
WMT	Wal-Mart Stores, Inc.	75.43	75.43
NKE	NIKE, Inc.	55.16	55.16
TRV	The Travelers Companies, Inc.	122.01	122.01
AAPL	Apple Inc.	143.68	143.68
MCD	McDonald's Corporation	140.84	140.84
CVX	Chevron Corporation	106.08	106.08
MRK	Merck & Co., Inc.	62.70	62.70
GE	General Electric Company	29.26	29.26
DD	E. I. du Pont de Nemours and Company	81.61	81.61
HD	The Home Depot, Inc.	154.22	154.22
BA	The Boeing Company	181.71	181.71
UTX	United Technologies Corporation	118.20	118.20
VZ	Verizon Communications Inc.	47.36	47.36
PG	The Procter & Gamble Company	87.74	87.74
	Sum of 1 of each share:	3,062.81	2,881.85
	Index Value:	20,975.09	20,975.09
	Divisor:	0.1460213	0.1373939

Fig. 8.2 Example calculation of the DJIA divisor before and after a stock split

find it easier to buy all 30 stocks directly rather than pay for an ETF to own the same 30 shares.

The other major price-weighted index still widely used as of 2017 is the Nikkei 225 index, tracking the prices of 225 Japanese stocks listed on the first section of the Tokyo Stock Exchange. Japan is covered in more detail in Chap. 10 on international investing, but in this paragraph on price-weighted versus market cap-weighted indices, it is worth noting that the Nikkei 225 remains by far Japan's most traded index, as measured by futures and ETF volume compared with the market cap-weighted TOPIX and MSCI Japan indices.

8.2   MARKET CAP WEIGHTING

As mentioned, most of the world's trillions of dollars of indexed equity assets are benchmarked not against price-weighted indices but against market capitalization or "cap-weighted" indices. While slightly more complicated to calculate, market cap-weighted indices are based more purely on ideas of passive investing, owning the same portfolio everyone else owns, and not trying to beat an efficient market. Cap-weighted indices, by design, own proportionately more of larger companies as measured by market capitalization (calculated as price per share times number of shares outstanding, a measure of the "total value" of all a company's listed equity), so that an investor would have 100× as much money invested in a $100 billion company as in a $1 billion company. Cap-weighted indices can be "float adjusted", meaning weights take into account which of the outstanding shares are actually available for public trading (as opposed to "non-floating" shares which are technically outstanding, but held by long-term insiders or other large holders who won't sell their positions), or in some cases "capped" (to prevent a company from having too large a percentage weight in an index, as exemplified by Nortel in Canada's TSX indices in 1999–2000).

In the United States, the most widely used benchmark indices are the S&P 500 index and the Russell 1000 and Russell 3000 indices. These indices, respectively, are meant to represent a size-weighted investment in the 500, 1,000, and 3,000 largest US-based and traded companies, and the Russell 3000 is often considered "the universe" or list of stocks from which US-focused equity fund managers are supposed to choose their stocks. Although the S&P 500 is also the largest benchmark tracked by "passive" index funds, it is worth noting that the S&P 500 index and its components are still manually selected by a committee at Standard & Poor's, arguably making it an actively managed index to whom the decision-making has been outsourced. Russell indices, on the other hand, are based more on rules that periodically cut off and define which are the largest 1,000 US companies and to be included in the "R1000" or "R1K" index. The 2,000 smaller companies in the Russell 3,000 index make up a separate index known as the "Russell 2000", which is currently the most widely used benchmark for US "small cap" companies. Size and the performance of small vs large companies will be examined later in this chapter.

Below is a snapshot of the names and weights of the top 30 components of the S&P 500 as of April 2017. These 30 components together make up about 37% of the value of the entire S&P 500 index, and include a balance of names traded on both the New York Stock Exchange (NYSE) and Nasdaq, unlike the Dow which has long favored NYSE-traded companies and the Nasdaq indices which only include Nasdaq-traded companies (Fig. 8.3).

One feature of cap-weighted indices, at least those not focused on smaller companies, is that they tend to be dominated by industries with extremely large companies. In many countries, the major benchmark indices are often mostly made up of shares of banks and very large resource companies, and while the United States arguably has one of the more diversified economies and stock markets, the S&P 500 in 2017 has been largely weighted in information technology and financial giants, with relatively little direct exposure to hospitals, real estate, transportation, food and beverage, or other sectors which employ a large share of the population and make up a large share of consumers' expenses. Some of the other major market cap-weighted indices around the world include (Fig. 8.4):

In addition to the S&P 500 and the Nikkei 225, the above international indices also underlie some of the most actively traded futures contracts in each of their respective markets. Equity index futures trading was described in Chap. 7 on how to implement a mean-variance optimized portfolio financed at institutional rates.

One key assumption underlying the choice of market cap-weighted indices is the efficient market hypothesis or "EMH". The EMH reasons that there is so much competition to buy undervalued stocks and sell overvalued stocks that the market efficiently sets the prices of stocks right around their fair value so that there is no added value in trying to evaluate one stock versus another.

Another line of reasoning for the EMH is that all investors in the world, collectively, own all the stocks in the world in proportion to their market cap, and so in aggregate earn the return of a market cap-weighted total stock market index, net of any costs and fees paid to or through their fund managers. Those who invest in actively managed funds will necessarily, on average, underperform passive funds by the amount of those extra expenses, and so many investors would be better off simply buying the whole market in proportion rather than wasting time and money picking winners versus losers. There is of course plenty of money still being made by active fund managers charging much higher management fees than passive funds; it

Ticker	Name	Weight (%)	Sector	Exchange
AAPL	APPLE INC	3.69	Information Technology	NASDAQ
MSFT	MICROSOFT CORP	2.55	Information Technology	NASDAQ
AMZN	AMAZON COM INC	1.75	Consumer Discretionary	NASDAQ
FB	FACEBOOK CLASS A INC	1.68	Information Technology	NASDAQ
XOM	EXXON MOBIL CORP	1.65	Energy	NYSE
JNJ	JOHNSON & JOHNSON	1.63	Health Care	NYSE
BRKB	BERKSHIRE HATHAWAY INC CLASS B	1.55	Financials	NYSE
JPM	JPMORGAN CHASE & CO	1.53	Financials	NYSE
GOOGL	ALPHABET INC CLASS A	1.28	Information Technology	NASDAQ
GOOG	ALPHABET INC CLASS C	1.25	Information Technology	NASDAQ
GE	GENERAL ELECTRIC	1.25	Industrials	NYSE
WFC	WELLS FARGO	1.19	Financials	NYSE
T	AT&T INC	1.19	Telecommunications	NYSE
BAC	BANK OF AMERICA CORP	1.17	Financials	NYSE
PG	PROCTER & GAMBLE	1.12	Consumer Staples	NYSE
CVX	CHEVRON CORP	0.98	Energy	NYSE
PFE	PFIZER INC	0.98	Health Care	NYSE
VZ	VERIZON COMMUNICATIONS INC	0.93	Telecommunications	NYSE
HD	HOME DEPOT INC	0.91	Consumer Discretionary	NYSE
CMCSA	COMCAST A CORP	0.89	Consumer Discretionary	NASDAQ
PM	PHILIP MORRIS INTERNATIONAL INC	0.85	Consumer Staples	NYSE
INTC	INTEL CORPORATION CORP	0.85	Information Technology	NASDAQ
V	VISA INC CLASS A	0.83	Information Technology	NYSE
MRK	MERCK & CO INC	0.83	Health Care	NYSE
DIS	WALT DISNEY	0.81	Consumer Discretionary	NYSE
UNH	UNITEDHEALTH GROUP INC	0.81	Health Care	NYSE
CSCO	CISCO SYSTEMS INC	0.81	Information Technology	NASDAQ
C	CITIGROUP INC	0.81	Financials	NYSE
KO	COCA-COLA	0.81	Consumer Staples	NYSE
PEP	PEPSICO INC	0.79	Consumer Staples	NYSE
MO	ALTRIA GROUP INC	0.68	Consumer Staples	NYSE

Fig. 8.3 Top 30 largest components of the S&P 500 index, with weights, sectors, and exchanges as of April 2017. (Source: iShares)

Country / Region	Cap-weighted Benchmark Index
Canada	S&P/TSX 60
United Kingdom	FTSE 100
Eurozone	Dow Jones Euro STOXX 50
Germany	DAX
Singapore	Straits Times Index / MSCI Singapore
Hong Kong	Hang Seng Index
China (H-share)	Hang Seng China Enterprises Index
China (A-share)	FTSE/Xinhua A50 / CSI 300
Korea	Kospi 200
India	Nifty
Australia	S&P/ASX 200

Fig. 8.4 Major traded market cap-weighted national benchmark indices

would seem to make sense that there need to be at least some of these active managers to keep markets even partly efficient. If all money were invested passively in a market cap-weighted portfolio, there is likely to be profit opportunities for active managers to enter the market and exploit mispricings no one else is competing to pay attention to, which would be an inefficient or under-efficient market. Many passive investors would argue that the US market is currently hyperefficient, in the sense that the returns from investing in research or other efforts to try and beat the market are likely to be negative, but it makes sense that markets need at least some active managers to remain critically efficient.

A popular test of the EMH is to construct a portfolio at random (say by throwing darts at the stock list in *The Wall Street Journal*) and compare the returns of the randomly selected portfolio to a professionally managed portfolio or a benchmark index. While not completely random, one example of this for which 55 years of data is readily available is to compare the returns of the DJIA versus the S&P 500 index. Although the two indices contain many of the same companies, the Dow excludes many of the S&P 500's most heavily weighted components entirely, and, as seen earlier, weights the index by the somewhat more random factor of the stock's price per share (which is largely uncorrelated with market cap), so the Dow can be considered a partially random portfolio for this experiment. As seen in the chart below, and might be surprising given these differences, the Dow and the S&P have tracked each other surprisingly closely over the 55-year period from 1961 to 2016. A significant portion of the difference between the two can be explained by the Dow's dividend yield being higher than the S&P's on average, so the total returns of the two indices are even closer than this chart would indicate (Fig. 8.5).

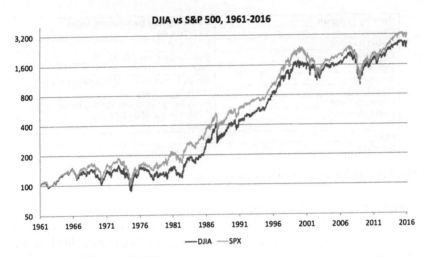

Fig. 8.5   Price return of the DJIA (price-weighted) versus S&P 500 (market cap-weighted), 1961–2016. (Source: Yahoo Finance)

8.3   Price Return Versus Total Return

Many of the most widely quoted stock indices are "price return" indices, meaning that they track the weighted average price of the stocks in the index and the returns that would come from stock splits, but they do not track or adjust for dividends. If an investor bought the 30 stocks of the Dow when the Dow was at 22,000, and held the stocks for one year where that year ended at 22,000, the investor's price return would have been zero, but the investor still would have earned dividends from the stocks, producing a few percentage points of total return. The effect of dividends is especially significant when factoring the effects of compounding of those few percentage points over many years.

To address the question of what an investor's total return would be from investing in the stocks of an index, many index providers have created total return indices or total return versions of their price return indices. Some of the non-obvious questions that make calculating total return indices more complicated than price return indices are:

A. Are dividends to be immediately reinvested in stocks on each respective dividend's payment date, or aggregated and reinvested in some other way?

B. Should the dividends be reinvested in the stock paying the dividend, or should this reinvestment be spread among all the stocks in the index?

C. How should the effect on taxes on those dividends be factored in, if at all?

The S&P 500 has a total return version called "SPTR", which is often used as a benchmark by institutional investors, and ignores any tax effect on dividends given that many of these institutions, or the retirement accounts they manage, can defer taxes on reinvested dividends as the money later taxed when withdrawals are made. Many of MSCI's international total return indices have two versions "gross" and "net" total return, with the latter being after deduction of withholding taxes on dividends from the source country to where the benchmark investor is based. Withholding taxes on dividends paid from one country to another often vary both on the source and destination country and any double-taxation treaty that may prescribe any such withholding rate between them.

When choosing or observing the index, it is important to watch for these differences between price return and total return indices. Price return indices are clearly simpler because they assume that dividends are either spent or reinvested elsewhere, net of any taxes the individual investor may be subject to, but total return indices may be built on assumptions different to those that apply to the investor.

Although dividends affect the returns from investing in components of an index, dividends may also be a factor used to weight an index and is one of the many factors of alternative weighting described in the next section.

8.4 Alternative Weighting and "Smart Beta": Growth vs Value, Size, Momentum, and Quality

Many investors find the passive strategy of owning all stocks in the market in proportion to their size unsatisfying, and instead would prefer to focus their capital on the fastest-growing companies, the highest-yielding companies, or some other well-defined, rule-based factors. These factors form a whole series of sub-index portfolios based on, but with the hope of outperforming, the major market cap-weighted benchmarks based on one or more driving factors. Portfolios based on these factors have been increasingly marketed as "smart beta" in the mid-late 2010s and are the basis of many ETFs. As will be explained in the next section, "smart beta" refers to how these funds retain beta exposure to the market while aiming to add "alpha" outperformance over a pure beta investment.

In order to have significantly different returns than the benchmark, a smart beta portfolio must either hold different stocks than the benchmark or weight the same stocks differently.

The first and perhaps most fundamentally promising factor is size, namely, tilting investment away from larger companies and toward with a smaller market capitalization (or "small caps", which have no set definition of size but can refer to those not among the 10–20% largest in a given market). A small cap factor bias makes sense for several reasons, two of the most obvious being:

A. Upside: There is more room for a $100 million company to become a $1 billion company than for a $100 billion company to become a $1 trillion company.
B. Competition: Smaller companies have less institutional coverage and ownership, often disproportionately less. This means the big and smart money is more likely to overlook a good opportunity in a smaller company and less likely to bid up its price/lower its return.

Some statistics to give an idea of the level at which institutional money is less invested in small cap companies from Bloomberg as of 2015:

- Bloomberg only listed 342 small cap Asia funds, vs 847 large cap funds
- The 18 largest small cap funds had AUMs of US$700–3,000 million each, while
- The 18 largest large cap funds had AUMs of US$150–600 billion each

The first statistic may not have seemed so disproportionate except when considering how much more numerous small cap stocks are than large caps. As one example, when the above statistics were taken in 2015, the Tokyo Stock Exchange was listing about 200 stocks with a market cap larger than US$5 billion and about 2,500 with a market cap less than US$5 billion, and the 200 large caps had over twice the combined market cap of the smaller 2,500 (US$3.3 trillion vs US$1.5 trillion).

One perception of small caps is that they are riskier than large caps. The scatterplot below shows a snapshot of how returns from the 52-week low vs 52-week high (y-axis) are distributed among stocks of different market cap sizes (x-axis). As expected, there are far fewer companies larger than $62.5 billion in market cap than smaller, and these larger companies are both far less likely to have fallen more than 50% from their highs or have risen more than 100% from their lows compared with smaller companies. The distribution of both large gains and large losses widens as the companies get smaller (Fig. 8.6).

Besides specifically small cap indices like the Russell 2000 or TOPIX small cap indices, one of the simplest "smart beta" strategies for capturing the higher expected returns from small companies over large companies is one that owns the same 500 stocks of the S&P 500 index, but weighting them equally rather than by market cap. This is what the ETF "RSP" does, and below is a chart of how this equal-weighted S&P 500 index ETF has performed against the "traditional" market cap-weighted SPY (Figs. 8.7 and 8.8).

The outperformance of RSP can partly be explained by the higher return from small caps, but also from the rebalancing the fund needs to perform to maintain an equal weight across the 500 names, which involves

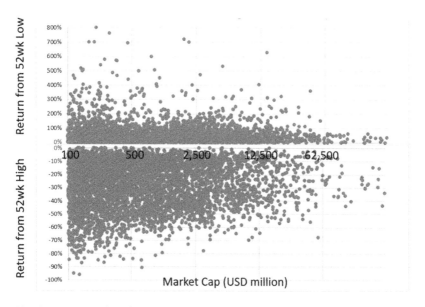

Fig. 8.6   Scatterplot of stock returns from 52-week low/high vs USD market cap

Fig. 8.7 Chart of S&P 500 equal-weighted (RSP) vs market cap-weighted (SPY) ETFs. (Source: Google Finance)

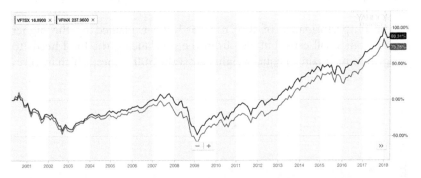

Fig. 8.8 Chart of Vanguard's FTSE socially responsible fund vs the Vanguard 500 Fund

selling those that have risen and buying names that have fallen since the previous rebalancing in a disciplined manner.

A second, also very widely used, factor is that of value versus growth. Value, as measured by the ratio of a company's book value to its market value, was, along with size and the performance of the overall market, the third factor identified by economist Kenneth French and Nobel laureate Eugene Fama as being significant determinants of stock returns. In addition to the Fama-French use of book-to-market ratio as a value factor (more often calculated by practitioners as a "price to book" ratio or "P/B"), investors also look at price-to-earnings ("P/E"), price-to-cash-flow

("P/CF"), and price-to-revenue or price-to-sales ("P/S") as a quick measure of how cheap or expensive a stock is. As a "smart beta" factor, "value" is generally considered the opposite of "growth", based on the understanding growing companies should trade at higher multiples to current earnings, cash flows, revenues, and book value as investors expect these underlying numbers to increase and translate into higher present value, as explained in Sect. 4.4. Value factor investors generally buy stocks with low P/B, P/E, P/CF, or P/S multiples which may imply but not necessarily be correlated with higher growth rates in book value, earnings, cash flows, or revenues. These factor splits can be seen in growth vs value versions of many benchmark indices, such as the Russell 1000 Growth and Russell 1000 Value indices, both tracked by ETFs. One challenge with P/E ratios is that many stock screeners that use them are highly sensitive to short-term changes in earnings that might not be a good indicator of a company's long-term earning power, and longer-term or other adjusted P/E ratios are examined in the book *The Essential P/E: Understanding the Stock Market through the Price/Earnings Ratio* by Keith Anderson. The field of "value investing", however, can go far deeper than simply looking at a few ratios and include far deeper analysis into the sustainable intrinsic value of a company.

Related to the value factor is the idea of weighting companies according to some measure of fundamental value, rather than by market cap or price. WisdomTree tested this idea with its ETFs weighting components by earnings or dividends, which has met with some success. The rationale of earnings or dividend weighting does make intuitive fundamental sense: rather than investing 10× more in one stock than another just before the former is 10× larger by market cap does not sound like as good a value as investing 10× as much in a company that earns 10× as much profit or pays out 10× as much in dividends. While factor investors may see this WisdomTree weighting approach as a step in the right direction, this methodology still invests more of a portfolio in larger companies than in smaller companies. That is, rather than just buying "the biggest" companies, an investor may prefer to tilt investments toward "the cheapest" (value), "the fastest" (growth), or "the best" (quality).

A third factor is momentum, which is simply based on the assumption that a price in motion will remain in motion long enough to generate some extra profits from following trends. Momentum strategies have the advantage of being relatively easy to define, calculate, and implement, but that also means many momentum traders are likely to be competing to implement similar momentum strategies, which would tend to make results riskier and less stable.

"Quality", defined in a number of ways, could be considered a fourth factor. Quality factors generally define how good the underlying business of a stock is compared to its competitors, or to other listed stocks as a whole. Fundamental metrics indicating quality often include having a higher return on assets (ROA) or return on investment (ROI) ratio (indicating the ability to make more profits with less capital invested), higher gross margins (indicating having a profitable product competitors haven't been able to squeeze much yet), and declining debt ratios (indicating healthy cash flows and/or a lower likelihood of financial distress). On a deeper level, Warren Buffett has been described as shifting from a Graham style buyer of "cheap" companies to preferring "great companies at a fair price over fair companies at a great price". Combining quality and value might be described as a two-factor investing approach: "the cheapest of the best" and "the best of the cheap".

A fifth factor is "low beta", which filters for companies with relatively low volatility and low sensitivity to market ups and downs, as will be described in the next section on alpha and beta.

While there are several other factors that can be used to filter or alternatively weight companies in a stock portfolio or index, these have been some of the most widely used alternatives to market cap weighting in fund and ETF portfolios.

8.5   THE ALPHA AND BETA OF OUTPERFORMANCE
AND RELATIVE PERFORMANCE

Chapter 7 examined investment performance with absolute metrics: total return, volatility, VaR, and Sharpe ratio—all numbers that can be calculated individually on an asset, portfolio, or index without regard to how any other investment is doing. Here, the metrics of alpha, beta, and epsilon are introduced, which measure the relative performance of an investment or investment portfolio of a benchmark. Alpha and beta are often applied to funds, so funds will be used as an example.

Beta is simply a measure of how much a fund is expected to move up or down, on average, relative to its benchmark. For example, a stock fund benchmarked to the S&P 500 with a beta of 0.8 would be expected to return, on average, about 8% in a month the S&P rises 10% and lose, on average, 8% in a month the S&P falls 10%. Beta is calculated as a combination of correlation and the ratio of the volatility of the fund to that of the benchmark, but it is important to remember that it is still possible to have a high beta and a low correlation, and this noise is measured by epsilon, defined after alpha below. The following scatterplot shows the monthly returns of the Fidelity Contra Fund (mutual fund ticker: FCNTX) against those as the S&P 500, and shows the beta of the fund as approximately 0.8 based on the slope of the best fit red line (Fig. 8.9).

Alpha is defined as the average extra return a fund averages after subtracting out the effect of beta. With the increasing availability of low-cost index funds and ETFs, investors are increasingly realizing that alpha is what is worth paying fund managers to produce, as beta exposure (returns from just passively owning the market) can be accessed for a very little cost. Fund alpha should, in theory, be produced by a fund manager's additional skill and information advantage over competitors, but in practice competition makes many markets so efficient it is difficult for most managers to even keep up with, let alone outperform, market benchmarks and index funds by actually producing alpha. With the benefit of hindsight, below is the scatterplot of the monthly returns of Apple Inc. against the S&P 500 from 1993 to 2017, including its explosive outperformance over the benchmark after its world-changing release of the iPhone. The alpha measure can be seen as the point at which the "best fit" red line intersects the y-axis, about 1.5% in the below chart. While alpha is an average, it is meant to represent the consistent average return a fund or stock produces above or below market averages, whether the market goes up or down. Continuing the above example, a fund with a beta of 0.8 but an alpha of 2% should, on average, be expected to rise 10% when the market rises 10%, but only fall 6% when the market falls 10% (Fig. 8.10).

Epsilon represents what is left over in the returns of a fund after subtracting out the effects of alpha and beta, and in the above two charts can be visualized by the average distance of the blue dots from the red line. Epsilon is also a measure of tracking error or "noise", and, unlike alpha or beta, always has an average of zero and is instead defined by its standard deviation. This means that epsilon is pure risk with no added edge or return, and ideally is a factor that should be minimized and diversified away by risk-averse investors, and definitely not confused with

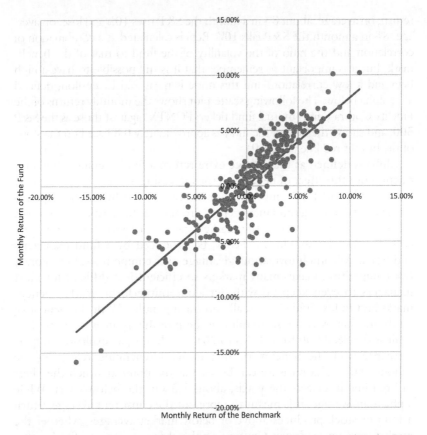

Fig. 8.9 Scatterplot of monthly returns of the Fidelity Contra Fund vs the S&P 500, 1993–2017, beta = slope of the red line

alpha (which can be statistically challenging). Funds that track an index closely are designed to have very low epsilon, meaning very low tracking error.

As a formula, a fund's monthly return can be broken down as:

$$\text{Fund return} = \text{Alpha} + \text{Beta} \times (\text{Benchmark return} - \text{interest rate}) + \text{Epsilon}$$

Alpha, beta, and epsilon can be calculated in Microsoft Excel by passing series of historical returns through the LINEST() function.

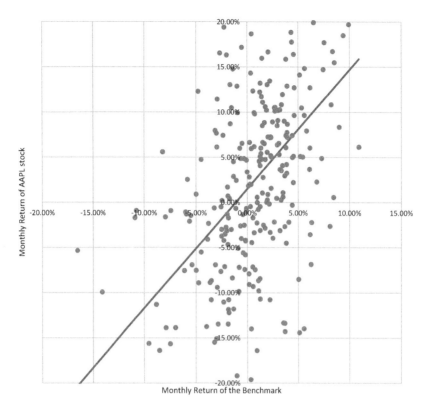

Fig. 8.10 Scatterplot of monthly returns of Apple Inc. stock vs S&P 500, 1993–2017, showing a monthly alpha of 1.5%

8.6   Closed-Ended Funds

Closed-end funds ("CEFs") are the oldest, simplest, and least scalable form of mutual funds and are similar to the BDCs introduced in Sect. 6.6. These funds raise money once in an initial offering to invest in their stated strategy, and then are closed to any new money entering or any capital leaving except on "special occasions". To enable existing investors to cash out and new investors to buy in, closed-end funds are generally listed on stock exchanges so that investors can sell their shares to one another without capital having to enter or leave the fund.

Because of their closed-end structure, closed-end funds often trade at a significant discount (and sometimes premium) to the net asset value ("NAV") of the stocks, bonds, or other assets in their fund. Historically, most funds have traded at a discount often around 5–10% and sometimes as high as 50%, as there is no arbitrage trade that would allow an investor to buy the fund and short the underlying assets without significant risk or holding period. While there is some debate as to why these discounts persist, a main reason is often said to be that closed-end funds spend all their distribution and marketing budgets on the initial offering, and so there is an imbalance when the retail investors come back to sell on the stock exchange to a more limited number of buyers that marketing dollars haven't been spent to attract. These discounts can be attractive for investors who understand and can accept that these discounts may persist or get even deeper, but can result in attractive dividend yields for those willing to take the risk.

As with other mutual funds, closed-end funds are generally categorized investing in stocks, bonds, or alternatives. Closed-end stock funds may be set up for a variety of reasons, but for many foreign stock markets, this vehicle was the earliest form of access product many foreign investors could use to access that market. For example, the Morgan Stanley China A-share fund (ticker: CAF) was set up many years before any true China A-share ETFs were possible. The fund sponsor used its Qualified Foreign Institutional Investor (QFII, described in Chap. 10) quota to convert US dollars into Chinese yuan renminbi (CNY or RMB) which allowed it to purchase A-share stocks listed in Shanghai and Shenzhen that were restricted to local or QFII investors. Investors in CAF in this way had access to a fixed pool of mainland Chinese stocks, which they could then trade with each other on a US stock exchange at a premium or discount to the pool's actual value.

In this way, the discount or premium of a closed-end fund can be read as a useful sentiment indicator of how much investor interest there is in a particular theme or keyword. For example, in 2006 the India Fund and Morgan Stanley India Fund (tickers: IFN and IIF) were trading at significant premiums to NAV, as the Indian stock market was doing well, but there was not yet an ETF allowing foreign investors ready access to the market. Similarly, before ETNs and ETFs tracking MLPs were launched, closed-end funds holding MLPs were trading at a premium to NAV, even though these CEFs had the disadvantage of being taxable at the fund level. With more and more ETFs covering more and more of these difficult markets that once required CEFs for access, stock CEFs have lost favor as an access products and now many trade at long-term discounts. Below is a snapshot from the January 2017 *Wall Street Journal* page on emerging market closed-end funds (Fig. 8.11).

As a general rule, one can read that when several closed-end funds on a given country or theme are trading at a premium, that is an indicator that investors are especially "hot" on that area at the moment. While a deep discount can also be read as a contrary indicator, the fact that many closed-end funds typically trade at a 5–15% discount anyway makes a modest discount less significant as an "out of favor" indicator. This article is an example of how relative discounts on different country CEFs were read as an outlook for 2017: http://seekingalpha.com/article/4041896-10-emerging-markets-watch-2017-closed-end-fund-sentiment-indicator.

Aside from stocks, closed-end funds retain some advantages in the field of bond funds and in the United States hold significant amounts of assets in both US taxable and tax-exempt municipal bonds. Here the two advantages of CEFs are in their holding of illiquid assets that only need to be

CLOSED-END FUNDS: Emerging Markets Funds | Return to Major Categories | About Closed End Funds

Wednesday, February 1, 2017

Fund	NAV	Weekly Statistics (as of 1/27/2017)		NAV	Daily Statistics (as of 2/01/2017)		52 Week Market Return %
		Mkt Price	Prem/Disc %		Mkt Price	Prem/Disc %	
Aberdeen Chile (CH)	7.53	6.36	-15.54	7.49	6.25	-16.56	22.82
Aberdeen EM SmCo Opptys (ABE)	13.63	11.74	-13.87	13.82	11.83	-14.40	13.91
Aberdeen Greater China (GCH)	11.02	9.20	-16.52	11.00	9.21	-16.27	19.96
Aberdeen Indonesia (IF)	7.68	6.44	-16.10	7.70	6.48	-15.84	19.66
Aberdeen Latin America (LAQ)	24.69	21.45	-13.12	24.49	21.19	-13.47	49.69
BMO LGM Frontier ME (N/A)	9.05	N/A	N/A	9.14	N/A	N/A	N/A
Central Euro Russia & Tu (CEE)	24.56	21.45	-12.66	24.33	21.42	-11.96	34.34
China Fund (CHN)	18.46	15.87	-14.03	18.47	15.78	-14.56	21.18
First Tr/Abrdn Emerg Op (FEO)	16.74	14.55	-13.08	16.77	14.48	-13.66	27.03
Herzfeld Caribbean Basin (CUBA)	7.71	6.84	-11.28	7.64	6.75	-11.65	27.39
India Fund (IFN)	25.31	22.96	-9.28	25.56	22.61	-11.54	15.12
JPMorgan China Region (JFC)	17.94	17.10	-4.68	17.91	16.98	-5.19	33.98
Latin American Discovery (LDF)	11.67	10.30	-11.74	11.53	10.10	-12.44	45.17
Mexico Equity & Income (MXE)	10.75	9.20	-14.42	10.77	9.24	-14.21	-10.94
Mexico Fund (MXF)	16.31	14.45	-11.40	N/A	14.40	N/A	-6.57
Morg Stan China A (CAF) ᴶ	21.62	18.04	-16.56	21.61	17.98	-16.80	18.36
Morg Stan Emerg Mkts (MSF)	16.06	14.00	-12.83	16.02	13.91	-13.17	18.21
Morg Stan India Inv (IIF)	31.65	28.32	-10.52	32.19	28.05	-12.86	25.62
Taiwan Fund (TWN)	19.40	16.90	-12.89	19.40	16.64	-14.23	16.71
Templeton Dragon Fund (TDF)	20.36	17.50	-14.05	20.41	17.57	-13.91	21.29
Templeton Emerging Mkts (EMF)	14.75	12.92	-12.41	14.76	12.90	-12.60	40.90
Turkish Investment Fund (TKF)	7.80	6.66	-14.62	8.31	7.00	-15.76	-13.72
Voya Em Mkts Hi Div Eqty (IHD)	9.04	8.10	-10.40	9.00	8.09	-10.11	34.57

Source: Lipper Inc.

Fig. 8.11 Snapshot of emerging market stock closed-end funds with their discounts, from January 2017 WSJ.com

bought once (and may be expensive or impossible to trade in any secondary market), and in their ability to leverage up these fixed income assets to multiply the income yield they can pay out. Bond CEFs often employ leverage by issuing senior preferred shares, including variable rate preferred and auction rate securities. As with the examples of Simple Sample Bank in Chaps. 2 and 4, these preferred shares allow the fund to, for example, raise $50 million from fund investors and another $50 million in preferred shares to invest $100 million in bonds that may yield, say, 4%. If the preferred shares only need to pay out an interest or dividend rate of 1% (which their investors may be happy to accept, as they only risk loss of capital in the extreme event the whole bond portfolio loses over 50%), then the closed-end fund would earn $4 million/year in bond yield while paying out only $500,000 year on the preferred shares, leaving $500,000 for fund management fees and $3 million to be paid out to the investors in the $50 million of common fund shares, a 6% dividend yield in a 4% environment. A few months after launching, the fund may trade down to a discount, reducing the total return of the seller while offering the buyer an even higher yield. In addition to the NAV discount/premium risk, such leveraged funds also face the risk that the rate they need to pay on the preferred shares rises and even exceeds the yield from the assets, which is what happens when the yield curve flattens or inverts. For this reason, leveraged closed-end bond funds, like leveraged bond trades, are most attractive when the yield curve is steep and allows borrowing at low, short-term rates to invest in high-, long-term rates.

Leverage has also become increasingly popular in ETFs, but with a daily rebalancing requirement that incurs high trading costs. ETFs will finally be covered after the next section on open-ended mutual funds.

8.7   Open-Ended Mutual Funds

For decades, open-ended mutual funds (often what is meant when people say "mutual funds") have been the main way individual retail investors have accessed stock and bond markets. In the days before ETFs and low-cost online brokers, mutual funds were the most accessible and cost-effective way for millions of people to own a diversified, professionally managed portfolio of stocks and bonds almost as easily as putting money in a time deposit. By 2017, mutual funds still manage many times more assets than ETFs, and a cynic might say mutual funds stick around primarily as a legal structure for siphoning fees from investors' money on its way to and from a stock exchange or bond market.

What makes open-ended mutual funds more scalable, and operationally more complicated, than closed-end funds is their openness to taking in new money from new investors (creating more shares), or allowing investors to redeem and cash out their shares directly with the fund company at NAV. For example, an investor can put $1,000 into a mutual fund and, subject to meeting that day's cut-off, will have that money invested in that mutual fund's pool of stocks or bonds at that day's closing price. Similarly, the investor can cash out part or all of the fund, based on the cut-off day's closing price, based on the value of stocks or bonds the fund values that day without any regard to premium or discount to NAV. This requires the significant administrative work of calculating the value of each share of the fund at the close of each business day, and accounting to ensure that incoming and outgoing investors have their shares allocated and redeemed at prices fair to all investors in the fund, including those who remain in the fund. Although the pricing and allocation of gains and losses may be done to ensure fairness to all its investors, the fund's requirement to buy stocks or bonds when money comes in or sell stocks or bonds when investors redeem can generate capital gains tax events to US investors even if they don't buy or sell any shares of the fund that year.

In addition to being classified by what they invest in, mutual funds are also divided into active and passively managed funds. Actively managed funds have a professional management team tasked with selecting and executing investments in the fund to meet the goals stated in the fund prospectus, while passively managed funds simply buy and hold the assets in proportion to their weights in an index, with the simpler goal of tracking the index as closely as possible. Due to the costs of hiring professional fund managers, research analysts, and a marketing team to sell their experience to investors, actively managed funds generally charge much higher management fees, often over 1% of assets under management per year, while passively managed funds often charge less than 0.1% of AUM per year. Jack Bogle is the legendary name in the development and popularization of passive index investing, with his low-cost Vanguard mutual funds now being one of the largest asset managers in the world. As described in the section on alpha and beta, actively managed mutual funds as a whole underperform passive funds by the amount of their additional expenses (i.e. their alpha is negative), which has led to increasing preference of low-cost passive index funds over more expensive actively managed funds, but as of 2017, the share of funds invested passively is arguably still well below the level of a "critically efficient" market as described in Sect. 8.2.

In addition to higher management fees and possible taxes, mutual funds often also have sales charges and other expenses which can be charged either up front, at redemption, or on an ongoing basis. Up-front charges, often called a front-end load or "A-share" in many mutual fund channels, are preferred by many advisors in that it cleanly pays a commission to the mutual fund salesperson up front. A 5% front-end load means that an investor must pay $105,000 to buy shares of a mutual fund that have an NAV of $100,000, which is the amount of money that would be invested and returned to the investor when redeemed. While front-end loads are simple, they obviously produce an incentive for advisors to churn sales in funds more often to earn more commissions. A back-end load allows $100,000 invested in a mutual fund to initially show an NAV equal to the $100,000, but charge the $5,000 if the fund is redeemed in the first year, and often reduce this amount if the fund is redeemed later. Some funds impose a charge for fund shares redeemed before a certain period of time which is not a sales charge but an incentive to hold the funds in the longer term. Back-end loads are made possible by higher ongoing charges which allow funds to pay the selling advisor a "trailer" or ongoing commission, which provides an incentive to keep the investor invested in the same fund. One of the most important lessons on Wall Street or many other industries is that to understand why one product sells more than another, start by looking at how those selling it get paid.

Below is a snapshot of some of the largest US mutual funds by assets as of March 2017. Note that some funds are listed more than once due to different share classes, which may differ by the minimum initial investment amount and whether any sales charges are paid up front (e.g. AGTHX) versus as a trailer (e.g. GFACX), which is reflected in the different expense ratios these different classes of the same funds charge (Fig. 8.12).

The turnover ratio in the above table also shows the difference between relatively passive buy and hold funds, such as the Vanguard or Fidelity S&P 500 index funds or American Funds EuroPacific Growth Funds, versus the more actively traded and rebalanced funds which sell and recycle a higher percentage of their assets in the market each year.

In addition to being purchased directly by investors, open-ended mutual funds are often wrapped in variable annuities, indexed universal life policies, or other insurance products. These insurance savings plans may have some bona fide insurance component but are generally sold for one of the following reasons:

Name	Inception	Assets (US$ million)	Turnover Rate	Min Initial Investment	Expense Ratio
$ Vanguard Total Stock Market Index Fund Investor Shares (VTSMX)	04/27/1992	$ 541,309	4.0%	$3,000	0.16%
$ Vanguard 500 Index Fund Investor Class (VFINX)	08/31/1976	$ 306,379	4.0%	$3,000	0.16%
$ Vanguard Total International Stock Index Fund Investor Shares (VGTSX)	04/29/1996	$ 251,607	23.9%	$3,000	0.18%
$ Vanguard Total Bond Market Index Fund Investor Shares (VBMFX)	11/12/1986	$ 176,037	61.0%	$3,000	0.16%
$ American Funds The Growth Fund of America® Class A (AGTHX)	11/30/1973	$ 155,096	31.0%	$2,500	0.66%
$ American Funds The Growth Fund of America® Class C (GFACX)	11/30/1973	$ 155,096	31.0%	$2,500	1.46%
American Funds The Growth Fund of America® Class F-1 (GFAFX)	11/30/1973	$ 155,096	31.0%	$2,500	0.71%
Fidelity® Government Cash Reserves (FDRXX)	10/5/1979	$ 136,008	--	$2,500	0.37%
$ American Funds EuroPacific Growth Fund® Class A (AEPGX)	04/16/1984	$ 127,750	0.3%	$2,500	0.83%
$ American Funds EuroPacific Growth Fund® Class C (AEPCX)	04/16/1984	$ 127,750	0.3%	$2,500	1.62%
Fidelity® 500 Index Fund - Institutional Class (FXSIX)	02/17/1988	$ 116,613	4.0%	$5,000,000	0.04%
Fidelity® 500 Index Fund - Institutional Premium Class (FXAIX)	02/17/1988	$ 116,613	4.0%	$9,999,999	0.02%
Fidelity® 500 Index Fund - Investor Class (FUSEX)	02/17/1988	$ 116,613	4.0%	$2,500	0.09%
Fidelity® 500 Index Fund - Premium Class (FUSVX)	02/17/1988	$ 116,613	4.0%	$10,000	0.05%
Fidelity® Contrafund® (FCNTX)	05/17/1967	$ 107,415	41.0%	$2,500	0.68%
$ American Funds American Balanced Fund® Class A (ABALX)	07/25/1975	$ 106,720	79.0%	$2,500	0.59%
$ American Funds American Balanced Fund® Class C (BALCX)	07/25/1975	$ 106,720	79.0%	$2,500	1.38%
$ American Funds The Income Fund of America® Class A (AMECX)	11/30/1973	$ 105,184	52.0%	$2,500	0.56%

Fig. 8.12 Largest US mutual funds by assets as of March 2017, according to Fidelity

A. Advisors can often earn much higher commissions selling mutual funds within an insurance product than outside of one.

B. Advisors without a securities license can sell an insurance-wrapped produce if they only have an insurance license.

C. The insurance companies providing the wrapper are often big, trusted names many investors may feel more comfortable with, and many buyers do not understand how the underlying monies are invested or charged.

D. Advisors often sell the tax treatment of the insurance wrapper as an advantage.

One reason the commissions and fees can be higher in an insurance-wrapped savings plan is because it is possible for the cash value of an insurance product to be zero or only a fraction of what the value would have been if invested in the underlying mutual funds directly. Part of this difference may go to paying for a bona fide insurance death benefit, but most of the difference is simply kept by the insurance company and other fee-takers in the value chain. The insurance component can often be purchased separately through a low-cost term life insurance policy, and the difference invested directly in a strategy called "buy term and invest the difference", which often results in lower fees and higher returns to the investor. While there can be genuine tax differences between investing in mutual funds directly versus through an insurance wrapper, tax reforms in the United States, and likely to be implemented in other countries with capital gains taxes, are likely to minimize the difference between the two. Prudent investors should do the math comparing the after-tax expected returns of the two options, and will often find that the non-insurance option is more transparent, is more flexible, and provides better returns at lower costs.

The next section introduces ETFs, which provide many of the best advantages of closed-end and open-ended mutual funds.

8.8   EXCHANGE-TRADED FUNDS (ETFs)

Exchange-traded funds, or ETFs, are one of the most important financial technologies of the late twentieth and early twenty-first centuries. ETFs have been referenced throughout this book, as for many investors they are the most direct, scalable, and cost-effective way to observe, access, and trade many market indices and asset classes as easily as they would any stock.

ETFs, like closed-end funds, are exchange traded on a stock exchange, but unlike CEFs, ETFs are open-ended and can be created and redeemed to minimize tracking error and ensure they trade close to NAV without much discount or premium. Unlike open-ended mutual funds, which investors can buy or redeem directly with the fund management company, ETFs can only be created or redeemed in blocks called creation units by institutional traders called authorized participants ("AP"). For example, the creation unit of the ETF "DIA" that tracks the Dow Jones Industrial Average (DJIA) is 50,000 shares of DIA, which would be exchangeable by the AP for about 3,000 shares of each of the 30 Dow component stocks.

If DIA ever traded much below the NAV of the Dow 30 stock portfolio, the AP could buy 50,000 DIA shares, exchange them for the 3,000 shares each of the Dow 30 stocks, and then immediately sell them for a riskless arbitrage profit. Conversely, if the ETF ever traded at a premium, the AP could buy the 3,000 shares of each of the 30 stocks and exchange them for 50,000 shares of DIA which could be immediately sold for a risk-free profit. This ETF arbitrage trade is extremely efficient and competitive between APs and ensures that most investors need not worry than most ETFs they would trade are fairly priced in the market at any time. Because this creation and redemption mechanism is done in kind and in the form of shares, it also removes from the fund any explicit need to handle cash coming in or out of the fund by buying or selling any fund assets, which both simplifies the accounting and minimizes possible tax events to long-term fund investors.

Investors in ETFs remain mostly made up of institutions and fee-based advisors, and US retail investors are increasingly learning how to include them in their accounts. In many markets, however, the big speedbump to broader adoption of ETFs is that they do not pay distribution commissions like mutual funds. This is especially noticeable in Asia, where the asset base is large but the ETF market still relatively small, because a large share of individual wealth is invested in relatively high-fee mutual funds and insurance-wrapped investment products which pay armies of agents to sell them. As markets become more open, as the United States has done over the past few decades but is still far from perfecting, ETFs are likely to replace many more expensive or exclusive funds as the core tool for asset allocation.

ETFs have come to represent a wide variety of asset classes, from major national, regional, or global stock indices, sector indices including technology or real estate, bond indices tracking government or corporate portfolios, and commodities ranging from gold to natural gas futures. While ETFs are often considered low-cost, passive, index tracking investments and compared with passive index mutual funds, the only primary requirement of an ETF is to have a daily published portfolio that an AP can create or redeem shares against. This portfolio often represents an index but can also represent an actively managed portfolio so long as it meets this requirement for AP creation/redemption. This same requirement applies to bond funds, which are created or redeemed in exchange for portfolios of the underlying bonds which the AP must source and trade, or physical gold ETFs, which are created or redeemed against delivery of physical gold. While there are entire books written on the subject of ETFs, understanding them as a wrapper around an asset or portfolio of assets that can be traded on a stock exchange as a single stock is most of what one needs to know about them.

Below is a list of the 20 largest US listed ETFs by assets as of March 2017. Three of the five largest and most actively traded ETFs remain those that track the S&P 500 index by the three US ETF giants: State Street's SPDRs, Blackrock's iShares, and Vanguard. These ETF companies have been waging a price war which has pushed down the cost of investing in a passive benchmark portfolio of large US stocks to record low levels below 0.1% per year, and may continue to push these closer to zero. Of these, the oldest, largest, and still most expensive of these three ETFs are the "Spyders", traded in the United States under the symbol "SPY" and originally standing for Standard & Poor's Depositary Receipts (SPDR). SPY works very similarly to the DIA example illustrated above, although the number of shares of each of the 500 component stocks will vary as the underlying index is market cap weighted, rather than price weighted. The higher fee is due to SPY being set up in an older structure which does not allow the shares in SPY to be lent out, which would raise stock loan fees that are not currently required to be disclosed to investors as part of the net expense ratio, and may be accepted by investors (and especially by traders) as long as SPY remains more liquid and less expensive to trade (Fig. 8.13).

The above table would indicate that investor interest, at least in the United States, is still especially concentrated and lopsided toward domestic large stocks and domestic bonds. While this certainly has resulted in the benefit of much lower costs for investors seeking simply this core exposure to the mainstream assets everyone else owns, it also highlights the opportunity of where else an "outside the box" investor can focus in smaller, foreign companies or other less traded bonds and alternatives.

The major indices and asset classes tracked by ETFs are often also tradable as cash-settled or physically settled futures contracts. As illustrated in the example in Sect. 7.3, large cap US stock exposure can be just as easily accessed by buying CME S&P 500 e-mini futures contracts as by buying SPY, and medium-term US government bond exposure can as easily be traded with CME ten-year treasury note futures as with the iShares 7- to 10-year bond ETF with symbol "IEF". Around the world, liquid futures contracts exist on stock indices including the DJ EuroSTOXX 50, Nikkei 225, and the Hang Seng Index, and on benchmark government bonds in

Symbol	Name	Net Assets (US$ billion)	Net Expense Ratio	Asset Class	Inception Date
SPY	SPDR S&P 500 ETF	$ 235	0.09%	Equity	01/22/1993
IVV	iShares Core S&P 500 ETF	$ 98	0.04%	Equity	05/15/2000
VTI	Vanguard Total Stock Market ETF	$ 76	0.05%	Equity	05/24/2001
EFA	iShares MSCI EAFE ETF	$ 64	0.33%	Equity	08/14/2001
VOO	Vanguard S&P 500 ETF	$ 63	0.05%	Equity	09/07/2010
VWO	Vanguard FTSE Emerging Markets ETF	$ 49	0.14%	Equity	03/04/2005
QQQ	PowerShares QQQ	$ 45	0.20%	Equity	03/10/1999
VEA	Vanguard FTSE Developed Markets ETF	$ 44	0.09%	Equity	07/20/2007
AGG	iShares Core U.S. Aggregate Bond ETF	$ 42	0.05%	Fixed Income	09/22/2003
IJH	iShares Core S&P Mid-Cap ETF	$ 39	0.07%	Equity	05/22/2000
IWD	iShares Russell 1000 Value ETF	$ 37	0.20%	Equity	05/22/2000
IWM	iShares Russell 2000 ETF	$ 37	0.20%	Equity	05/22/2000
VNQ	Vanguard REIT ETF	$ 35	0.12%	Real Estate	09/23/2004
GLD	SPDR Gold Trust	$ 34	0.40%	Commodity	11/18/2004
IWF	iShares Russell 1000 Growth ETF	$ 34	0.20%	Equity	05/22/2000
BND	Vanguard Total Bond Market ETF	$ 32	0.06%	Fixed Income	04/03/2007
LQD	iShares iBoxx $ Investment Grade Corpora	$ 31	0.15%	Fixed Income	07/22/2002
VTV	Vanguard Value ETF	$ 30	0.08%	Equity	01/26/2004
IJR	iShares Core S&P Small-Cap ETF	$ 30	0.07%	Equity	05/22/2000
EEM	iShares MSCI Emerging Markets ETF	$ 28	0.72%	Equity	04/07/2003

Fig. 8.13 20 largest US listed exchange-traded funds (ETFs) by assets

Canada, Britain, Germany, France, Italy, Japan, Korea, and Australia. Some differences between trading stocks and bonds via ETFs vs futures include:

A. ETFs incur fund management fees in addition to trading costs, while futures only incur trading costs.
B. Futures positions would need to be rolled quarterly, while ETFs can be held in the long term.
C. ETFs may pay dividends, while any implied dividend would be realized only on the roll with futures contracts.
D. Futures can be traded long or short with only a few percent of its notional value in a margin account, without requiring margin loans or securities lending as with an ETF.
E. Futures contracts and ETFs are taxed differently under US tax law.

In practice, the difference between futures and ETFs can be somewhat blurred by traders that fluently participate in both markets, and both have their uses with both short-term traders and long-term investors.

Using an analogy to music recording technology, one might draw the following parallels:

- Closed-end funds are like vinyl records: They can't be changed once they're recorded, were expensive in their day, and are increasingly hard to find, but some old classics are best heard on vinyl or owned via a CEF.
- Open-ended mutual funds are like cassette tapes: Mass-produced, but can be re-recorded and re-used, made some new things possible (like the Walkman® or 401(k)), but had several problems leaving users looking for better solutions.
- ETFs (and financial futures) are like compact disks: All-digital, smaller, lighter, and cheaper than vinyl or cassettes, and with several advantages like the ability to skip or randomize tracks, and copy tracks to a computer.
- The future of portfolio investment may come through electronic streamlining of direct portfolio curation and trading, like how iTunes and Spotify have already replaced CDs in recording technology.

Blockchain is one technology that is likely to streamline transactions and settlements in both fund-like and futures-like instruments and is the subject of the next chapter.

CHAPTER 9

Blockchain and Cryptocurrencies

Blockchain technology is likely to transform the world of banking and signed documents in the coming decades, similar to how e-mail and mobile messaging transformed post offices, telephones, and photography over the past few decades. Blockchain applications development in the 2010s has so far been comparable to how web pages evolved in the 1990s. By 2017, markets in Bitcoin and other cryptocurrencies and tokens have grown to a value of over US$100 billion to levels many consider a manic bubble. This chapter aims to explain the essentials of blockchain, cryptocurrencies, and the example case of Bitcoin to hopefully help these technologies understood for some of their many excellent potential applications rather than as simplistic vehicles of speculation. In other words, investing "outside the box" in blockchain does not mean simply buying into an ICO or cryptocurrency with the blind hope of making money, but rather in understanding how blockchain applications work and should be valued.

The author holds a strong view that simply buying units of Bitcoin, Ethereum, or other cryptocurrency tokens with the hope of selling them later for a profit is not investing, but speculation. Doing so would be similar to seeing development of Internet companies in the late 1990s and early 2000s and putting money into buying up domain names rather than investing in shares of Amazon or Priceline. The latter would have invested in capital used to develop online services that actually served and benefited people, while the former is simply a "buy and hope" punt on future prices. The record rise in ICOs (initial coin offerings) in 2017, described later in this chapter, are a first but primitive step to using cryptocurrency technol-

© The Author(s) 2018   209
T. Dennison, *Invest Outside the Box*,
https://Doi.org/10.1007/978-981-13-0372-2_9

ogy to actually fund the development and maintenance of economically useful services. If a technological visionary were to imagine a future solution to a problem like payments using electronic blockchain software, chances are a token with an extremely volatile value against currencies actually used in the real world would not be a necessary or desired feature, and the different interests in the solution versus the volatility can largely be explained by psychological drivers discussed in Chap. 11.

9.1   The Basics of Public Key Cryptography on Which Blockchain and Cryptocurrencies Are Based

Although it may be boring, it is important to understand at least some of the basics of public key infrastructure ("PKI") cryptography as the technology underlying all blockchains and cryptocurrencies. PKI is what allows the transactions on a blockchain to be both public and secure. The two main functions of PKI are to *encrypt* and *sign* transactions.

Encryption means to scramble information so thoroughly that only the holder of a specific key can decrypt and read it. For example, a customer typing a credit card number into a web browser may understand that the Internet signal may be passing through several different computers between the customer and the processing bank, but is assured that the encryption allows only the receiving bank with its key to unscramble and read the credit card number, so that none of the computers in between may be able to use it. In other words, encryption ensures that only the intended recipient of a piece of information, the one who holds the key, will be able to decrypt and read it.

Digital signatures, on the other hand, ensure that the key holder is the only one who could have sent the information, and that it has not been tampered with since it was sent. This may be valuable in a document that includes, say, a bank account number into which the recipient should transfer funds, and of course the sender would want to be sure it was evident if the messenger somehow changed the bank account number the recipient saw.

Information can be both encrypted and signed, or just encrypted or just signed, but the free and open availability of algorithms and software and the falling cost of computing power have made it worthwhile to make encryption and signature a standard part of many electronic transactions. Perhaps the most widely seen application of encryption and digital signa-

> 🔒 Secure | https://**www.amazon.com**

Fig. 9.1   Example of HTTPS and secure lock on the site Amazon.com using the Google Chrome web browser

tures is the HTTPS protocol used in web browsers that assures users that (Fig. 9.1):

A. The website content comes from the source in the navigation bar and has not been tampered with, and
B. Information entered on that site will be sent securely to the source of the website.

The green lock showing that the above site has been certified as coming from the domain amazon.com is currently verified by a certificate authority, of which a few large ones (with names like VeriSign and Godaddy) are trusted by major web browsers including Mozilla Firefox, Google Chrome, and Internet Explorer. These certificate authorities currently act similar to banks as centralized recordkeepers, as opposed to a blockchain that polls a decentralized number of "witnesses" on a network to validate a certificate through consensus.

Many children practice the basics of encrypting messages using private keys, for example a decoder ring that translates each letter of the alphabet into another cryptic one and back, but only as secure as the decoder ring can be kept secret. Scaling encryption and signing requires the math of public keys, also known as asymmetric cryptography. Public keys are ones that can be shared publicly, since they can be used by anyone to encrypt messages that can only be decrypted by the owner of the private keys, and the public keys can be used to verify signatures (and lack of tampering) that could only have been signed by the owner of the private keys.

There are several algorithms for PKI, but some of the easiest to understand involve very large numbers which even today's most powerful computers are unable to break down into prime numbers within any practical time limit. Prime numbers are numbers greater than 1 that are only divisible by 1 and itself: for example, $7 or $19 cannot be divided evenly into whole dollars between any number of friends greater than one and different than 7 or 19, respectively, without splitting a dollar into cents. The fundamental theorem of arithmetic is that every whole number greater than 1 can be uniquely broken down as a product (multiplication) of a unique combination of prime numbers, which effectively form the number's "signature". For example, the number 60 can be broken down as 2 × 2 × 3 × 5, and no other product of any other prime numbers. A common basis for public keys is that it is generally far easier to multiply prime numbers to form their product than it is to break down a large number into its prime numbers. For example, in one basic PKI algorithm, I could share my public key as the number 1,720,501, and use this number to encrypt any message, or verify the signature of any message, which can only be decrypted, or could have only been signed, using the prime numbers that multiply out to this number: 853 × 2017. Multiplying the private keys 853 × 2017 to get the public key 1,720,501 is relatively easy as it is only one multiplication, but figuring out the private key from the public key for a seven-digit number could take up to 500 operations. The strength of a public key relies on using numbers large enough that even the fastest and most powerful computers and algorithms would take hundreds of years or longer to crack the public key into the private keys, keeping the private keys and what they can secure in that time.

9.2   BLOCKCHAIN BASICS: BITCOIN, CRYPTOCURRENCIES, AND PAYMENTS

A *blockchain* is simply a distributed, encrypted ledger that keeps track of transactions in a public but secure way. Blockchains publish, online and in plain sight, on a public network as with any blog post or public website, transactions which can be executed, secured, and verified using the public key infrastructure described above. Two key buzzwords many blockchains aim to follow is being *open-source* (meaning anyone can view, and even submit modifications to, the software source code) and *decentralized* (meaning records are redundantly stored on many different computers with no one institution having control over them). The first and arguably simplest implementation of a widely used blockchain is the cryptocurrency Bitcoin.

Bitcoin is purely an Internet-based, electronic form of cash that can be sent from one Bitcoin address to another in a way similar to how an e-mail is sent from one e-mail address to another. A Bitcoin address, also known as a Bitcoin wallet, is a cryptic string of about 34 case-sensitive alphanumeric characters that acts as a public key. For example, the non-profit Free Software Foundation (www.fsf.org) publishes the Bitcoin address

---

fsf.org/about/ways-to-donate

- Via Bitcoin, the peer-to-peer virtual currency. The FSF's Bitcoin address is "1PC9aZC4hNX2rmmrt7uHTfYAS3hRbph4UN". Note that since we are using a single address for receiving all contributions, we are not providing full anonymity.
- Via Litecoin, the peer-to-peer virtual currency. The FSF's Litecoin address is "LPttYC3GoXNrBqGfLT7tTbNHm8SiUpBwYz". Note that since we are using a single address for receiving all contributions, we are not providing full anonymity.

Fig. 9.2 Example of how the Free Software Foundation accepts donation in Bitcoin

"1PC9aZC4hNX2rmmrt7uHTfYAS3hRbph4UN" at which it accepts donations in Bitcoin. Anyone with this address can send Bitcoin units to this address, but only the holder of the private keys (in this case, the treasurer at the FSF) can send Bitcoin units from this address (say, to an exchange to cash them into US dollars). Note the FSF also publishes a Litecoin address, which is another cryptocurrency competing with Bitcoin (Fig. 9.2).

Unlike a bank transfer, where transfers of money are kept on the records of a single centralized institution, the Bitcoin ledger is decentralized and stored on multiple computers in many locations, with the most up-to-date version verified by checking the consensus of what is the latest version of the ledger on the network across those computers. The ledger stores the entire transactional history, from wallet to wallet, of a given Bitcoin (and each tiny fraction of each Bitcoin) ever since its initial "mining" (described two paragraphs later). Below is an example of an information page on the website blockchain.info, showing the lifetime number of transactions and volume received, current balance, and most recent transaction of the FSF Bitcoin wallet (Fig. 9.3).

Anyone can create any number of Bitcoin wallets as easily as (or, arguably, even more easily than) creating a Gmail or Yahoo e-mail address, and in practice many individuals and organizations use multiple wallets for security, privacy, or accounting purposes because they are easy to create and manage than multiple bank accounts.

The scarcity value of Bitcoin comes from the fact that the algorithm limits, by design, the number of Bitcoins to a total of about 21 million Bitcoins that will ever be allowed to exist. Bitcoins are created through a process called "mining", where powerful computers compete to solve math problems (comparable to finding the next prime number with a bil-

Fig. 9.3 Blockchain.info page showing lifetime transaction volume, current balance, and latest transaction of FSF's Bitcoin wallet

lion digits) where the solution is the basis of a new Bitcoin. All the other computers in the network then record the consensus of the chain of transactions from the miner that originally generated the Bitcoin through each wallet that receives and sends it up to its current holder. Each transaction, where Bitcoins are sent from one wallet to another, is signed with the private keys of the sending wallet in the same way that a bank check is signed, and the consensus of the Bitcoin network on the record of signed transactions acts as the decentralized replacement of a bank's ledger. As will be listed in the list of advantages below, these Bitcoin transactions have the advantage over paper banknotes, checks, and signatures in that digital signatures are almost impossible to counterfeit or forge.

Bitcoin's most obvious application is as an electronic form of cash or payment with its ability to operate at lower cost and with less overhead than credit cards or bank transfers. E-mail users, who have seen the savings of time and money from no longer having to mail letters at the post office, should see this the obvious way forward in a world where banks can still charge US$15 or more for an international money transfer in 2017, even though a barrel of crude oil can be sent around the world for only US$2–4. Bitcoin wallets do not require any permission, documentation, in-person branch visits, or other expensive overhead of opening a bank or credit card account. As a digital currency, Bitcoin also has the benefit of being divisible into very small fractions of a whole Bitcoin. As of late 2017 with the price of 1 Bitcoin hitting US$7,000, this divisibility is essential for Bitcoin to be useful enough to send ฿0.0005 as payment for, say, a US$3.50 cup of coffee.

The pure computational foundation of Bitcoin's value as a stake in a scarce share of a fixed pool of solutions to math problems may be seen by some as an advantage, in that it is not tied to any country's fiat currency or government policy, but this lack of connection to any physical or legal anchor of value makes Bitcoin's exchange rate against real currencies so volatile it is unusable for many mainstream applications. While someone who bought a Bitcoin at US$1,000 may be happy to see the ability to sell it for US$7,000 less than a year later, merchants selling real products or services would not be able to maintain stable prices in Bitcoin nor would likely want to keep their working capital in such a volatile unit of account. That in mind, merchants may still find it handy to accept payment in Bitcoin, as the FSF has done with donations, due to advantages that include:

A. Anyone with an Internet connection can pay in Bitcoin from anywhere in the world, whether they have a bank account/credit card or not.
B. The Bitcoin network fee for processing a transaction is much lower than bank or credit card fees.
C. Like cash, and unlike credit card and bank transfers, Bitcoin transactions are immutable and cannot be reversed.
D. Unlike cash, Bitcoin is nearly impossible to counterfeit, tear, or stain, but the keys can be backed up on a separate drive in case the original is lost or damaged.

Besides its price volatility, Bitcoin does have a few other disadvantages as a payment technology, including the inability to recover lost keys (a security feature some might say is too secure), and the limitations on how quickly the network can process transactions (currently a fraction of what Visa or MasterCard can do without breaking a sweat). The network capacity is one reason there was a debate in late 2017 over whether to "fork" the Bitcoin protocol into two networks: "Bitcoin" and "Bitcoin Cash", with the latter focused more on fast and low-cost payments. It will be interesting to see how the world's first cryptocurrency fares against others in the coming years and decades. While there have already been many other cryptocurrencies launched with varying degrees of success (including Litecoin, seen on the FSF donation page), one of the more promising is a blockchain platform called Ethereum, which, in addition to allowing transfers of value, has the ability to encode *smart contracts*, described in the next section.

9.3   ADVANCED BLOCKCHAINS: SMART CONTRACTS

Being able to send money securely, cheaply, and nearly instantly over a computer network through a technology like Bitcoin is already pretty awesome (at least compared with paying US$15 for a bank transfer), but as with e-mail and the Internet, it is only the first of many possibly applications blockchain technology is capable of. Some of these applications may already be as obvious today as video calls were to science fiction writers of the 1950s, while many more are likely to be as unimaginable today as *Gangnam Style*'s billions of YouTube views would have been as recently as 1992.

As with the ability to write code that powers web pages that can collect information and interact with users, blockchains can encode *smart contracts* that program much of the logic currently entrusted to banks, government offices, and other human institutions to be executed without human delay or error. One blockchain platform rising to compete with Bitcoin, especially on its support for smart contracts, is called Ethereum, on which many initial coin offerings ("ICOs", described later in this section) have so far been based.

As many transactions, financial and non-financial, involve more details and steps than a simple transfer of value from one wallet to another, the smart contract functionality allows such transactions to be programmed on a blockchain. This may be best understood by a series of examples to be described below:

A. Settlement of a bond trade
B. Offering a blockchain-traded fund ("BTF")
C. Leaving shares of a BTF to heirs in a will

Example A is only slightly more complicated than the simple Bitcoin transaction of transferring ฿0.02 from one wallet to another. In the example of a bond trade in Sect. 2.3, Tracy the trader bought bonds from Delia the dealer. The "contract" in the bond trade was that after saying "done", Delia would deliver the bonds to Tracy and Tracy would deliver the cash to Delia on the following business day based on the numbers agreed. As of 2017, settling transactions in the multi-trillion-dollar bond market still involves the following five steps:

1. Tracy must have an account open with a bank or broker. Opening an account can take as little as two to three hours, but in many cases, the paperwork can still take a month or longer.
2. Tracy must then fund this account with money, which can involve more paperwork and/or checking or wire transfer fees, and, if the transfer needs to be made in another country or currency, may be at the mercy of uncompetitive exchange rates or high fees of the sending or receiving bank.
3. Then, Tracy is ready to place an order to buy the bond from Delia. Many bond trades are still executed over the phone, but there has been an increasing use of proprietary electronic systems which can selectively show prices and handle trade execution, often for a large fee.
4. Once Tracy and Delia execute the bond trade order by saying "done" on the phone or US$2,000/month Bloomberg messenger service, the trade is passed to their respective back offices of both sides for settlement, a process of exchanging the funds versus securities which still takes between one and three business days.
5. The bonds are then typically held in custody by the bank or broker, or at a separate custodian firm. Transferring cash or securities to another custodian involves repeating step #2 in reverse, often with significant costs in time and money. This is still accepted as the cost of safekeeping of very valuable paper certificates of ownership of securities, which might otherwise be easily lost, stolen, damaged, destroyed, or forged.

Now consider instead that a few simple advances in blockchain wallet technology would allow Tracy and Delia to hold both the cash and securities as secure electronic keys, which can be backed up on cloud drives, flash drives, or advanced "cold storage" setups, and could allow Tracy and Delia to trade as follows:

1. Tracy has money in "crypto" form on one digital wallet, and wants to use that money to buy bonds from Delia, who holds those bonds in another digital wallet on the same blockchain platform. They agree on price and exchange their "wallet addresses" (public keys), which act like exchanging e-mail addresses that are much longer and more cryptic (but still effortless to copy and paste).

2. Tracy's software verifies the digital signatures on Delia's wallet address, confirming that (a) Delia's bonds are genuine and (b) Delia has pre-signed a "smart contract" trusted to release the bonds to a sending wallet address that delivers the right amount of cash against them and otherwise return any extra cash it receives. Similarly, Delia's software verifies the digital signature on Tracy's wallet address, confirming that (a) there is enough cash in the wallet to buy the bonds and (b) the wallet is capable of receiving and holding the bonds Delia is selling.

3. The trade is settled over the network in minutes if not seconds: Tracy has the bonds, Delia has the cash, and now both have plenty of time to go to the museum and see how bond traders were still using back offices and paper back in 2017.

4. The issuer of the bonds can send coupon interest payments directly over the blockchain network to verified holders of the bonds— almost literally "e-mailing" the money directly back to bondholders.

While electronic processing of financial transactions is not new, standardizing their execution over a public, secure network like a blockchain would truly revolutionize financial back office work the way e-mail revolutionized post offices.

Blockchain settlement of bond trades does not immediately solve the *price discovery* problem of OTC bond markets, but arguably is easier to integrate into electronic quotation systems.

The "only" prerequisite for bonds and other securities to start trading this way is for both the currency and the securities denominated in that currency to both be implemented on a blockchain. This may seem like a long way off, but the Bank of Canada and People's Bank of China have both been reported to be looking into putting their currencies (the Canadian dollar and the Chinese yuan renminbi) on blockchains to both reduce friction between banks and the central bank and to better track currency flows and eliminate counterfeiting. Placing a national currency on a blockchain is simply an online, secure version of the serial numbers already on paper money, and could be implemented gradually while phasing out paper and non-blockchain units of currency, just as many central banks issue new editions of paper banknotes every few years already. Coding securities on a blockchain is arguably an even less monumental transition, as many securities already exist in registered form (or bearer form with serial number), and issuing securities this way would almost immediately reduce issuance and administrative costs.

A second application of a blockchain smart contract, example B above, would be a blockchain-traded fund or "BTF". Tracy at this point has developed quite the track record and reputation as an excellent bond trader, and now many investors would like to invest in a bond portfolio professionally managed by Tracy. Tracy registers the prospectus for the planned bond fund with the appropriate regulators as a security, but instead of using the traditional fund administrators, custodians, distribution networks, and exchanges, Tracy simply lists a public wallet address for investors who would like to create or redeem units of the fund versus a published "creation unit" of bonds (as described in Sect. 8.8 on ETFs). The public wallet would function like the custody account of a traditional ETF and hold all the bonds against which units of the fund were created, and Tracy would trade this portfolio of bonds the same way as if they were at a custodian, but with the second set of blockchain steps described in the second example above with Delia. Investors could then freely trade units of the BTF with each other (or with other traders acting as "APs" as with an ETF), also with the same price discovery, execution, and settlement steps Tracy and Delia illustrated on the blockchain. Embedded in the BTF "smart contract" are also terms Tracy defined in the prospectus for the fund, including the management fee to be paid to her personal wallet quarterly, restrictions in how much can be invested in any one bond or sector, automatic publication and verification of fund holdings, and automatic notifications and filings of many compliance reports. In many ways, regulators and compliance officers should be some of the biggest fans of encoding financial industry rules and their implementation onto blockchains, as the technology greatly reduces the human paperwork and associated error, delays, interpretation uncertainty, and opportunities for fraud.

A third blockchain application (example C above) would be executing the will of an investor, Ingrid, who wishes to leave her 3,000 share investment in Tracy's BTF to her three children "per stirpes". (Per stirpes means that the heirs of one heir must share the parent heir's share of the inheritance, rather than being counted as separate heirs for dividing an estate.) Ingrid writes this will onto the blockchain in the year 2020, but in 2022 her eldest child is killed in a self-driving car incident, and she is left by two children. When Ingrid passes away in 2023, her death is certified on the blockchain by the pre-required two or three witnesses (by digitally signing with their pre-verified wallets), which then triggers the release of the BTF shares to her heirs' wallets: 1,000 shares each to her two younger children, and 500 shares to each of her grandchildren through her eldest child (which would be automatic, if that eldest child's death was already signed on the same blockchain). Requiring multiple signatures, for example, to witness the execution of a will, or to certify the death of the testator, is what blockchain technologists refer to as "multi-signature" or "multisig" features of a transaction of smart contract. Note that the "smart contract" framework and terminology are used in this example of a will, even though under common law, wills are not technically contracts (as their consideration is generally not required, and the will only kicks in when the testator dies) but rather referring to the feature of requiring a specific number of a specific class of signatures to trigger an action by the blockchain, in this case the release of assets.

While many people today may not be rushing to replace their paper wills at their trusted lawyer's offices with a digital will on a blockchain, the steps to set this up are far more private and small scale than requiring central banks or securities issuers to set up on a blockchain. Last will and testament documents have legal requirements which vary by jurisdiction, stating how many witnesses are required, what makes a will valid, and which heirs or assets may be excluded. Like other good software applications, an application that encodes a will on a blockchain could automatically verify that each of these steps is done correctly, in order, and serve as a redundant, secure platform whether authorized wallets can view, witness, and execute the will as needed. This example of a will is one where, it might be argued, a blockchain solution may not provide many advantages over a soft copy will, written on a computer by a trusted lawyer, and electronically signed and backed up on a platform like Adobe Sign or DocuSign. It took over a decade for many individuals to switch from sharing photos in paper albums to sharing more of their photos on online platforms like Facebook, so it is likely to take another decade or more before online platforms, whether centralized like Adobe Sign or decentralized like a blockchain, replace most paper documents and signatures, but the advantages against lost, damaged, or forged documents or signatures are clear.

These blockchain applications may feel more tangible to more people as they cross from being purely electronic information verification applications to signing transactions in the real world. Perhaps the most obvious "physical" blockchain application is a land or real property register, where ownership of an apartment or piece of land is recorded on the decentralized, redundant, digitally secured ledger anyone can verify, as opposed to using paper deeds or court records. As with the example of a will, the different computers on the land registry blockchain serve as digital "witnesses" to the transfer of chain of transfers from buyer to seller, and proof of the current owner's legal title. Digital ownership in this way also make it easy to imagine a large tract of land or valuable buildings getting divided up and issued in fractional ownership tokens on a blockchain, effectively acting as a real estate-backed digital currency or blockchain-traded REIT.

Beyond real estate, everyday supply chains could also be supported by blockchain applications verifying authenticity and chain of custody of physical items sold in stores or on international website. One of the first examples this may be worth implementing for is valuable watches, which are widely known to have a parallel market of fakes. A digital code imprinted on a watch could allow a buyer to not only verify whether a watch is a genuine Rolex® or Omega® but also see the chain of ownership from each seller to each buyer while allowing the watchmaker or warranty provider to prove the same. Again, all the computers on the blockchain serve as digital witnesses to the history of sales of each watch through a set of transactions than could only have been signed off by each seller, and can be verified by the buyer as not having been faked or tampered with.

9.4   VALUING CRYPTO ASSETS

2017 marked an explosion not only in the prices of Bitcoin and Ethereum but in the launches and funds raised in initial coin offerings ("ICOs"), with well over US$1 billion raised in ICOs in the first three quarters of 2017.

As an example, imagine that a law firm wrote the software for the will execution application described at the end of the last chapter and launched it on an open blockchain network like Ethereum. The law firm could then sell digital tokens on the network to use this software application in an ICO, similar to how an IPO (described in Chap. 4) would sell shares in a company running such software in a stock market. While there is still much debate on whether and how regulators will treat ICO tokens legally as securities, the tokens in this example are programmed to be spent by users of this blockchain network on services including:

- Paying to have a will drafted/reviewed by an experienced lawyer or will writer on the blockchain.
- Paying (likely an extremely small amount) to have the will contract stored and maintained on the blockchain.

- Verifying a signature, either of a witness or of an authorized issuer of a death certificate.
- Paying for services of the testamentary trustee.

Besides buying tokens to use this application in the ICO (so far mostly using Bitcoin or Ether), users of this application can also earn tokens on this network by providing services to the network, including:

- Drafting, reviewing, or encoding a will on the blockchain for a client.
- Providing storage space on a hard drive to store (one of many) encrypted copies of the will.
- Providing a death certificate or other professional witnessing/verification services.
- Providing the services of a testamentary trustee.

These tokens then effectively become the "currency" of this application, and this decentralized application basically operates like an open digital economy for this specific type of service. The application is decentralized in that it is hosted on a large number of different computers in many different locations, and transactions on the application are verified by checking the consensus of the latest timestamps and digital signatures of the computers on the network participating in a given transaction (including those who simply store a copy of the record of a witness's signature).

What makes these tokens different from a traditional security (and in some ways more like shares in a Vanguard fund, as Vanguard is a mutual organization) is that the application is no longer owned or maintained by the law firm but rather by the owners of the tokens. All governance and operations of this application are encoded on the network, from voting on software updates to issuing any dividends for profits from the network.

In many other ways, valuing a network application like this one is similar to valuing a network application like Facebook or Twitter. Facebook offers its users the ability to post and share messages, photos, videos, and other content to their network of friends at no charge, and makes its money by charging advertisers to post their content for these users to see. In 2016, Facebook's revenue from this business model was US$27.6 billion, on which it made a US$10 billion net profit, and currently trades at over 50x that annual profit with its stock market capitalization at over

US$500 billion. Facebook shareholders value the stock at such a high multiple because they expect its earnings to continue to grow, as illustrated in Sect. 4.4, and the market value for the tokens of the will execution application would be determined by similar supply and demand mechanics, hopefully against its fundamentals. The major difference that might be seen so far is that Facebook earns its revenue and issues its shares in dollars, while all activity on the will application would take place in tokens, and there would need to be a separate market for exchanging those tokens for dollars or other cryptocurrencies.

It is quite easy to imagine a blockchain version of the Facebook developing where advertisers pay to place ads in crypto tokens, which may be bought or sold on exchanges against Bitcoin, Ether, or other crypto currencies or assets. With an ecosystem of enough blockchain applications providing wills, social networking, search engine, online shopping, real estate title transfer, watch repair certification, and other services that can be encoded in smart contracts, cryptocurrencies might start being valued against a "basket of blockchain service tokens" similar to how inflation-indexed currencies are valued against a "basket of goods" in the offline world. If the blockchain applications and tokens start including more and more government services, for example applying for a driver's license or filing a tax return, a critical component in the value of a cryptocurrency could be the government service value and taxing power of the same treasuries fiat currencies are based on today.

This author believes that much of the 2017 trading activity in Bitcoin, Ether, and ICO tokens is a speculation with little regard for fundamentals, in many ways similar to the .com bubble of 1999–2000, and history will see which of these blockchain technologies and units of account succeed like eBay or Priceline and which fail like Pets.com. In 2017, the SEC rejected an application to launch a mainstream ETF holding Bitcoin, while later this year the CME announced plans to launch futures contracts on Bitcoin. While some believe such steps help "legitimize" this space, the author has argued against the idea of a Bitcoin-specific ETF for reasons including:

- Reason #1: A Bitcoin ETF would wrap a twenty-first-century technology in twentieth-century overhead. Technologically, a Bitcoin ETF makes as much sense as printing out an e-mail to deliver at the post office, rather than scanning and e-mailing a letter. Rather than wrap Bitcoin in an ETF, existing funds should be wrapped as BTFs (described in Sect. 9.3).

- Reason #2: A Bitcoin ETF diverts investor focus to price speculation, rather than how to invest in productive applications of the technology.
- Reason #3: This trading and more volatility makes it harder for the mainstream to actually use Bitcoin.
- Reason #4: Currency ETFs, even cryptocurrency ETFs, may be less efficient than direct currency markets, but the successful ones are at least based on solid money markets. One reason to buy some currency ETFs is to get a better interest rate of a foreign currency deposit than one might get at a bank. Before a Bitcoin ETF would make sense, a Bitcoin money market should develop and efficiently set rates of interest one might earn on Bitcoin deposits, or, more likely, repos of Bitcoin against dollars. Repos are described in Sect. 2.4, and in this case one would replace bonds with Bitcoin.
- Reason #5: Many IPOs (and even ICOs) have a "use of proceeds" to invest in growing a real business. The only use of proceeds from launching a Bitcoin ETF would be to help current Bitcoin holders cash out from unsuspecting money held in traditional funds and brokerage accounts. The initial sources of Bitcoin "wealth" were early miners and adopters, and it is easy to see that the Bitcoin economy is currently less based on economic productivity than even some of the most corrupt economies in the world.
- Reason #6: Cryptocurrencies and blockchain platforms should be selected by users for their utility and efficiency, not by regulators or speculators. Approving a Bitcoin ETF would steer institutional money into one cryptocurrency based on raw computing power, rather than at some of the many ICOs which might be building actually useful applications. A BTF of blockchain applications would more closely resemble the ETF of the future, rather than a pure bet on the price of one cryptocurrency.

There are many more sources of information and viewpoints on the fascinating space of blockchain and cryptocurrencies, and this chapter only aims to provide the most basic introduction in the context of an investor. As the Internet changed how information is broadcast and shared, so will blockchain technology likely streamline how signed documents and the value they transfer are safeguarded and moved around. Some may imagine a world in the not-too-distant future where code on a blockchain replaces many of the manual and paper-based process currently dominating many banks, courts, and government offices, but for now, most of the world still lives within a framework of geographic differences between cities and nation states. The next chapter looks at international investing, and how investing outside one's home country will be the most important box to break out of for years, if not decades, to come.

Part III

The "Where" Boxes and "Why Break the Boxes"

Investing within boxes described in parts I and II can be done entirely within the boundaries of a single country, and assume that markets are perfectly rational and always fairly priced. Chapter 10 surveys several international markets where investors are likely to find diversification of risk and return sources versus an all-domestic portfolio. Despite all the data, many investors are likely to not venture into many foreign markets or diversification strategies for emotional or agency reasons which will be among those surveyed in the final chapter on behavioral investing.

International Investing and the Importance of Breaking the Country Box

For many investors, the hardest boxes to think outside of are the geographic ones. American investors still mostly invest in American assets, Chinese investors still focus on Greater China, and even Australian investors keep a majority of their assets in the 2% of the world's market that is Australia. Even many advisers who do highlight the importance of international diversification often suggest only a small fraction of one's portfolio (often up to one-third) be invested internationally, while this author argues for higher international allocations (often more than half) for many investors.

As outlined in Chap. 7, diversification across assets that don't all go up or down together is key to enhancing investment returns and reducing risk. Although correlations between countries have risen with the rise in international futures and ETF trading, diversifying into foreign assets that relatively few compatriots, especially institutional ones, are competing for has clear advantages over tying one's entire fortune to a single country. Many English-language investment books only cover the US market, or the UK, Canadian, or Australian markets, but very few cover more than one of these markets, and fewer compare these markets with major non-Anglophone markets side by side. This chapter aims to be one of the most important guides to help investors take advantage of the benefits of foreign diversification.

The advantages of investing in foreign markets include at least three:

© The Author(s) 2018
T. Dennison, *Invest Outside the Box*,
https://doi.org/10.1007/978-981-13-0372-2_10

- Foreign markets offer sources of return that may be greater than, or at least different from, those available domestically.
- Being based on a different economy's fundamentals, foreign assets are likely to have a lower correlation with domestic assets than two assets are likely to have with each other.
- In extreme cases, owning assets overseas provides protection against a collapse of one's home country, currency, or property rights.

The last advantage is perhaps most obvious to citizens of countries known for unstable currencies or a lack of good property protections, including Venezuela and Zimbabwe in the early twenty-first century, but even in countries like the United States, where the government confiscated gold from citizens in the early twentieth century. As mentioned in Chap. 3, many Chinese and Russian investors have been buying up apartments in the United Kingdom, Canada, and Australia mostly as a way of safely storing money overseas, while more financially savvy investors have been learning about REITs and other instruments for diversifying across countries with greater liquidity and flexibility.

The first two advantages can largely be compared in terms of expected return and expected risk (with volatility being only one measure of risk), as described in Chap. 7. Expected returns are largely driven by a combination of underlying economic fundamentals (described in Chaps. 2, 3, 4, 5, and 6), and market sentiment driving what multiples of those economic fundamentals investors will pay for financial assets. One factor keeping correlations low are limits on how freely investors can move money from one market to another to pursue opportunities. Investors are increasingly able to move money from, say, US Treasury bills to Japanese REITs to Chinese A-share stocks with just a few computer key clicks, but as with the move to ETFs and digital signatures, many investors still stick to what they know and what is close to home. Just as economic returns are driven by a combination of local fundamental and global flow factors, both factors also drive the volatility of each asset class and the correlation of between their returns. As the below chart shows, average correlations between the United States's S&P 500 and Japan's Nikkei 225 stock market indices have steadily risen from a range of +0.2 to +0.4 in the 1960s and 1970s to between +0.5 and +0.8 for much of the 2000s and 2010s. This higher correlation has reduced the risk diversification benefit of holding both US and Japanese stocks in a portfolio, but such benefit is still significantly positive enough to warrant higher international allocations (Fig. 10.1).

As mentioned in Chap. 8, and will be outlined later in this chapter, MSCI publishes one of the most standardized and widely used set of international stock indices to track returns of investing in many different markets. Below is a table showing how MSCI classifies the national stock markets it tracks into developed, emerging, and frontier markets as of late 2017 (Fig. 10.2):

While it may seem overwhelming to try and keep track of all these different national markets, the MSCI indices, and the funds that benchmark to them, largely weight exposure to these different companies by size, so that far more would be invested in large US and Chinese stocks than in smaller Belgian companies. As discussed in Sects. 7.3 and 8.4, this market cap weighting approach does not necessarily ensure the optimal mix of risk versus return but does represent what shareholders own globally in the aggregate, and so owning this allocation serves as insurance against falling behind. National markets are also often grouped into categories for easier top-down classification: for example, the "G7" developed markets of the United States, Canada, the United Kingdom, France, Germany, Italy, and Japan, and the "BRIC" list of Brazil, Russia, India, and China, later expanded into "BRICS" to include South Africa.

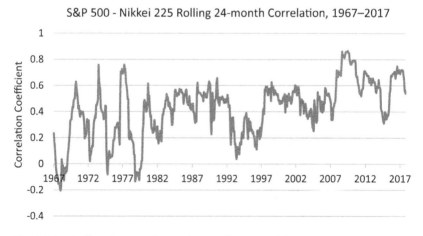

Fig. 10.1 Rolling 24-month correlation of returns of the US S&P 500 vs Japan's Nikkei 225 stock indices, 1967–2017, date from Yahoo Finance

MSCI ACWI & FRONTIER MARKETS INDEX

- **MSCI ACWI INDEX**
  - **MSCI WORLD INDEX**
  - **MSCI EMERGING MARKETS INDEX**
- **MSCI EMERGING & FRONTIER MARKETS INDEX**
  - **MSCI FRONTIER MARKETS INDEX**

DEVELOPED MARKETS

Americas	Europe & Middle East	Pacific
Canada	Austria	Australia
United States	Belgium	Hong Kong
	Denmark	Japan
	Finland	New Zealand
	France	Singapore
	Germany	
	Ireland	
	Israel	
	Italy	
	Netherlands	
	Norway	
	Portugal	
	Spain	
	Sweden	
	Switzerland	
	United Kingdom	

EMERGING MARKETS

Americas	Europe, Middle East & Africa	Asia
Brazil	Czech Republic	China
Chile	Egypt	India
Colombia	Greece	Indonesia
Mexico	Hungary	Korea
Peru	Poland	Malaysia
	Qatar	Pakistan
	Russia	Philippines
	South Africa	Taiwan
	Turkey	Thailand
	United Arab Emirates	

FRONTIER MARKETS

Americas	Europe & CIS	Africa	Middle East	Asia
Argentina	Croatia	Kenya	Bahrain	Bangladesh
	Estonia	Mauritius	Jordan	Sri Lanka
	Lithuania	Morocco	Kuwait	Vietnam
	Kazakhstan	Nigeria	Lebanon	
	Romania	Tunisia	Oman	
	Serbia	WAEMU[2]		
	Slovenia			

MSCI STANDALONE MARKET INDEXES[1]

Americas	Europe & CIS	Africa	Middle East	Asia
Jamaica	Bosnia Herzegovina	Botswana	Palestine	Saudi Arabia
Panama[3]	Bulgaria	Ghana		
Trinidad & Tobago	Ukraine	Zimbabwe		

Fig. 10.2 MSCI country classifications as of 2017. (Source: https://www.msci.com/market-classification)

Below are a pie chart and table showing the relative sizes of 11 of the world's largest stock market compared with the rest of the world (Figs. 10.3 and 10.4).

These relative sizes of course do not remain constant over time, and while the United States remains the largest, China has remarkably risen from a country with no stock market in the late 1980s to the world's second largest market by 2017 (Fig. 10.5).

World Stock Market Capitalization 2017

Fig. 10.3 Pie chart showing the world's largest national (+Eurozone) stock markets by size, 2017. (Source: World Bank)

Stock Market	% of World Market Cap	Market Cap (US$ trillion)
United States	42.2%	$ 27.35
China	11.3%	$ 7.32
Euro area	9.6%	$ 6.22
Japan	7.6%	$ 4.96
Hong Kong SAR, China	4.9%	$ 3.19
United Kingdom	4.7%	$ 3.06
Canada	3.1%	$ 1.99
India	2.4%	$ 1.57
Switzerland	2.2%	$ 1.40
Australia	2.0%	$ 1.27
Singapore	1.0%	$ 0.64
Rest of World	9.1%	$ 5.88

Fig. 10.4 Table showing the world's largest national (+Eurozone) stock markets by size, 2017. (Source: World Bank)

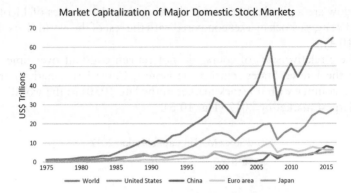

Fig. 10.5 Relative market caps of the world vs four large markets, 1975–2017. (Source: World Bank)

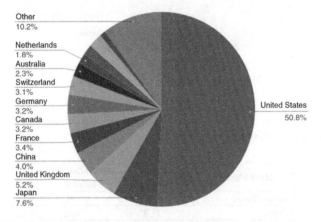

Fig. 10.6 Country weights in MSCI ACWI index as of mid-2017. (Source: iShares.com)

The relative weightings will of course also vary based on which markets are included or excluded. The MSCI All Countries World Index ("ACWI"), for example, has long included China as an emerging market, but only the "H-shares" of Chinese companies traded in Hong Kong, and only in 2017 did MSCI announce plans to start including Shanghai and Shenzhen listed "A-shares" of Chinese companies in its benchmark emerging market and ACWI indices. As a result, the relative weightings of countries in the MSCI ACWI index differ from the table above and were, as of mid-2017, as follows (Fig. 10.6):

The following sections survey each of some of these largest markets, introducing what makes each of them worth considering by an outside the box investor.

10.1   THE US MARKET

Although China's economy surpassed that of the United States as measured by purchasing power parity gross domestic product ("PPP GDP", basically the size of an economy comparing the values of similar baskets of goods and services), the United States remains the largest economy in terms of GDP measured in nominal exchange rate terms, and by far the largest domestic equity market and a top choice among foreign investors. It is worth emphasizing that the above statistic of the US stock market making up over 42% of the world's total refers only to domestic US companies, and does not even include the large number and value of foreign companies and funds investing in foreign assets that are listed in the United States.

Economics 101 courses often show that foreign capital invested into a country tends to be the flip side of that country having trade deficits. This means that because the United States imports more than it exports, foreign firms selling to the United States are left holding a balance which needs to be placed somewhere, either into US assets, or deposited into or exchanged with banks or other financial institutions, who in turn invest those US dollars into US assets. Below is a chart of the current account balances of the United States, Japan, and China, showing the US persistent trade deficits against its East Asian trading partners' surpluses since 1980 (Fig. 10.7).

The US dollar remains the world's reserve currency as of 2017, meaning it is the main second choice of currency many foreigners choose to hold and use after their own currency. An Indian or Brazilian company doing business with a Japanese or Russian company is more likely to contract the transaction in US dollars than in rupees, reals, yen, or rubles. As a result, the US Treasury bond market is very heavily invested in by foreign banks and governments that keep US dollars in reserve for transactions and as a store of value. As explained in Chap. 3, some countries (most notably China and many GCC countries) use US dollar reserves to stabilize their national currency. Below is a table of some of the major foreign holders of US Treasury debt. As explained in the previous paragraph, this list is understandably topped by China and Japan, who have maintained some of the largest trade surpluses with the United States for decades (Fig. 10.8).

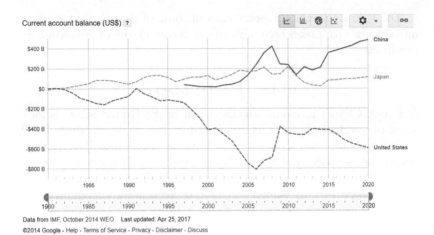

Current account balance (US$) ?

$400 B
$200 B
$0
-$200 B
-$400 B
-$600 B
-$800 B

China
Japan
United States

1985   1990   1995   2000   2005   2010   2015   2020

1980   1985   1990   1995   2000   2005   2010   2015   2020

Data from IMF, October 2014 WEO   Last updated: Apr 25, 2017
©2014 Google - Help - Terms of Service - Privacy - Disclaimer - Discuss

Fig. 10.7 US trade deficits vs China and Japan trade surpluses since 1980, according to the IMF

Back on stocks, comparing the S&P 500 or even Nasdaq 100 to other broad market indices like the Japan's Nikkei 225, China's CSI 300, Europe's STOXX 100, or Canada's S&P/TSX Composite, the US market is not only large but diversified and home to many of the world most valuable and respected brands in many different industries, including Apple, Coca-Cola, Google (Alphabet), McDonald's, and Microsoft, many of which have no close analogue or competitor in most other markets outside of China. Just as foreigners invest their dollars into US Treasuries and Manhattan apartments, many buy shares in Amazon or Tesla as a high-quality place to park millions, or even billions, of dollars. Because the US market is so large and advanced, it may almost be excusable than many American investment advisers see no need to diversify their allocations to foreign assets outside the United States. The broader market indices of the Russell 3000 contain a wide variety of investible names across many different industries, beyond the big household names. US-based companies benefit from what is still the world's largest and wealthiest domestic economies, supported by strong legal protections, and high investor disclosure standards on the SEC Edgar website. The United States was one of the first markets to standardize electronic filing of financial statements in the machine-readable XML-based eXtensible Business Reporting Language (XBRL). XBRL has made it easier for analysts to crunch large volumes of

	August 2017	August 2016
China, Mainland	$ 1,201	$ 1,185
Japan	$ 1,102	$ 1,144
Ireland	$ 307	$ 266
Brazil	$ 274	$ 256
Cayman Islands	$ 260	$ 264
Switzerland	$ 248	$ 238
United Kingdom	$ 225	$ 205
Luxembourg	$ 213	$ 221
Hong Kong	$ 197	$ 192
Taiwan	$ 180	$ 190
India	$ 139	$ 123
Saudi Arabia	$ 138	$ 93
Singapore	$ 120	$ 106
Russia	$ 105	$ 88
Belgium	$ 97	$ 157
Korea	$ 95	$ 90
France	$ 76	$ 71
Canada	$ 74	$ 82
Germany	$ 73	$ 104
Thailand	$ 72	$ 51
Total Foreign Holdings	**$ 6,270**	**$ 6,199**

Fig. 10.8   Top 20 and total foreign holders of US Treasury debt (in US$ billions). (Source: http://ticdata.treasury.gov/Publish/mfh.txt)

financial numbers by computer and trade on them quickly, which has arguably made the US markets hyper-efficient, where it is one of the most difficult places for active managers to outperform.

Data in Jeremy Siegel's classic book *Stocks for the Long Run* mostly focus on US data, and indeed, an investor buying only US stocks and ignoring the rest of the world would have done very well over the past century; however, looking forward, even the fourth edition of this book has placed greater emphasis on foreign stocks as the United States represents a declining share of the world economy, market cap, and future return. Investors may also consider whether the US record fiscal and trade deficits may be reaching a peak with adverse consequences for the value of the US dollar in the twenty-first century. Also, enough books have been written on how to invest in the US market that it may be better to refer to those rather than try and go into more detail in a book about investing outside the box.

Traditionally, American investment advisers have considered four levels of "foreign exposure" in their stock portfolios:

1. Buying stocks in US companies with a significant portion of their business overseas, especially revenue in foreign currency from sales abroad.
2. Buying funds or ETFs that invest in foreign stocks.
3. Buying shares of foreign stocks listed in the United States, mostly as American depository receipts (ADRs).
4. Buying shares of foreign companies directly on foreign stock exchanges.

The first one may seem like the most diluted form of foreign exposure, and indeed the author was surprised to hear a New York broker once say "when a client wants foreign stock exposure, I sell them shares in Coca-Cola and Caterpillar" (both are US companies with significant foreign sales). This approach may be most appropriate to an investor holding relatively few stocks they know relatively well, and can keep track of which countries each of their stocks earn what percentage of their revenue in.

The second approach may seem more pure and complete, as allocating 10% of one's portfolio to a Japan fund is clearer than figuring out which percentage of the S&P 500's revenue comes from Japan. Funds investing in foreign markets may be single country or regional (some even global or global ex-US) and may be actively or passively managed. Some may hedge out currency risk (like DXJ below), but most are fully exposed to the ups and downs of the foreign currency against the dollar. Below is a list of some of the largest single-country foreign stock ETFs listed in the United States (Fig. 10.9):

The third way for US investors to get foreign stock exposure is by buying shares in foreign companies listed on US exchanges, either as a direct listing or in the form of American depository receipts (ADRs). Direct listings are of companies, that have no foreign listed shares, but rather list their shares directly in the United States, for example, Alibaba as of this writing. ADRs, on the other hand, are shares of foreign listed companies held at a large global

Symbol	ETP Name	Net Assets (US$ million)	Net Exp Ratio	Country Objective
EWJ	iShares MSCI Japan ETF	$ 16,300	0.48%	Japan
DXJ	WisdomTree Japan Hedged Equity Fund	$ 8,600	0.48%	Japan
EWZ	iShares MSCI Brazil Capped ETF	$ 5,500	0.63%	Brazil
INDA	iShares MSCI India ETF	$ 4,200	0.71%	India
EWG	iShares MSCI Germany ETF	$ 4,100	0.48%	Germany
EWC	iShares MSCI Canada ETF	$ 3,500	0.48%	Canada
EWY	iShares MSCI South Korea Capped ETF	$ 3,200	0.64%	South Korea
FXI	iShares China Large-Cap ETF	$ 3,100	0.74%	China
EWT	iShares MSCI Taiwan Capped ETF	$ 3,000	0.64%	Taiwan
RSX	VanEck Vectors Russia ETF	$ 2,600	0.67%	Russia
EWU	iShares MSCI United Kingdom ETF	$ 2,500	0.48%	UK
MCHI	iShares MSCI China ETF	$ 2,300	0.64%	China
DBJP	Deutsche X-trackers MSCI Japan Currency-Hedged Equity Fund	$ 2,200	0.45%	Japan
EWA	iShares MSCI-Australia ETF	$ 2,000	0.48%	Australia
EWW	iShares MSCI Mexico Capped ETF	$ 1,600	0.48%	Mexico
EWH	iShares MSCI Hong Kong ETF	$ 1,600	0.48%	Hong Kong
EPI	WisdomTree India Earnings Fund	$ 1,500	0.84%	India
EWL	iShares MSCI Switzerland Capped ETF	$ 1,100	0.48%	Switzerland
HEWJ	iShares Currency Hedged MSCI Japan ETF	$ 961	0.49%	Japan
GXC	SPDR S&P China ETF	$ 861	0.59%	China
INDY	iShares India 50 ETF	$ 797	0.94%	India
EWP	iShares MSCI Spain Capped ETF	$ 747	0.48%	Spain
EWS	iShares MSCI Singapore Capped ETF	$ 545	0.48%	Singapore
DFJ	WisdomTree Japan SmallCap Dividend	$ 539	0.58%	Japan
EWI	iShares MSCI Italy Capped ETF	$ 530	0.48%	Italy
HEWG	iShares Currency Hedged MSCI Germany ETF	$ 486	0.53%	Germany
EIDO	iShares MSCI Indonesia ETF	$ 470	0.63%	Indonesia
ERUS	iShares MSCI Russia Capped ETF	$ 430	0.64%	Russia
TUR	iShares MSCI Turkey ETF	$ 418	0.64%	Turkey
EZA	iShares MSCI South Africa ETF	$ 404	0.64%	South Africa
ASHR	Deutsche X-trackers Harvest CSI 300 China A-Shares Fund	$ 403	0.65%	China
THD	iShares MSCI Thailand Capped ETF	$ 403	0.63%	Thailand
ECH	iShares MSCI Chile Capped ETF	$ 391	0.64%	Chile
EWQ	iShares MSCI France ETF	$ 325	0.48%	France
EWD	iShares MSCI Sweden Capped ETF	$ 294	0.48%	Sweden
FXB	CurrencyShares British Pound Sterling Trust	$ 291	0.40%	UK
VNM	VanEck Vectors Vietnam ETF	$ 288	0.67%	Vietnam
GREK	Global X FTSE Greece 20 ETF	$ 267	0.62%	Greece
EWM	iShares MSCI Malaysia ETF	$ 259	0.48%	Malaysia
EPU	iShares MSCI All Peru Capped ETF	$ 250	0.63%	Peru

Fig. 10.9 Largest US-listed single-country ETFs as of 2017. (Source: Fidelity)

custodian firm (often BNY Mellon or JPMorgan Chase), who then issues receipts to be traded on US exchanges representing ownership in the foreign shares. Due to the depth and efficiency of the US market, many ADRs are actually more liquid than the underlying shares in their home market. Converse to the first approach, many foreign companies large enough have US listings, or ADRs are also likely to have a significant share of their sales in the United States, which may counter some of the foreign exposure. Below are lists of the countries most represented by individual names (direct and ADR) listed in the US market, and a list of the 25 largest US-listed foreign shares by market cap. As of November 2017, there are over 900 foreign names listed in the United States with a total market cap of over US$10 trillion (Figs. 10.10 and 10.11).

Fig. 10.10 Countries most represented in the US ADR market, by market cap and number of issues. (Source: Nasdaq.com)

Country	Number of ADRs	Total Market Cap (US$ bio)
United Kingdom	72	$ 1,606
Canada	171	$ 1,308
China	142	$ 1,165
Japan	14	$ 708
Switzerland	32	$ 606
Brazil	29	$ 534
Netherlands	32	$ 495
France	15	$ 398
Australia	13	$ 285
Taiwan	12	$ 267
Hong Kong	20	$ 264
Mexico	13	$ 263
Ireland	25	$ 258
Belgium	7	$ 231
Spain	8	$ 215
India	12	$ 203
Germany	9	$ 202
Bermuda	70	$ 138
Denmark	5	$ 129
South Korea	10	$ 129
Singapore	7	$ 122
Italy	3	$ 79
Israel	93	$ 76
Norway	1	$ 69
Argentina	15	$ 65

Symbol	Name	Market Cap (US$ billion)		Industry	Country
BABA	Alibaba Group Holding Limited	$	477	Business Services	China
BUD	Anheuser-Busch Inbev SA	$	228	Beverages (Production/Distribution)	Belgium
TSM	Taiwan Semiconductor Manufacturing Company Ltd.	$	216	Semiconductors	Taiwan
CHL	China Mobile (Hong Kong) Ltd.	$	211	Telecommunications Equipment	Hong Kong
HSBC	HSBC Holdings plc	$	195	Savings Institutions	United Kingdom
NVS	Novartis AG	$	193	Major Pharmaceuticals	Switzerland
TM	Toyota Motor Corp Ltd Ord	$	185	Auto Manufacturing	Japan
UN	Unilever NV	$	165	Package Goods/Cosmetics	Netherlands
BTI	British American Tobacco p.l.c.	$	149	Farming/Seeds/Milling	United Kingdom
TOT	Total S.A.	$	142	Oil & Gas Production	France
SAP	SAP SE	$	135	Computer Software: Prepackaged Software	Germany
BP	BP p.l.c.	$	133	Integrated oil Companies	United Kingdom
PTR	PetroChina Company Limited	$	131	Oil & Gas Production	China
NVO	Novo Nordisk A/S	$	127	Major Pharmaceuticals	Denmark
RY	Royal Bank Of Canada	$	115	Commercial Banks	Canada
BHP	BHP Billiton Limited	$	114	Precious Metals	Australia
SNY	Sanofi	$	113	Major Pharmaceuticals	France
AVGO	Broadcom Limited	$	108	Semiconductors	Singapore
TD	Toronto Dominion Bank (The)	$	106	Commercial Banks	Canada
SAN	Banco Santander, S.A.	$	104	Commercial Banks	Spain
LFC	China Life Insurance Company Limited	$	100	Life Insurance	China
BBL	BHP Billiton plc	$	100	Coal Mining	United Kingdom
MTU	Mitsubishi UFJ Financial Group Inc	$	93	Commercial Banks	Japan
DCM	NTT DOCOMO, Inc	$	92	Radio And Television Broadcasting And Communications Equipment	Japan
ACN	Accenture plc	$	91	Business Services	Ireland

Fig. 10.11 25 largest foreign companies listed in the United States, by market cap, as of November 2017. (Source: Nasdaq.com)

While ADRs provide the investor far more flexibility to choose which individual foreign companies to own, only a few large companies from each market are available to trade in the United States as ADRs. For maximum choice, an investor would consider buying foreign shares directly on the foreign exchange where they trade. This may be operationally more difficult and requires the services of a global custodian, and one or more brokers with memberships on the foreign exchanges or other access to said markets, but has been increasingly available through international online firms like Interactive Brokers.

The rest of this chapter will survey some of the major non-US market foreign investors are likely to consider accessing directly.

10.2   THE EUROZONE

The history of the twentieth century was heavily defined by two world wars, which might be oversimplified as centering around the fight between Germany and US allies primarily led by France and Britain. Post-World War II European history has been a far happier story with Western Europe seeing rapid reconstruction and economic recovery in the decades of the 1950s through the 1980s, and then joined by the opening and catching up of the formerly communist countries of Eastern Europe after the collapse of the Berlin Wall in 1989 and the Soviet Union in 1991. By the end of the twentieth century, and early twenty-first century, the continent seemed well on its way to forming a prosperous "United States of Europe" with many of the trade and movement barriers between countries eliminated, and even a common currency, the euro, removing the friction of currency exchange and FX risk from trade between Eurozone members. The European Union is often said to be defined by "four freedoms": the free movement of goods, services, capital, and persons between member nations, all freedoms long taken for granted in the United States where the individual states surrendered regulation of interstate commerce to a federal government.

One consequence of the euro is that government bonds issued by Eurozone members no longer behave like "treasuries" issued in a government's own currency but rather more like "sovereign" bonds issued in a foreign currency (even though that "foreign" currency is now the nation's only official currency). Before the euro, whenever Spain or Italy had too much debt denominated in pesetas or lira, the currency had the ability to devalue before Spain or Italy have had to default on any post-war debt. (Spain famously defaulted on its debts six times in the eighteenth century and seven times in the nineteenth century, source: https://www.cnbc.com/id/47814564.) The tendency of some countries to devalue their currency to manage local currency debt did result in those currencies having higher interest rates, but the flexible exchange rate did act as a safety valve. After joining the euro, however, Spain and Italy were no longer able to devalue the currency of their euro-denominated debt, and so what used to be currency risks now became sovereign credit risks of buying these countries' government bonds. As with other foreign currency borrowers, these countries would need to earn as much "foreign" currency as they spent in order to be able to pay off their debts. As seen in the chart below, this was a problem for Spain, Italy, and even France which all started recording trade deficits between joining the euro in 1999 and the austerity measures taken in response to the Eurozone sovereign debt crisis of 2012. Germany, by contrast, saw its trade surplus soar after joining the euro (which effectively kept Germany's currency weaker than if the deutsche mark kept floating independently from other European currencies), which only started to plateau around 2012 (Fig. 10.12).

Germany's relatively strong trade and fiscal balances have made German government bonds the benchmark for euro-denominated debt. Like the CME US Treasury futures, the Eurex futures exchanges list futures contracts on the German "Schatz" (2-year notes), "Bobl" (5-year), "Bund" (10-year), and "Buxl" (30-year) benchmark debt securities. Eurex also lists futures contracts on the French Obligations Assimilables du Trésor (OAT), Italian Buoni del Tesoro Poliannuali (BTP), and Spanish Bonos, mostly as a way of trading or hedging the credit spreads of these sovereign issuers against the German benchmark. As explained in choice (E) in Sect. 5.4, a foreign investor can earn the carry, roll, and appreciation on these European bonds by buying one of these futures contracts, and only being exposed to euro FX risk on the amount of euros in the margin account.

Ten-year Bund yields briefly went negative in mid-2016, and are still relatively low in absolute terms, reflecting the abundance of cash and retirees and long-term low expectations of growth and inflation across the Eurozone (Fig. 10.13).

While the countries within the Eurozone continue to retain their own national stock markets and benchmark indices, the euro and EU harmonization rules have made it far easier to trade stocks listed on different exchanges across the Eurozone. The mutual fund market has also been opened across the EU through a harmonized set of rules known as the "Undertakings for Collective Investment in Transferable Securities" or "UCITS". The major national benchmark indices of Eurozone member states include Germany's DAX, France's CAC-40, Italy's FTSE/MIB, Spain's IBEX, and the Netherlands' AEX; by far the most liquid European equity index futures contract is that on the EURO STOXX 50® index of 50 of the largest blue chip companies across the Eurozone. STOXX also

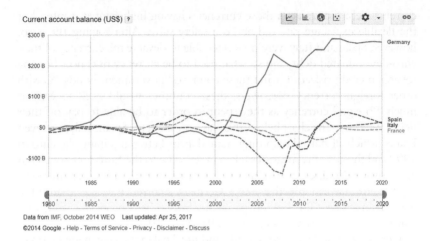

Fig. 10.12 Trade deficits of France, Italy, and Spain vs surpluses of Germany after the euro

Fig. 10.13 Ten-year German Bund yields, 2012–2017. (Source: Bloomberg)

includes a range of indices that are broader, some including non-Eurozone European firms (like those in the United Kingdom, Norway, or Switzerland), as well as sector indices (the most liquid being the EURO STOXX® Banks index), but none are as liquid a benchmark as the EURO STOXX 50® (Fig. 10.14).

Name	Headquarters	Industry
Adidas	Germany	Sportwear
Ahold Delhaize	Netherlands	Retail
Air Liquide	France	Chemistry
Airbus	Netherlands	Aerospace
Allianz	Germany	Insurance
Anheuser-Busch InBev	Belgium	Food and beverage
ASML Holding	Netherlands	Technology
AXA	France	Insurance
Banco Bilbao Vizcaya Argentaria	Spain	Banking
Banco Santander	Spain	Banking
BASF	Germany	Chemistry
Bayer	Germany	Chemistry
BMW	Germany	Automotive industry
BNP Paribas	France	Banking
CRH	Ireland	Construction and materials
Compagnie de Saint-Gobain	France	Construction and materials
Daimler AG	Germany	Automotive industry
Deutsche Bank	Germany	Banking
Deutsche Post	Germany	Logistics
Deutsche Telekom	Germany	Telecommunication
Enel	Italy	Electric utility
Engie	France	Electric utility
Eni	Italy	Petroleum
E.ON	Germany	Electric utility
Essilor International	France	Pharmaceutical industry
Fresenius SE	Germany	Health care equipment
Groupe Danone	France	Food and beverage
Iberdrola	Spain	Electric utility
Inditex	Spain	Retail
ING Group NV	Netherlands	Banking
Intesa Sanpaolo	Italy	Banking
L'Oréal	France	Personal and household goods
LVMH Moët Hennessy Louis Vuitton	France	Personal and household goods
Munich Re	Germany	Insurance
Nokia	Finland	Technology
Orange S.A.	France	Telecommunication
Philips	Netherlands	Personal and household goods
Safran	France	Aerospace
Sanofi	France	Pharmaceutical industry
SAP SE	Germany	Technology
Schneider Electric	France	Goods and Services
Siemens	Germany	Goods and Services
Société Générale SA	France	Banking
Telefónica	Spain	Telecommunication
TOTAL S.A.	France	Petroleum
Unibail-Rodamco	France	Real estate
Unilever	Netherlands / UK	Food and beverage
Vinci SA	France	Construction and materials
Vivendi	France	Media
Volkswagen Group	Germany	Automotive industry

Fig. 10.14 Components of the EURO STOXX® 50 Index as of June 2017. (Source: Investing.com via Wikipedia)

As in the United States, many of the best opportunities investing in European stocks are in looking past the biggest and most liquid names, and to the smaller- and medium-sized companies, for example, the *Mittelstand* companies in Germany. The STOXX 600 still does not cover many of these opportunities, which are best sought out market by market.

Europe's aging population and low growth rate make it comparable with another advanced, mature, and low-growth market on the other side of the Eurasian land mass: Japan.

10.3   JAPAN

Japan remains one of the biggest and most important stock and bond markets in the world, but one where relatively few foreign investors have been well allocated since the great decline in the Nikkei from almost 40,000 in 1989 to around 20,000 in early 2017, followed by over a decade of zero to negative interest rates. Post-war Japanese stock and bond market history can basically be divided into two eras: from about 1950 to the peak of the stock market and real estate bubble in 1989 marked by rapid growth, and the era since then and including this writing (late 2017) marked by low to zero growth, deflation, and market maturity. Despite the lack of growth, Japan remains a country with enormous amounts of money, a wide variety and variety of listed stocks in highly profitable businesses, and one of the biggest examples of where low growth can mean high investor returns. First, this chapter will begin by describing some of the main stock and bond benchmarks of Japan.

One way to put Japan's market in perspective: Japan has almost as high a per-capita GDP as the United States, and just under half the population, but Japanese have about four times the savings rate of Americans. As a result, Japan may have as much as double the amount of investible assets as US investors do. As some of these assets are in foreign currency due to Japan's trade surpluses, a large share of Japanese-owned assets are invested overseas, but a large amount is still invested domestically with little foreign competition. This last point is in contrast to how US trade deficits have meant a large share of US assets are owned by foreign investors.

Japan's main stock market is the Tokyo Stock Exchange (TSE), which is owned by the Japan Exchange Group (JPX) along with the Osaka Securities Exchange. Stocks listed on the TSE are divided into three sections: the first section, including roughly 1,600 of the largest listed companies, the second section with about 400 smaller companies, and the Market Of The High growth and EmeRging Stocks (MOTHERS) section of about 200 stocks. Like the Russell indices, the TSE maintains a series of market cap-weighted benchmark indices tracking stocks on the first section of the TSE called the Tokyo Price Index (TOPIX), where the TOPIX 30, 100, 500, and 1,000 represent the largest 30, 100, 500, and 1,000 TSE-listed companies, respectively. Between these, there is the TOPIX Mid 400 index of companies in the TOPIX 500 but not the TOPIX 100, and the TOPIX small cap index of stocks smaller than those in the TOPIX 500. As a sample, below are 30 of the largest TSE-listed stocks as of October 2017 (Fig. 10.15).

The relative weights of different industry sectors in the Japanese stock market are shown below, based on the MSCI Japan index (Fig. 10.16).

Although the TOPIX indices are very well organized, and market cap weighted like most other major benchmark indices around the world, the older and price-weighted Nikkei 225 index remains the main benchmark index followed and traded in Japan. For comparison, below are the top ten components and sector weights of the Nikkei 225 index (Fig. 10.17).

As mentioned earlier, the history of the post-war Japanese stock market can be defined by two eras: before 1989 and since 1989. Below is a chart of the value of the Nikkei 225 price index from 1950 to 2017 (Fig. 10.18).

The above long-term chart is simple, but the milestones and driving factors of the Nikkei's rise and range trading are better appreciated in a decade-by-decade comparison between the Dow Jones Industrial Average and the Nikkei 225:

- In 1950, the Dow was around 220, while the Nikkei was around 100.
- The Nikkei first crossed 1,000 in 1960, while the Dow was still at 680.
- Nikkei then rose to 2,400 by 1970 over two years before the Dow first crossed 1,000 in 1972.
- In 1980, the Nikkei hit new highs of 6,500 and 7,000, while the Dow was still below its 1973 high of 1,051.71, even though the dollar weakened from 360 yen to 240 yen over the previous decade.

RIC	Name	Industry	Market Cap (JPY trillion)
7203.T	Toyota Motor Corp	Auto & Truck Manufacturers	¥ 22.8
9432.T	Nippon Telegraph And Telephone Corp	Integrated Telecommunications Services	¥ 11.3
9984.T	SoftBank Group Corp	Wireless Telecommunications Services	¥ 11.2
8306.T	Mitsubishi UFJ Financial Group Inc	Banks	¥ 10.8
9437.T	NTT Docomo Inc	Wireless Telecommunications Services	¥ 10.5
9433.T	KDDI Corp	Wireless Telecommunications Services	¥ 7.8
2914.T	Japan Tobacco Inc	Cigars & Cigarette Manufacturing	¥ 7.6
6861.T	KEYENCE CORPORATION	Electrical Components & Equipment	¥ 7.4
8316.T	Sumitomo Mitsui Financial Group, Inc.	Banks	¥ 6.4
7182.T	Japan Post Bank Co Ltd	Commercial Loans	¥ 6.3
7267.T	Honda Motor Co Ltd	Auto & Truck Manufacturers	¥ 6.2
6178.T	Japan Post Holdings Co Ltd	Life Insurance	¥ 6.1
7974.T	Nintendo Co., Ltd	Games, Toys & Children Vehicles	¥ 6.0
7751.T	Canon Inc	Office Equipment	¥ 5.6
6758.T	Sony Corp	Household Electronics	¥ 5.4
8411.T	Mizuho Financial Group, Inc.	Banks	¥ 5.2
6954.T	Fanuc Corp	Industrial Machinery & Equipment	¥ 5.1
4502.T	Takeda Pharmaceutical Co Ltd	Pharmaceuticals	¥ 5.0
4063.T	Shin-Etsu Chemical Co Ltd	Commodity Chemicals	¥ 4.7
6098.T	Recruit Holdings Co Ltd	Outsourcing & Staffing Services	¥ 4.6
6902.T	Denso Corp	Auto, Truck & Motorcycle Parts	¥ 4.6
7201.T	Nissan Motor Co Ltd	Auto & Truck Manufacturers	¥ 4.6
5108.T	Bridgestone Corp	Tires & Rubber Products	¥ 4.5
9022.T	Central Japan Railway Company	Passenger Transportation, Ground & Sea	¥ 4.2
8058.T	Mitsubishi Corp	Diversified Trading & Distributing	¥ 4.2
6594.T	NIDEC CORPORATION	Electrical Components & Equipment	¥ 4.2
9020.T	East Japan Railway Company	Rail Services	¥ 4.2
3382.T	Seven & i Holdings Co., Ltd.	Food Retail & Distribution	¥ 4.2
6501.T	Hitachi, Ltd.	Industrial Conglomerates	¥ 4.1
6503.T	Mitsubishi Electric Corporation	Industrial Conglomerates	¥ 4.1

Fig. 10.15 30 of the largest TSE-listed stocks as of October 2017. (Source: Reuters, Interactive Brokers)

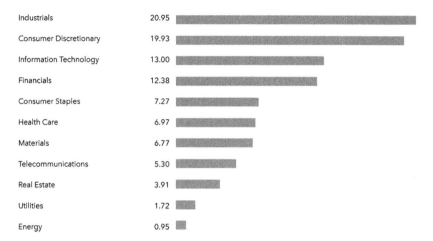

Industrials	20.95
Consumer Discretionary	19.93
Information Technology	13.00
Financials	12.38
Consumer Staples	7.27
Health Care	6.97
Materials	6.77
Telecommunications	5.30
Real Estate	3.91
Utilities	1.72
Energy	0.95

Fig. 10.16 Sector weights of the MSCI Japan index. (Source: iShares. com)

https://indexes.nikkei.co.jp/nkave/archives/file/nikkei_stock_average_factsheet_en.pdf

■ Top 10 Components by weight (Dec/30/2016)

Company	Code	Sector	Nikkei Industry Classification	Weight (%)	ParValue (yen)	Price (yen)	PER	PBR	Dividend Yield (%)
Fast Retailing	9983	Consumer Goods	Retail	8.40	50	41830	42.65	7.42	0.84
Softbank Group	9984	Technology	Communications	4.68	50/3	23295	9.55	3.69	0.57
Fanuc	6954	Technology	Electric Machinery	3.98	50	19815	36.90	2.95	1.63
KDDI	9433	Technology	Communications	3.56	25/3	17757	13.47	2.13	2.70
Kyocera	6971	Technology	Electric Machinery	2.33	25	11624	25.14	0.94	1.72
Tokyo Electron	8035	Technology	Electric Machinery	2.22	50	11045	18.12	3.14	2.76
Daikin Industries	6367	Capital Goods/Others	Machinery	2.15	50	10735	21.64	3.24	1.12
Shin-Etsu Chemical	4063	Materials	Chemicals	1.82	50	9067	24.14	1.96	1.32
Nitto Denko	6988	Materials	Chemicals	1.80	50	8969	29.12	2.46	1.67
Terumo	4543	Technology	Precision Instruments	1.73	25	8630	32.97	3.28	0.95

■ Sector Weight (Dec/30/2016)

Weight

- Technology — 43.51%
- Financials — 3.03%
- Consumer Goods — 22.56%
- Materials — 16.35%
- Capital Goods/Others — 11.39%
- Transportation and Utilities — 3.16%

Number of Issues

- Technology — 58
- Financials — 21
- Consumer Goods — 30
- Materials — 61
- Capital Goods/Others — 35
- Transportation and Utilities — 20

Fig. 10.17 Top ten components and sector weights of the Nikkei 225 index

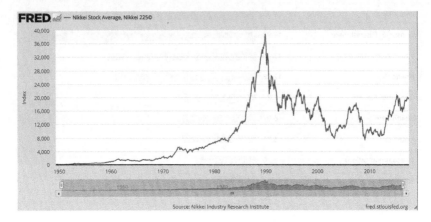

Fig. 10.18   Chart of Nikkei 225 price index, 1950–2017. (Source: fred.stlouis-fed.org)

- Later in the 1980s, the Nikkei first crossed 20,000 in January 1987, and then reached its historic high of 38,915.87 in December 1989. Meanwhile the Dow began a great bull market in the 1980s, rising from 1,000 to 2,800 over the decade, while the dollar fell from 240 yen to around 150 yen.
- In 1990, the Nikkei crossed back below 30,000 and traded between 15,000 and 25,000 for most of the rest of the 1990s, crossing 20,000 both ways several times. In the United States during the 1990s, the Dow rose from 2,800 in 1990 to crossing 10,000 and then 11,000 in late 1999. The currencies traded more sideways with each other this decade, ending at around 120 yen to the US dollar.
- Both the Dow and the Nikkei plummeted in the early 2000s with the collapse of the dotcom bubble and post-9/11 recession in the United States, paired with not just recession but deflation in Japan where short-term rates first hit zero in 2001. Both indices spent much of the decade recovering, with the Dow hitting new highs of 12,000 through 14,000 in 2006, and the Nikkei never nearing the 20,000 level where it started the decade for the rest of the 2000s, but rather hitting a 30+-year low of 7,054.98 in early 2009. The dollar moderately weakened in the 2000s from 120 to 90 yen.

- So far in the 2010s, we have seen a steady bull market in the Dow as it has recovered from its 2008–2009 sub-10,000 lows and hit new highs from 15,000 in 2013 to 20,000 in early 2017, while the Nikkei also recovered from below 10,000 to hit 20,000 in early 2015. Abenomics and reflation have been drivers weakening the yen back to around 120 to the dollar twice so far this decade.

The above bullets on the history of the two indices put an order of magnitude on the relative scale of Japan's economic boom in the 1950s through the 1980s, and how it took about 50 years for the indices to cross again, even ignoring the roughly 3× strengthening of the yen in that period.

In addition to its stock market, Japan also has a very large bond market, although one far more dominated by Japanese government bonds (JGBs), with a relatively low percentage of corporate bonds. Japanese debt reached the landmark level of ¥1 quadrillion in the mid-2010s, which at over 200% of GDP makes Japan one of the most indebted governments in the world. The rise in debt has coincided with continuing trade surpluses (like Germany, but unlike the United States or many other European countries), an aging populating with a soaring demand for fixed income investments (even at very low interest rates), and the Bank of Japan's (BOJ) policies of quantitative easing, which has meant most Japanese debt has been funded and owned domestically rather than by foreigners. Below is a graph of the USD value of outstanding Japanese bonds, where the decline in value since June 2012 has had more to do with the decline in the yen against the dollar than any decline in debt levels (Fig. 10.19).

Below are the yield curves of Japanese government bonds in 1987, 1997, 2007, and 2017. In 1987, Japan was still in the middle of its stock and real estate bubble described above, and the yield curve at the time reflected this in "normally" high interest rates between 4% and 6%. 1997 and 2007 surrounded the years of the 2000s with one of the modern world's first zero interest rate policies (ZIRP), accompanied by relatively low long-term rates, but a yield curve that was still attractively steep. The 2017 JGB yield curve shows the BOJ's negative interest rate policy (NIRP), which has so far had the effect of weakening the yen and driving the Nikkei above 20,000 for the first time since the mid-1990s.

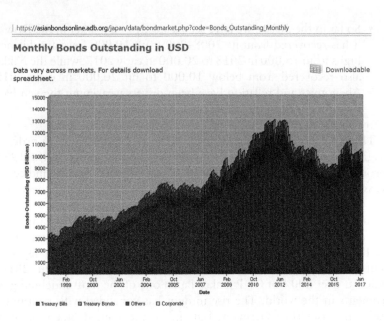

Fig. 10.19 USD value of Japanese bonds outstanding, showing an enormous rise in government debt and crowding out of corporate bonds

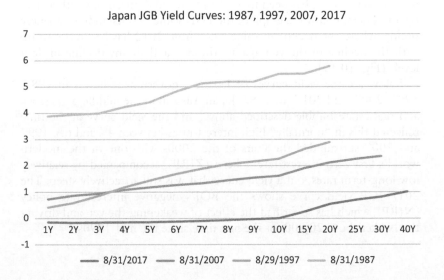

As illustrated at the end of Sect. 2.6, low absolute interest rates do not necessarily imply low excess returns from investing in bonds, and JGBs have in fact delivered some of the best Sharpe ratios of any major asset class over the past three decades, especially over periods of crashes of financial crises. Part of this has been due to falling rates, but also due to the carry difference between short-term and long-term rates, the roll-down return on a steep yield curve, and the very low volatility of Japanese rates. Below is a chart of the excess return (after subtracting the interest on cash) of investing ¥100 in rolling nine-year JGBs from 1974 to 2017 (Fig. 10.20).

Just as S&P 500 and US Treasury futures trade in Chicago, not New York, futures on the Nikkei and ten-year JGB trade in Osaka with competing contracts listed in Singapore (SGX, formerly SIMEX) and Chicago on CME GLOBEX. Below is a snapshot of the prices and trading volumes of some of these different contracts on a typical trading day (Fig. 10.21).

The above contracts differ in that:

Excess Return of 100 Invested in Rolling 9 Year JGBs

Fig. 10.20 Excess return from investing ¥100 in rolling nine-year JGBs, 1974–2017, calculated from MoF data

254   T. DENNISON

	LAST	VLM	TRDN...
SGXNK ∞ Dec07'17 @SGX	20140	54.7K	JPY
SGXNKM ∞ Dec07'17 @SGX	20139	930	JPY
N225 ∞ Dec07'17 @OSE.JPN	20140	5.42K	JPY
N225M ∞ Dec07'17 @OSE.JPN	20140	77.6K	JPY
NIY ∞ Dec07'17 @GLOBEX	20145	11.5K	JPY
NKD ∞ Dec07'17 @GLOBEX	20180	4.66K	USD
N225U ∞ Dec07'17 @SGX	c20175		USD
JGB ∞ Dec13'17 @OSE.JPN	150.80	2.97K	JPY
SGB ∞ Dec12'17 @SGX	150.79	994	JPY
JPY ∞ Dec18'17 @GLOBEX	0.00901...	71.2K	USD
ISN ∞ Dec18'17 @ICEUS	c111.030		JPY
UJ ∞ Oct16'17 @SGX	c111.145		JPY
UY ∞ Oct16'17 @SGX	c111.145		JPY
AJ ∞ Oct16'17 @SGX	c89.50		JPY
KJ ∞ Oct16'17 @SGX	c98.57		JPY

Fig. 10.21 Prices and volumes of futures contracts on Nikkei 225, JGBs, and yen on an Interactive Brokers trading screen

- The SGX Nikkei futures are ¥500 (SGXNK) vs ¥100 (SGXNKM, "mini") per point.
- The OSE Nikkei futures are ¥1,000 (N225) vs ¥100 (N225M, "mini") per point.
- GLOBEX has a ¥500/point contract traded in yen, and a US$5/point contract traded in US dollars. The dollar contract tracks the Nikkei index point for point in dollars with no direct currency risk, which is sometimes called a "quanto".
- The JGB futures trade at ¥1,000,000 per point on the OSE vs ¥100,000 on SGX.
- Futures on the Japanese yen currency trade on GLOBEX and on the SGX against the US dollar and other currencies.

In terms of economic fundamentals, Japan remains one of the wealthiest countries in the world on a per-capita GDP basis. As the following two charts show, Japan's relatively slow overall economic growth has not been due to a lack of growth in per-capita output but rather in a lack of population growth and an aging population with a frighteningly low ratio of working-age to retirement-age citizens. In many ways, Japan's demographics and its impact on economic growth, interest rates, and stock returns across different sectors are a look into the future of other countries whose declining population growth rates follow Japan's path (Figs. 10.22 and 10.23).

The following two charts compare the growth paths of Japan and China, and how the relationship between economic growth rates and stock market returns has compared across developed and emerging markets (Fig. 10.24).

The source link for the above chart is https://www.minneapolisfed.org/publications/the-region/how-rich-will-china-become.

Perhaps the most important factor to keep in mind when comparing Japan vs China as places to invest is to consider the relationship between growth and investment returns. As mentioned in Sect. 8.4, investors may naturally prefer to invest in a company, sector, or country's economy that is rapidly growing, but high economic growth empirically seems to be negatively correlated with economic returns. Below are two charts from Jeremy Siegel's *Stocks for the Long Run* showing how slower-growing

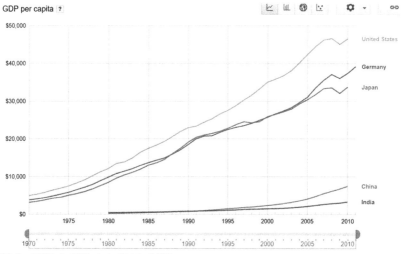

Fig. 10.22 Per-capita GDP growth of Japan vs the United States, Germany, China, and India

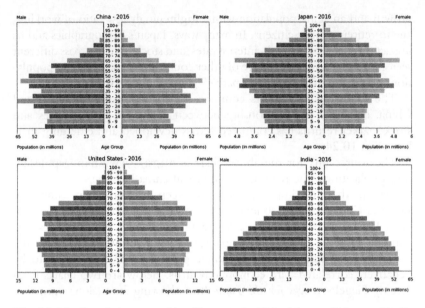

Fig. 10.23 Population pyramids of Japan vs the United States, China, and India. (Source: CIA World Factbook)

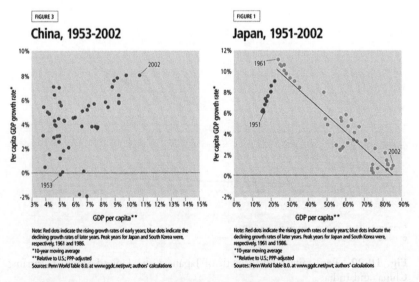

Fig. 10.24 China's per-capita GDP growth rates since 2000 resemble those of Japan in the 1950s, long before Japan approached US levels

countries have averaged higher rates of return for stock investors across decades, both in developed and emerging markets (Fig. 10.25). The next section crosses the Sea of Japan to China, where a heavily export-oriented, government- and bank-driven economy seems on track to follow Japan's post-war path as it has been transitioning from communism to a guided market economy, but with distinctly Chinese characteristics.

Fig. 10.25 Charts from Jeremy Siegel's book *Stocks for the Long Run* (5e, p. 197), showing the weak inverse relationship between economic growth and stock returns

10.4   GREATER CHINA

French poet and 1952 Nobel laureate (literature) François Mauriac report-edly wrote "J'aime tellement l'Allemagne que je suis heureux qu'il y en ait deux" ("I love Germany so much, I'm glad there are two of them"), and might say something similar about "One China, Two Systems".

The term "Greater China" refers collectively to Mainland China, Taiwan, Hong Kong, and Macau. As of 2017, these four entities have different currencies, issue different passports with different immigration systems, and effectively have separate, but increasingly inter-connected, legal and financial systems. Hong Kong and Macau are "Special Administrative Regions" of the People's Republic of China, while the government in Taipei refers to itself as the "Republic of China", although it has been replaced by Beijing at the United Nations since 1971. One might naturally ask why this isn't called "One China, Four Systems", other than perhaps considering the number four is considered unlucky in Chinese.

The rise of China from a closed and almost internationally negligible communist economy to a global superpower in less than 40 years is hard to exaggerate, having lifted more people out of poverty in a generation than almost any country has ever been able to count as their entire population. Below is a chart from the International Monetary Fund's World Economic Outlook database showing the PPP GDP share of the world's ten largest economies as of 2017, and the rise of China from 2% to over 20% of the world economy (Fig. 10.26).

Just as Greater China has multiple currencies and legal jurisdictions, it quite uniquely has multiple parallel stock markets:

- "A-" shares refer to shares of Chinese companies listed in Mainland China, traded in local currency Chinese Yuan (renminbi or RMB).
- "H-" shares are shares of Chinese companies listed in Hong Kong, traded in Hong Kong dollars. There are also "Red Chip" stocks listed in Hong Kong, which are similar to H-shares except that Red Chips refer to mainland-run businesses legally incorporated outside of Mainland China, often in the Cayman Islands.
- There are also "B-" shares available to foreigners listed in US dollars in Shanghai and Hong Kong dollars in Shenzhen, but fewer and fewer investors are following this market and it may phase out.
- QFII stands for "Qualified Foreign Institutional Investor", which is a program for foreign institutional investors to receive a quota to convert US dollars into RMB capital for buying A-shares or listed

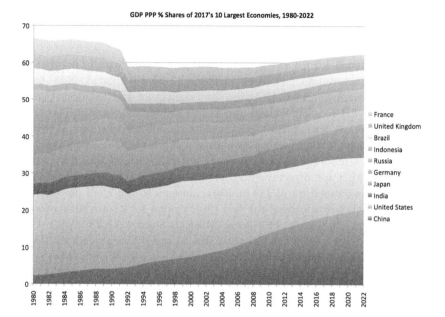

Fig. 10.26 % of world GDP (PPP) of 2017's ten largest economies, with China's rise from 2% to 20% in 40 years

bonds. QFII has limited investors from using this quota to buy inter-bank bonds (most of the Chinese bond market) or from trading futures (including the CSI300 stock index futures).

- QDII stands for "Qualified Domestic Institutional Investor" and is a program for Chinese investors to receive a quota to invest abroad.
- "RQFII" (R for renminbi) is a relatively new program which provides asset managers (so far mostly Chinese-sponsored ones) to use offshore RMB to purchase onshore investments.

From the point of the view of a US-based or Hong Kong-based investor (or more generally, investors outside Mainland China), access to Mainland Chinese shares, and especially A-shares, can be viewed as a series of steps, both looking back and projecting into the future:

1. In the 1990s, foreign investors wanting to invest in onshore listed Chinese companies were limited to the B-share market. China was still seen as a relatively closed, poor, and communist country of

little interest to US investors, so there were relatively few US funds and B-shares were a tiny slice of the investment fund space even in Hong Kong.

2. In parallel since 1993, there have also been a growing number of Chinese companies listed in Hong Kong (H-shares), New York (sometimes called N-shares), and Singapore and London (which could be called S-chips and L-shares). In time foreign investors seem to have greatly preferred these offshore listings over the B-share market (as seen by trading volume and fund assets), but all of these foreign-accessible shares still only covered a fraction of the number and diversity of companies listing on the A-share markets.

3. China joined the WTO in 2001, announced the QFII program in 2002, and approved the first QFII quotas to 12 foreign banks in 2003, including US firms Morgan Stanley (NYSE:MS), Citi (NYSE:C), Goldman Sachs (NYSE:GS), and JPMorgan (NYSE:JPM), providing foreign investors access to A-shares for the first time.

4. The first "China" ETFs were H-share ETFs: Hang Seng H-share ETF (2828.HK) in 2003 and the iShares China Large-Cap ETF (NYSEARCA:FXI) in the United States in 2004. For most of the 2000s, many foreign investors allocated "China equities" in their portfolios through H-share funds like these.

5. Also in 2004, the iShares FTSE Xinhua China A50 ETF (2823. HK) was listed in Hong Kong and was the first ETF to try and track the A-share market. It did this by holding China A-share Access Products (CAAPs), such as certificates issued by Citi against A-shares held with its QFII quota. These CAAPs were not freely convertible or widely accessible, making arbitraging the ETF very difficult, which allowed 2823.HK to have far wider premium/discount ranges than most ETFs.

6. In 2006 in the United States, Morgan Stanley launched the closed-end Morgan Stanley China A-share Fund (NYSE:CAF). The closed-end fund structure was a better fit than an ETF for the fixed QFII quota to buy A-shares, and the premium/discount reflected investor demand for this fixed pool of shares.

7. In 2009–2010, China slowly started allowing RMB settlement in Hong Kong, beginning a slow process of internationalizing the currency by developing an offshore RMB market (as there has been a global US dollar market for decades if not centuries). Hong Kong residents began being allowed to convert HK$20,000 (about

US$2,580) per day into or out of RMB, beginning a growing base of offshore RMB deposits.

8. In 2011, China began granting RQFII quotas to Chinese firms to allow this offshore RMB to be invested back into the onshore A-Share and interbank bond market. These quotas are approved more quickly than QFII quotas and may soon eclipse QFII in size and importance, because they mark existing offshore RMB rather than providing any new quota to convert RMB into USD.

9. In 2013, the Deutsche X-trackers Harvest CSI300 China A-share ETF (NYSEARCA:ASHR) was launched in the United States, following the 2012 launch of the similar ChinaAMC CSI300 ETF (3188.HK) in Hong Kong. Based on the more dynamic RQFII, this ETF is easier for dealers to arbitrage with quota shares and so provides tight NAV tracking more in line with other ETFs and unlike CAF or 2823.HK.

10. In November 2014, the Hong Kong-Shanghai Stock Connect was launched, allowing foreign investors access to A-shares ("northbound") for the first time without any QFII or RQFII quota requirement (and similarly, allowing mainland investors access to Hong Kong shares "southbound" without any QDII requirement). This still provides access to only a fraction of the A-share market (570 eligible A-shares as of the 2014 launch, with the list updated on the HKEX website), and uses a "closed-loop" system to ensure cross-border funds are kept invested in the shares traded on the connect. Still, this is another huge step forward in foreign accessibility to A-shares and eventual convergence of A-shares and H-share markets. In 2016, a similar Stock Connect link was opened with Shenzhen.

This ten-point history lesson is meant to show how slowly and gradually the Chinese equity markets are converging in a tightly controlled set of patient steps. With this timeline in mind, range trading the A-H premium index is a medium- to long-term play on the order of months or years rather than days or weeks, as can also be seen by the earlier chart on the Index.

Below are some statistics on the relative sizes of the stock markets in Hong Kong, Shanghai, and Shenzhen. Note that H-shares and Red Chips are far less numerous than Hong Kong stocks, but these mainland companies listed in Hong Kong are generally much larger than all Hong Kong companies (Fig. 10.27).

	Hong Kong Exchange (08/05/2018)		Shanghai Stock Exchange (08/05/2018)		Shenzhen Stock Exchange (08/05/2018)	
	Main Board	GEM	A Share	B Share	A Share	B Share
No. of listed companies	1,829	359	1,415	51	2,100	49
No. of listed H shares	230	24	n.a.	n.a.	n.a.	n.a.
No. of listed red-chips stocks	158	6	n.a.	n.a.	n.a.	n.a.
Total no. of listed securities	13,465	360	n.a.	n.a.	n.a.	n.a.
Total market capitalisation (Bil. dollars)	HKD 34,501	HKD 265	RMB 32,546	RMB 90	RMB 23,133	RMB 72
Total negotiable capitalisation (Bil. dollars)	n.a.	n.a.	RMB 27,686	RMB 90	RMB 16,680	RMB 71
Average P/E ratio (Times)	12.44	40.89	15.44	12.53	28.87	7.99
Total turnover (Mil. shares)	208,481	1,463	14,774	21	18,250	27
Total turnover (Mil. dollars)	HKD 103,161	HKD 639	RMB 189,660	RMB 124	RMB 256,042	RMB 164
Total market turnover (Mil. dollars)	HKD 103,800		RMB 190,095		RMB 256,206	

Fig. 10.27 Relative sizes of Hong Kong, Shanghai, and Shenzhen stock markets. (Source: HKEX)

Because A-shares and H-shares of the same company are not freely inter-tradable, and short selling A-shares ranges from extremely difficult to impossible, H-shares often trade at significant discounts in Hong Kong vs the same company's A-share in the Mainland. Below is a snapshot showing the discounts of a sample of Chinese companies with both A-shares and H-shares, with some H-shares trading at discounts as deep as 70% (Fig. 10.28).

What is especially surprising is that these significant discounts have not only persisted, but in many cases even widened after Stock Connect gave investors on both sides the ability to trade whichever share was cheaper. The above names that have the "CON" icon next to them are the names available to trade on Stock Connect. The Hang Seng China AH Premium Index, charted below, shows the market cap-weighted average premium of A-shares over H-shares, with A-shares going from a 5–10% average discount before the launch of Stock Connect in late 2014 to an average 20–30% premium after the launch of Stock Connect (Fig. 10.29).

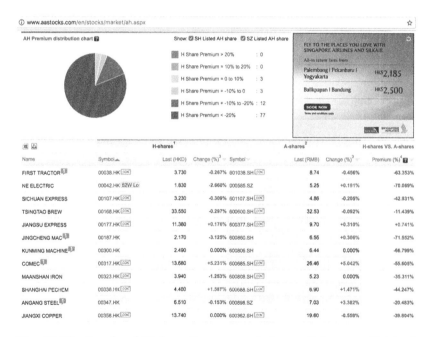

Fig. 10.28 Sample of H-share discounts vs A-shares of the same Mainland Chinese companies, with a pie chart of discount levels

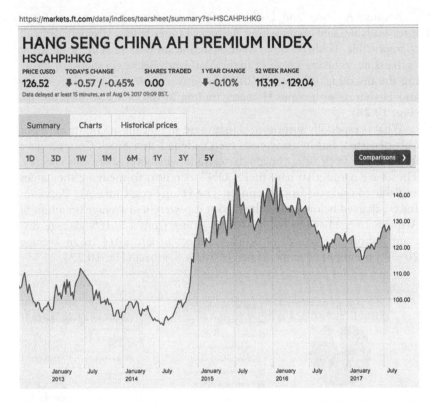

Fig. 10.29 Chart of the Hang Seng China AH Premium Index, showing the shift from A-share discount to A-share premium around the 2014 launch of Stock Connect

Greater China, with its rich variety of so many other things, naturally also has a rich variety of stock market indices. Perhaps the most internationally known index in this region is the Hang Seng Index, long an index of 30 blue chip Hong Kong companies, but expanded in the early twenty-first century to include 50 names, with an increasing percentage coming from Mainland China. One landmark example of this change was Hang Seng Indexes' November 2017 decision to drop Hong Kong flag carrier airline Cathay Pacific from the index and replace it with Mainland Chinese property developer Country Garden. The same index provider also maintained a separate Hang Seng China Enterprises Index, also known as "the

H-share Index", which along with the Hang Seng makes up the two most liquid equity index futures benchmarks in Hong Kong.

More broadly, MSCI has so far covered Greater China with three separate indices: the "China Free" index of mostly H- and N-shares, "Taiwan", and a separate "China A" index. In 2017, MSCI finally announced long-expected plans to include A-shares in its widely tracked Emerging Market index, which had been delayed due to concerns about openness of the A-share market to the foreign investors who use the index as a benchmark. Below are the sector weights and top components of the MSCI China Free and Taiwan Indices (Tables 10.1, 10.2, 10.3, 10.4 and 10.5).

As can be seen above, both the MSCI China Free and MSCI Taiwan Indices have the largest sector weighting in "information technology", but in two very different types of IT companies: Taiwan remains focused on the competitive production of back-end hardware, while the top H- and N-share IT companies are the Mainland Chinese Internet giants Baidu, Alibaba, Tencent, and JD.com, together known as the "BAT-J" rivaling the United States's "FANG".

As MSCI was relatively late to include A-shares in its major benchmarks (despite maintaining a separate but less used A-share index), other index

Table 10.1 Top holdings of the iShares MSCI China A-share Index ETF, note the large share of banks and alcoholic beverage makers

Ticker	Name	Weight (%)	Sector	Exchange
600519	KWEICHOW MOUTAI LTD A	4.6	Consumer Staples	Shanghai
601318	PING AN INSURANCE (GROUP) OF CHINA	3.5	Financials	Shanghai
600036	CHINA MERCHANTS BANK LTD A	3.2	Financials	Shanghai
2415	HANGZHOU HIKVISION DIGITAL TECHNOL	1.9	Information Technology	Shenzhen
333	MIDEA GROUP LTD A	1.8	Consumer Discretionary	Shenzhen
601166	INDUSTRIAL BANK LTD A	1.7	Financials	Shanghai
601398	INDUSTRIAL AND COMMERCIAL BANK OF	1.7	Financials	Shanghai
600000	SHANGHAI PUDONG DEVELOPMENT BANK L	1.7	Financials	Shanghai
858	WULIANGYE YIBIN LTD A	1.5	Consumer Staples	Shenzhen
2	CHINA VANKE LTD A	1.4	Real Estate	Shenzhen

Table 10.2 Top holdings of the iShares MSCI China Free ("H" and "N" shares) Index ETF, note IT firms Baidu, Alibaba and Tencent make up 35%

Ticker	Name	Weight (%)	Sector	Exchange
700	TENCENT HOLDINGS LTD	17.1	Information Technology	Hong Kong
BABA	ALIBABA GROUP HOLDING ADR REPRESEN	13.5	Information Technology	New York
939	CHINA CONSTRUCTION BANK CORP H	5.2	Financials	Hong Kong
BIDU	BAIDU ADR REPTG INC CLASS A	4.3	Information Technology	NASDAQ
1398	INDUSTRIAL AND COMMERCIAL BANK OF	3.8	Financials	Hong Kong
941	CHINA MOBILE LTD	3.5	Telecommunications	Hong Kong
2318	PING AN INSURANCE (GROUP) CO OF CH	3.0	Financials	Hong Kong
3988	BANK OF CHINA LTD H	2.5	Financials	Hong Kong
883	CNOOC LTD	1.8	Energy	Hong Kong
386	CHINA PETROLEUM AND CHEMICAL CORP	1.5	Energy	Hong Kong

providers took the lead in indexing the A-share market. Two of the most widely used A-share benchmarks are the FTSE/Xinhua China A50 and the Mainland's own CSI 300, tracking 50 and 300 of the largest A-shares, respectively. Both are tracked by ETFs, mostly traded in Hong Kong, and there are futures contracts on the CSI 300 traded in Shanghai in RMB by mainland investors, and futures on the A50 traded in Singapore in US dollars (quanto), allowing foreign investors to take long or short positions in the index. Below is a table of the top ten components of the A50 index, which has a 62% weight in financials, followed by the trading statistics on the SGX-listed A50 futures (Fig. 10.30).

For fundamental investors, China presents a diverse, challenging, and high-opportunity market requiring the understanding of many different legal, accounting, and financial reporting regimes running in parallel.

In addition to equities, China also has a large and diverse bond market. As with many other emerging markets, there is a separate onshore market

Table 10.3 Top holdings of the iShares MSCI Hong Kong Index ETF, dominated by financials and real estate

Ticker	Name	Weight (%)	Sector	Exchange
1299	AIA GROUP LTD	19.7	Financials	Hong Kong
388	HONG KONG EXCHANGES AND CLEARING L	7.1	Financials	Hong Kong
1	CK HUTCHISON HOLDINGS LTD	5.8	Industrials	Hong Kong
16	SUN HUNG KAI PROPERTIES LTD	4.2	Real Estate	Hong Kong
1113	CK ASSET HOLDINGS LTD	4.1	Real Estate	Hong Kong
27	GALAXY ENTERTAINMENT GROUP LTD	3.8	Consumer Discretionary	Hong Kong
2388	BOC HONG KONG HOLDINGS LTD	3.5	Financials	Hong Kong
11	HANG SENG BANK LTD	3.5	Financials	Hong Kong
823	LINK REAL ESTATE INVESTMENT TRUST	3.5	Real Estate	Hong Kong
3	HONG KONG AND CHINA GAS LTD	3.3	Utilities	Hong Kong

for Chinese debt denominated in RMB, and until the 2010s only available to Mainland Chinese banks, funds, and some private investors. Some foreign issuers have been able to issue RMB-denominated bonds in the domestic China market, which have been known as "Panda bonds". Offshore, the Chinese government and private companies have issued debt in US dollars, and the high-yield debt of Chinese property developers has been especially popular with private banks. In the 2010s, an offshore RMB market started developing and gave rise to the "Dim Sum bond" market for bonds issued in RMB, initially in Hong Kong and so named after the snacks eaten in Hong Kong. Later in 2010, China opened a "Bond Connect" program allowing registered accounts to trade onshore RMB-denominated bonds directly with Mainland banks in a closed-loop system similar to Stock Connect.

While many investors are likely to find these complexities a hassle, these many gradual steps and use of safeguards have arguably kept the Chinese

Table 10.4 Top holdings of the iShares MSCI Taiwan Index ETF, more focused on IT hardware and materials

Ticker	Name	Weight (%)	Sector	Exchange
2330	TAIWAN SEMICONDUCTOR MANUFACTURING	21.5	Information Technology	Taiwan
2317	HON HAI PRECISION INDUSTRY LTD	7.2	Information Technology	Taiwan
2454	MEDIATEK INC.	2.9	Information Technology	Taiwan
1301	FORMOSA PLASTICS CORP.	2.5	Materials	Taiwan
2882	CATHAY FINANCIAL HOLDING LTD	2.5	Financials	Taiwan
2412	CHUNGHWA TELECOM CO. LTD.	2.4	Telecommunications	Taiwan
1303	NAN YA PLASTICS CORP.	2.3	Materials	Taiwan
3008	LARGAN PRECISION LTD	2.3	Information Technology	Taiwan
2891	CTBC FINANCIAL HOLDING CO LTD	2.2	Financials	Taiwan
1326	FORMOSA CHEMICALS & FIBRE CORP.	2.0	Materials	Taiwan

Table 10.5 Weights by sector of these four iShares MSCI Greater China Index ETFs

Row Labels	China A	China H&N	Hong Kong	Taiwan
Consumer Discretionary	9.8	8.7	13.4	3.4
Consumer Staples	11.1	2.2	1.6	3.3
Energy	2.1	5.2		1.0
Financials	32.6	22.8	35.4	18.5
Health Care	5.8	2.7		0.5
Industrials	13.4	3.8	11.9	3.1
Information Technology	8.1	40.7	0.7	54.5
Materials	7.5	1.7		9.9
Real Estate	6.0	5.2	25.1	0.6
Telecommunications	0.1	4.4	1.4	4.3
Utilities	3.2	2.5	9.8	

market far more stable than many other emerging markets, and China's growth and opening story will continue to be one of the main shows of the early twenty-first century.

Weighting	NameEN	NameSC	ExchgTicker	TradExchg	GICSSectorEN	GICSSectorSC
10.9	PING AN INSURANCE GROUP CO-A	中国平安	601318 CG	SHAX	Financials	金融
6.8	CHINA MERCHANTS BANK-A	招商银行	600036 CG	SHAX	Financials	金融
5.5	INDUSTRIAL BANK CO LTD -A	兴业银行	601166 CG	SHAX	Financials	金融
4.7	KWEICHOW MOUTAI CO LTD-A	贵州茅台	600519 CG	SHAX	Consumer Staples	日常消费品
4.0	SHANGHAI PUDONG DEVEL BANK-A	浦发银行	600000 CG	SHAX	Financials	金融
3.9	CHINA MINSHENG BANKING-A	民生银行	600016 CG	SHAX	Financials	金融
3.2	MIDEA GROUP CO LTD-A	美的集团	000333 CS	SHEX	Consumer Discretionary	非日常生活消费品
3.0	CITIC SECURITIES CO-A	中信证券	600030 CG	SHAX	Financials	金融
3.0	AGRICULTURAL BANK OF CHINA-A	农业银行	601288 CG	SHAX	Financials	金融
2.9	BANK OF COMMUNICATIONS CO-A	交通银行	601328 CG	SHAX	Financials	金融
2.7	IND & COMM BK OF CHINA-A	工商银行	601398 CG	SHAX	Financials	金融

sgx.com/wps/portal/sgxweb/home/marketinfo/derivatives/delayed_prices/futures

Contract Month	Last	Bid Size	Bid	Ask	Ask Size	Open	High	Low	Screen Volume	Off-Exch Volume	Total Volume	Open Interest
Aug 17	▼11,745.00	36	11,745.00	11,760.00	560	11,852.50	11,872.50	11,742.50	138,800	5,000	143,800	615,566
Sep 17	▼11,730.00	1	11,727.50	11,750.00	2	11,840.00	11,850.00	11,715.00	8,437	5,000	13,437	18,914
Oct 17	▼11,745.00	1	11,735.00	11,982.50	3	11,745.00	11,745.00	11,745.00	1	-	1	5
Dec 17	▼11,775.00	1	11,765.00	11,895.00	1	11,830.00	11,915.00	11,775.00	29	-	29	704
Mar 18	▼11,810.00	1	11,762.50	11,950.00	1	11,945.00	11,945.00	11,810.00	7	-	7	231
Jun 18	▼11,800.00	1	11,750.00	11,950.00	1	11,810.00	11,810.00	11,800.00	2	-	2	24

Fig. 10.30 Top components of the FTSE/Xinhua A50 index and trading statistics of the SGX-listed A50 futures. (Source: CSOP, SGX)

10.5   The "ABCS" and Other Developed Markets

A globally diversified investment portfolio allocated to the United States, Eurozone, Japan, and Greater China would still be missing many important markets around the world, but would cover about 75% of the world's stock market capitalization and a similarly large percentage of the global tradable bond market, and would arguably be over 90% as diversified as most liquid investment portfolios would need to be, at least in terms of geographic risk measures.

Beyond these four "majors", one may supplement by adding four "minor" markets, each related to one of the majors, but with enough difference to its "major" analogue for the diversification benefit to justify additional currency risk and administrative effort. These four markets may be referred to as the "ABCS": Australia, Britain, Canada, and Singapore. Being English-speaking countries scattered globally on which the sun never sets, these four countries make up a balanced basket of small and different countries where an Anglophone can read financial statements and legal documents with minimal linguistic friction.

Britain is the largest of these four markets in its own right and should properly refer to the whole of the United Kingdom of Great Britain and

Northern Ireland other than the need for a "B" in the above acronym. The United Kingdom has a history of a global empire that connected it to many parts of the world and made English the international language of business (and the obvious language to write this book in), but after World War II became more focused on its economic relationship with continental Europe than with its former colonies. From the 1970s to the 2010s, the UK economy was focused on increasing trade with the European Union, but Britain long refused to merge its pound with the euro currency, and in 2016 voted in the "Brexit" referendum to leave the European Union, and there is debate on what trade barriers or deal will arise between the United Kingdom and the EU. The United States and the three other ABCS all happen to be former British colonies, and their connection through a common language and strong institutions based on English law are one reason these former colonies have economically outperformed many of their neighbors. As the largest and oldest of the ABCS, the UK economy and market, as one would expect, are the most diversified in the group, and represent not just resources and banks, and include more pharmaceutical and technology companies as well. The largest UK stock by market cap as of 2017 is The Hong Kong and Shanghai Banking Corporation ("HSBC"), which also used to be the largest HK stock in the Hang Seng Index until it was surpassed by Tencent. London remains one of the most important financial centers of the world and seems likely to continue this role even after Brexit and a scandal around rigging of the LIBOR index, and British government bonds ("gilts") remain popular with foreign investors willing to accept or hedge GBP currency risk.

Canada and Australia, to many foreign investors, may be seen as two similar and balancing components to their "major" counterparts (the United States and Japan) and to their ABCS counterparts (Britain and Singapore). What makes them similar to each other, and different from the aforementioned counterparts, is that Canada and Australia are both heavily resource-dependent economies, where the second most important industry is an oligopoly of banks that serve those resource companies. Both Canada and Australia have large industries in the mining of gold, base metals, and coal, and in the mid-2000s, Canada became one of the world's largest oil producers with development of the Alberta tar sands made economical by advancing technology and rising oil prices. Both have relatively small, but still liquid and tradable, currency and government bond markets, and the sensitivity of their economies and currency exchange rates to commodity prices became very visible in the mid-2010s when a slowdown in China's growth rate led to a fall in commodity prices.

Singapore is often compared to Hong Kong, and as Hong Kong is the English law-based gateway to Mainland China, Singapore is often seen as the AAA-rated gateway to Southeast Asia and South Asia (described below). Singapore differs from Hong Kong in that it is a sovereign nation with its own military, leading the island city-state to far higher debt-to-GDP levels than most countries outside Japan. Many investors may consider Singapore too small in its own right, as the island is only 700 sq. km in size and home to fewer than six million people, but remains one of the wealthiest cities in the world on a per-capita basis and one of the best places to do business. The SGX's lead as a regional futures trading hub, as seen with the above examples of Japan and China futures, is just one of the many signs of why investors may want to keep an eye here.

The ABCS, added to the major four, make an even more diversified portfolio but still have excluded even other developed markets: Korea, Switzerland, Norway, and Sweden, just to name a few. The final part of this chapter will do a similar survey of some of the remaining emerging and frontier markets not yet discussed.

10.6   EMERGING AND FRONTIER MARKETS

There are several debatable definitions about what makes a market "developed", "emerging", or "frontier", but generally these are categorized by level of foreign investor access, property right protection, and efficiency in fairly disseminating information and executing transactions. While China is still widely considered an "emerging" market, this book has categorized it as one of the "majors" along with three other "major developed" and four "minor developed" markets. Analogous to "Greater China", one might broadly look around the other three "BRIC" components for additional markets surrounding Brazil, Russia, and India, as well as three other major emerging and frontier regions of Southeast Asia, the Middle East, and Africa. Many of these markets are more difficult to access by foreign investors, and so are mostly referenced through ETFs traded in one of the major markets mentioned earlier.

India is the largest market not included in this chapter's classification of the four majors and four minor ABCS. Like the ABCS, South Asia is also made up of former British colonies. British India covered what now includes India, Pakistan, Bangladesh, Sri Lanka (formerly known as

Ceylon), and Myanmar (now considered part of Southeast Asia, Myanmar was split off as a separate colony "British Burma", many years before the rest of India's independence and partition). As China's long sphere of influence led to similar-sounding currency names in East Asia (the Chinese yuan, Japanese yen, and Korean won all have roots of the same Chinese word for money), the currencies of India, Pakistan, Sri Lanka, and Nepal are all called the "rupee", with only Bangladesh's currency called the "taka". The Republic of India is by far the largest and most open of these markets but is still not included in the top eight simply because of access: foreign investors still face difficulty converting foreign currency in and out of Indian rupees and registering for custody accounts to freely trade financial assets and repatriate profits. While progress has been made in replacing antiquated and corrupt paper systems with efficient and transparent electronic ones, and access products have long been available through a tax treaty with Mauritius, straight-through access as with China's stock connect still seems a long way off. Many foreign investors will access India through a series of ETFs covering large cap, small cap, and earnings-weighted strategies, through futures on India's Nifty 50 index listed in Singapore, or through a small handful of ETFs tracking large cap indices of Pakistan and Bangladesh. South Asian countries also have high local currency interest rates, and have often paid relatively wide credit spreads in US dollars, but ETFs tracking South Asian debt have yet to pick up.

Russia's historic sphere of influence might be considered to include the republics of the former Soviet Union, as well as some Eastern European countries that were in the Soviet sphere of influence during the Cold War of 1945–1991. Russia remains by far the largest of these economies and markets, followed distantly by Kazakhstan. Both Russia and Kazakhstan, like Canada and Australia, are dominated by resource extraction companies and the banks that serve them, and as seen in Sect. 6.2, Russian currency and equity markets tumbled in the mid-2010s with the fall in oil prices. Russia defaulted on its US dollar debt in 1998, but Russian debt has since been one of the best performers in the JPMorgan Emerging Market Bond Index (EMBI). Foreign investors can track Russian large cap and small cap indices through ETFs, and some individual Russian single stocks are traded as ADRs and GDRs in New York and London, respectively. Former Soviet state Estonia has joined the European Union and the Eurozone, while other formerly communist states that were not technically Soviet allies, like the former republics of Yugoslavia, remain outside the EU, though mostly with more diversified and less resource-dependent economies than Russia. Poland may be one market worth highlighting in this extended sphere of influence, as it was a Warsaw Pact Soviet ally, though not a Soviet state, and perhaps one of the better post-Cold War recovery stories with its membership in the EU while still remaining outside the Eurozone.

Brazil is the BRICS' cornerstone in Latin America and is the Portuguese-speaking country in a predominately Spanish-speaking region. Other major Latin American markets covered by ETFs include Mexico, Chile, Colombia, Peru, Argentina, and Venezuela, with the latter two suffering the most extreme debt crises as of this writing. Caribbean islands, for example, Trinidad and Tobago, Jamaica, and Cuba, plus the legal company structuring havens of the Cayman and British Virgin Islands (BVI), are sometimes included in the same geographic region as Latin America, though practically have little in common with most "mainland" Latin American countries financially. Brazil and Chile, like Russia, Canada, and Malaysia, also depend heavily on resource extraction, highlighted by Brazilian oil and mining giants Petrobras and Vale, and Chile's role as the world's #1 producer of copper. Many Latin American countries are considered by economists to have been caught in the "middle income trap", where their development seems to have plateaued below the potential levels achieved by the United States and China. Around the year 1900, Argentina (whose name means "silvery") was one of the wealthiest countries in the world, as evidenced by the beautiful architecture in Buenos Aires that the surrounding economy has not been able to keep up with. Currency controls and a lack of competitiveness in non-extractive industries are two main factors of this, as can be seen by the below examples of four Latin American currencies which have all been taken out of circulation due to hyperinflation. Within the lifetime of many readers of this book, Brazil has replaced the cruzeiro with the real, Peru the inta with the nuevo sol (meaning "new sun"), Argentina the austral with the peso, and Venezuela the bolivar with the "bolivar fuerte" ("fuerte" meaning "strong"). One advantage of hyperinflation in Latin America is that some of these countries have developed some of the world's most advanced markets for tracking inflation, as exemplified by Mexico's UDI and Chile's UF in Chap. 5. It has been said that "Brazil is the country of the future, and it always will be" (Fig. 10.31).

Beyond the BRICS, Southeast Asia is another large market, of which Singapore was the only one included in the eight most accessible markets above. Southeast Asia is often defined by the Association of Southeast

Fig. 10.31 Banknotes of Brazilian cruzeiros, Peruvian intas, Argentine australes, and Venezuelan bolivar, all of which have been replaced by new currency denominations due to hyperinflation

Asian Nations (ASEAN), made up of Singapore; the "M-TIP" markets of Malaysia, Thailand, Indonesia, and the Philippines; and Southeast Asia's frontier markets of Brunei, Vietnam, Myanmar, Cambodia, and Laos. With a combined population of over 600 million, a US$2.5 trillion GDP, and a 2000–2013 average GDP growth rate over 5% (surpassed only by India and China), ASEAN is too large and too fast growing a market to ignore completely. The Asian Financial Crisis, mentioned in Chap. 5 around the collapse of the Thai baht, still lingers in the mind of foreign investors with long memories, but bigger issues remain the lack of regional integration and free foreign exchange, which makes many of these markets not much easier to access than India. Each of the M-TIP markets, plus Vietnam, is accessible through US-listed and some non-US-listed ETFs, while the big frontier of Myanmar only got its first ATM in 2012 and first stock exchange in 2016. While the many linguistic, legal, and technical differences between the ASEAN markets continue to present friction and barriers, this diversity also makes the region a large and challenging opportunity for investors willing to learn and take advantage of these differences.

The Middle East and North Africa are often associated by foreign investors with Islam, the Arabic language, and geopolitical struggles over oil and Israel. So far, all US-listed ADRs of companies classified as "Middle East" (of which there were over 90 as of 2017) are actually based in Israel, which in some ways can be seen as a "silicon valley of the Middle East" with its proliferation of technology companies. In 2013, MSCI upgraded the United Arab Emirates and Qatar from "frontier" to "emerging" market status, and as of this writing, Saudi Arabia is in talks about listing its trillion-dollar state-owned oil company Saudi Aramco in an IPO to foreign investors, though likely will do so on the Saudi Tadawul stock exchange with limited allocations to a few large sovereign wealth funds. The Arab states of the Middle East also include Gulf Cooperation Council (GCC) members Bahrain, Kuwait, and Oman; the North African states from Egypt to Morocco; and in the middle the war-torn frontiers of Iraq and Syria. Beyond the Jewish and Arab states are Iran and Turkey, both of which have large, young populations with enormous potential as bridges between the Middle East, Europe, South Asia, and the Far East.

Africa, specifically sub-Saharan Africa, may be considered the final frontier of international investors with a variety of languages, colonial and tribal histories, and mineral and demographic wealth comparable only to that of Asia, but so far seeming to lag Asia in economic and financial development by several decades. Sub-Saharan Africa is home to one billion people as of 2017, projected to grow to two billion by 2050 and three billion by 2075 due to having many of the youngest population pyramids on the planet, as seen below in contrast to the earlier ones of Japan, China, India, and the United States (Fig. 10.32).

Although there is more to destiny than demographics, the question is whether Africa will be able to harness its mineral and demographic wealth

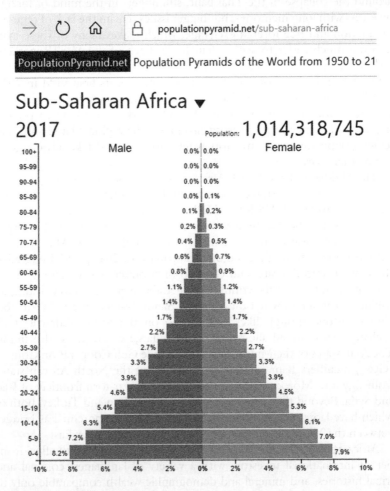

Fig. 10.32   Population pyramid of sub-Saharan Africa, showing a young population with enormous growth potential

to do in the coming decades what China and India have been doing. So far, the main investable market in sub-Saharan Africa is the Republic of South Africa, followed distantly by Nigeria. Some African companies and credits trade in some of the more developed markets, especially in London, but most of the continent remains a frontier, about which major updates will hopefully be written in the second edition of this book.

There is far more to learn and discover about the many different markets of the world than could possibly be covered in these few pages, but hopefully these summaries have been enough to whet the appetite of investors who have yet to fully maximize the potential benefits of diversification into foreign markets.

CHAPTER 11

Behavioral Investing That Breaks the Boxes

Chapters 1 through 10 defined many of the boxes different investments are often categorized in, and aimed to get readers comfortable diversifying into new boxes. This chapter steps outside these "textbook" investment boxes and discusses one of the most important differences between investment theory and investment practice affecting all these boxes: the fact that people don't always act rationally. A good understanding of the principles and pitfalls in behavioral investing can both help investors better avoid such mistakes themselves and find ways to profit from the irrational actions of other investors. While these behavioral anomalies may cover some of the most obvious ways for investors to outperform the benchmarks using 100% public information, it is important to remember the John Maynard Keynes quote that "Markets can remain irrational longer than you can remain solvent."

As of this writing, Vanguard is the world's leading brand in low-cost index funds, long advocating passive investment in the whole market rather than paying expensive managers to try and beat the marker, yet Vanguard still highlights measurable value from a professional advisor in their "Advisor's Alpha" methodology. Of the factors Vanguard lists as valuable to advisor clients, "behavioral coaching" is listed below as the most significant, typically adding 1.5% per year in value to an investor's returns. Here, behavioral coaching largely refers to calmly guiding an investor to have a rational investment plan and avoid performance chasing, buying on euphoric highs, and selling at depressing lows, which accounts

© The Author(s) 2018   279
T. Dennison, *Invest Outside the Box*,
https://doi.org/10.1007/978-981-13-0372-2_11

		Moving from the scenario described to Vanguard Advisor's Alpha methodology
Vanguard Advisor's Alpha strategy	Module	Typical value added for client (basis points)
Suitable asset allocation using broadly diversified funds/ETFs	I	> 0 bps*
Cost-effective implementation (expense ratios)	II	40 bps
Rebalancing	III	35 bps
Behavioral coaching	IV	150 bps
Asset location	V	0 to 75 bps
Spending strategy (withdrawal order)	VI	0 to 110 bps
Total-return versus income investing	VII	> 0 bps*
Total potential value added		About 3% in net returns

* Value is deemed significant but too unique to each investor to quantify.
We believe implementing the Vanguard Advisor's Alpha framework can add about 3% in net returns for your clients and also allow you to differentiate your skills and practice. The actual amount of value added may vary significantly, depending on clients' circumstances.
Source: Vanguard.

Fig. 11.1 Behavioral coaching is the largest value-add of a professional financial advisor, according to Vanguard

for much of the difference between invest*ment* returns and invest*or* returns described in Sect. 11.3. While the other factors spending order, cost-effective implementation, rebalancing, and asset location may involve more "inside the box" professional finance knowledge, actually acting on these also requires avoiding behavioral traps of procrastination and comfort zones (Fig. 11.1).

Classical finance theory makes several simplifying but almost laughably unrealistic assumptions about investor behavior. Some of these assumptions include:

1. Rational investors aim to maximize their overall lifetime happiness by balancing current consumption versus savings and investment risk.
2. Rational investors take into account all available, relevant information when selecting and valuing investments.
3. Rational investors do not invest in assets on which they lack enough information on which to base a calculated expectation of a worthwhile return.
4. Rational investors only care about the past decline in the value of an investment if it makes a difference that can be acted upon (say, harvesting a tax loss).
5. Rational investors diversify and lever/de-lever their portfolios for the optimal balance of risk versus return, using techniques like the mean-variance optimization framework described in Sect. 7.3.

Some patterns we might expect to see in a world where all investors behave as the perfectly rational *Homo Economicus* described in finance textbooks include:

1. Assets would always be priced rationally, and it would be virtually impossible to outperform a low-cost index fund on a risk-adjusted basis using public information. In other words, the efficient market hypothesis (EMH) would be true.
2. Actively managed mutual funds would struggle to raise or maintain assets or charge fees much above that of index funds. The aggregate amount of actively managed capital would be just enough to keep asset prices in line with fundamentals, and earn barely enough of a return for doing so.
3. Bubbles and crashes generally would not happen.
4. Pensions would rarely be underfunded or overfunded. Workers would save just enough money for their retirement, and invest it in a portfolio that indexes expected future costs of their standard of living.
5. No one would have any credit card or high-interest consumer debt. Borrowing would be at low, competitive rates for long-term assets whose value matches or exceeds how long the money is borrowed for.
6. Stores would not price products at $9.99, as this would cost more in ink and effort than the simpler price of $10 to be worth the extra sales from a 0.1% price cut.
7. Traders would not care about "getting even" nor perform any "revenge trades", but rather get out of a bad investment and move onto a better one if the underlying fundamentals deteriorate.
8. No one would buy an investment without a pretty good idea of how they would get their money back plus a worthwhile rate of return from it.
9. Only the most specialized of investors would not diversify outside their home country and industry.

11.1   Procrastination and "Analysis Paralysis"

For many people who need to invest, the first barrier to higher returns and lower risk is actually taking action. Whether an investor chooses one fund over another, uses a simple or more complex asset allocation model, or diversifies internationally is a far less significant factor in long-term wealth than whether or not the individual actually ever got around to putting money into an investment at all, and whether investing is habitual or not. Getting a larger share of the public to "just do it" when it comes to retirement investment decisions is a major reason more defined contribution plans are enrolling employees to set aside part of their pay in low-cost investments by default, meaning more and more workers would have to "opt out" of investing rather than have to take any active decision to "opt in" to an investment plan.

Putting off investing is naturally a problem for someone who is busy with life and does not feel they have time to think about investing but is also a problem for those who have the will, skill, and time to evaluate investments and instead delay action by thinking and talking about investments for longer than might be necessary. This is often known as "analysis paralysis" and is expensive both in the excessive time and effort spent overthinking it and in the opportunity cost of missing returns those who "just do it" enjoy in the meantime.

Conversely, some shareholders come to own a concentrated stock position that they become reluctant to sell even part of. These are often shares in a company they worked at for a long time, or inherited from a relative who worked there for the company for a long time, or in some other way accumulated and concentrated in the hands of an "accidental" investor as likely to have excuses for not reducing their exposure as many investors have for not initiating investment exposure. Some of the barriers to reducing exposure to concentrated stock positions are beyond individual behavior, and may be regulatory (restrictions against selling or hedging) or based on familial or peer pressure, but all make interesting challenges for advisors of many high net worth clients.

11.2   COMFORT ZONE AND BIASES

Many of the boxes in this book can also define comfort zones, and one of the main objectives of this book is to identify those psychological barriers and expand the reader's comfort zone to diversify into other boxes. Psychological comfort zones can be thought of as having multiple layers, with the largest being awareness (what we know exists or is possible), within which there is familiarity (knowing enough about an investment and how to execute on it), within which there is willingness and readiness (there are many investments you may understand and be set up to trade, but see no point in including in your portfolio) (Fig. 11.2).

The first few chapters in this book were roughly presented in the order the author has seen many individuals become aware of and familiar with these different boxes. In Hong Kong, where this author lives, a large percentage of individuals have a bank account and save a significant share of their salary in cash or bank deposits, and then are likely to buy some long-term fixed deposits or insurance-linked savings plans, and then they are likely to make their first significant investments in residential property. There are many wealthy individuals in Hong Kong who only keep money in cash, bank deposits, and physical property. While stock investing may seem like a popular pastime among Chinese, many individuals view the Hong Kong stock exchange as a legal casino for making fast money through short-term trades, rather than as a gateway to accumulating long-term wealth by owning profitable businesses. Although Hong Kong investors love investing in real estate, Hong Kong has only nine listed real estate investment trusts (REITs) as of this writing, partly due to a lack of special tax advantages for the REIT structure, but perhaps mostly due to a lack of awareness by many Hong Kong investors that it is even possible to own property through a REIT. This awareness gap may not be much a surprise to those observing how luxuriously property agents spend on catered events and glossy brochures to market off-plan apartments (even in far-off cities) compared with how much is spent marketing REIT investments. Once there is awareness, the investor needs to be familiar with how

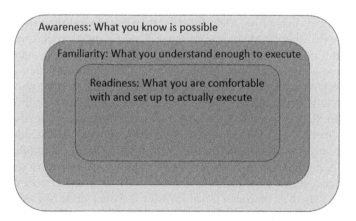

Fig. 11.2 Three layers of comfort zone: awareness, familiarity, and readiness

a brokerage account differs from a bank account, how to buy and sell shares on and exchange, and how owning shares of a REIT for long-term income and inflation protection is different than betting on whether Tencent stock will go up another ten points next week. Of all the assets and instruments an investor may be familiar with, they may only get around to actually trading and owning a small variety, and only a relatively small percentage of rational or well-advised investors tend to do so among a well-balanced portfolio of the different boxes.

Personal or institutional bias is one factor dividing familiarity and readiness. A somewhat timely example over the past two decades has been the significant difference in valuation ratios of Canadian vs Russian natural resource firms, where the Canadian firms have often traded at an average of three times the multiple to earnings or book value of comparable oil or mining companies. The major stock index benchmarks in Canada and Russia are surprisingly similar to each other in the size and importance of these extraction industries and the banks that finance them. It is understandable that different standards of accounting, rule of law, and transparency in business practices differ measurably between these neighbors across the Bering straits, but many purely quantitative valuation models would struggle to explain the difference without some attribution to a bias of G7-based investors against owning Russian companies.

The rational side of a comfort zone is what Warren Buffett and Charlie Munger refer to as an investor's "circle of competence". While many legendary investors, including Buffett and Munger, have chosen to concentrate their bets rather than diversify, they have found their investment edge in focusing all their investment efforts on assets they can deeply know and understand extremely well. These focused investors admit that they miss many great investment opportunities that have fallen outside their circle of competence, but with the trade-off that their hit rate within that circle is much higher than it would have been in a more diversified portfolio. Rather than being defined by comfort and bias, circle of competence is marked by a genuine edge in gathering, understanding, and interpreting investment opportunities within that circle. Optimistically, investors might seek to continuously broaden or deepen their circles of competence in ways not naturally expected of most comfort zones.

One of the best places to be an investor is with a circle of competence in an area most investors are unaware of, and few if any other investors have sufficient familiarity or interest to compete in. These areas are sometimes called "esoteric markets", as they are often for most trading conversations and activity. One example of an esoteric market is financing receivables for certain types of trading businesses, where opportunistic and well-organized investors have been able to earn secured double-digit returns providing a service to merchants that banks and other investors have failed to finance for some solvable reason.

11.3   FEAR AND GREED, FOMO, BUYING HIGH, AND SELLING LOW

Although supply and demand produce trading volumes, it is the forces of greed and fear that drive bubbles to dizzying heights and then sink prices to unbelievable lows long before and shortly after such bubbles develop and pop. There is plenty of literature on bubbles, the herd mentality, and the madness of crowds, but the underlying "physics" of bubbles still comes down to understanding and modeling the balance of these forces.

Greed often describes the side of the force that drives prices higher as new investors, who otherwise might have never entered an asset class and likely still don't have properly familiarity or understanding of it, pile in. The spectacular rise in the prices of several cryptocurrencies in 2017 (as described in Chap. 9) attracted many such retail investors who were as much driven by the greed of the chance of multiplying their money quickly as they were the fear of not keeping up with their neighbors and colleagues that did. This sort of greed has been widely labeled as the "fear of missing out" or "FOMO".

September 2008 to March 2009, on the other hand, was a period marked by the fear of a "melt down" of the global financial system (rather than the "melt up", which describes some contagious bull markets). In 2017 and 2018, it is already difficult for many to remember how desperate those months were following the collapse of Lehman Brothers, when Warren Buffett was able to command a 10% annual rate for capitalizing top-tier banks and many firms were trading at single-digit multiples to their long-term average earnings, all because many buyers were either too busy unwinding bad debts or too afraid that process might unwind the entire banking and economic system as they understood it.

One of the most repeated Warren Buffett quotes is to "be fearful when others are greedy and greedy when others are fearful". Naturally this is something most people won't be able to do either statistically, emotionally, or in terms of their own financial preparation, but those that do are seen as history's best market timers in hindsight.

11.4   Agency Problems

Over the past few decades, one of the biggest differences between the US equity market and China's onshore "A-share" market is that the former is heavily institutionalized and dominated by professional fund managers, while the latter is still dominated by relatively unsophisticated retail investors, and the higher volatility of China's A-share market, most recently exaggerated in the isolated bubble and crash in Chinese shares in the summer of 2015, lends some evidence to this. Even though unsophisticated retail traders fill the behavioral stereotype of the irrational investor, a market dominated by institutional investors has so far mostly codified rather than eliminated behavioral anomalies in markets.

One of the most important perspectives this author learned on Wall Street is that understanding what actions a Wall Street professional is likely to take and why is often as simple as understanding how that professional gets paid. Sales agents are paid a commission to sell a product, and no commission to not sell such products, so naturally they will focus their actions on what sells products, which may not always be in the buyer's best interest. Mutual fund managers are paid based on a percentage of the assets they manage, so their incentive is to increase the amount of assets they manage. This can be done through marketing or better describing performance in reports, rather than in producing what may be the best returns for a shareholder.

Speaking of fund managers, Howard Marks of Oaktree Capital summarized beautifully how outperformance in investing requires two things: (1) you have to be right, and (2) your view that was right must have been a contrarian view, otherwise you would have simply gotten the same result as everyone else. Research analysts get paid high salaries to produce reports that their readers hope to be right, but those highly paid analysts are more likely to lose their prestigious salaries and titles if they are wrong and alone versus if they are wrong with everyone else, so it is rational career risk management for research analysts not to stick their necks out too far (Fig. 11.3).

Arguably the greatest recent example of an institutionalized behavioral finance problem (or opportunity) was the chain of decisions that drove up and popped the 2006–2008 bubble in US residential housing and mortgage-backed bonds. Unlike the stereotypical bubble, which is driven by underinformed individual investors chasing performance on fear of missing out, mortgage-backed securities are bought by highly paid professionals acting on sets of rules in their job description:

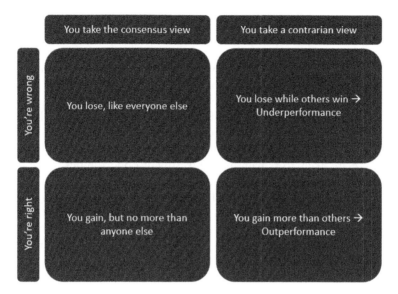

Fig. 11.3   The Howard Marks matrix of needing to be both right and non-consensus to outperform

1. Mortgage lenders originated mortgage loans based on a defined set of lending standards that had been loosened to promote home ownership. These lenders got paid to originate and service the loans, but then sold them to investors so they were not exposed to whether the loans were actually paid back.

2. Investment banks earned high fees from repackaging the loans into bonds that paid out the slice of cash flows from these mortgages that bond investors were looking for.

3. Bond investors eagerly bought these bonds, as many such investors were only allowed to buy bonds rated investment grade by a major rating agency, and these bonds paid a higher yield than other similarly rated bonds.

4. The major rating agencies, including S&P and Moody's, were paid by the bond issuers to rate the bonds, and based their ratings on models and data that underestimated the risk of a large percentage of the underlying mortgage loans not getting paid back.

5. Home buyers and investors saw it was easy to get a mortgage and that US house prices were rising quickly, so more and more rushed

to buy properties on borrowed money, with more and more such borrowers becoming unable to keep up with the mortgage payments.
6. As portrayed in Michael Lewis's 2010 book *The Big Short*, and dramatized in the 2015 movie of the same name, very few fund managers went out on a limb to bet against mortgage bonds, and those that did were ridiculed until they were right and they made enormous profits when most others were losing.

There are likely to remain many investment opportunities in the gaps left by rigid institutional rules guiding the behavior of finance professionals, even though many are far smaller and less dramatic than *The Big Short*. These gaps provide some of the best advantages smaller and more unconstrained investors have against larger institutions, though an interesting development in the twenty-first century will be if and how developments in areas like artificial intelligence (AI) close some or all of these gaps.

11.5   Gender, Age, and Artificial Intelligence (AI)

Although behavioral finance is often described in terms of individual and mass psychology, there is evidence that factors like gender and age can be used to explain some patterns in investment decisions. Just as population pyramids define how the balance between male vs female and young versus old drive much of what goes on in an economy, it remains to be seen whether developments in AI (robots arguably making up a "third gender of workers" in a population pyramid) may either mute or multiply the tail events caused by human behavior.

The *Financial Times* regularly publishes articles on how investment portfolios managed by women tend to generate better risk-adjusted returns than those run by men. As a benchmark, the *FT* references the HFRX Women index (a measure of female-run hedge funds) against the performance of the broader universe of HFR-tracked funds, of which roughly 19 out of 20 are managed by men. (As referenced in Chap. 6, HFR stands for "Hedge Fund Research" and is a Chicago-based firm that is one of the leading sources of data on hedge funds.) On a retail level, a study by the University of California at Berkeley found that the female individual investors in their study outperformed their male counterparts by an average of 1.4% per year, largely because the men trade more often and were more overconfident in their trades (source: https://www.ft.com/content/8bffa2c4-99f3-11e7-a652-cde3f882dd7b).

BEHAVIORAL INVESTING THAT BREAKS THE BOXES   289

Unlike gender, age acts as a different factor on investment behavior, as all 70-year-old investors have passed through every earlier age from 10 to 69 in order, though with very different experiences and lessons learned from them in the same years. Investors who have lived through a great crash or bear market are likely to have that experience embedded in their memories and influencing their actions in ways younger investors (without such first-hand memories) would have a hard time identifying with. Some of these memories bring back pain or fear, but ideally the lessons learned from them would be applied as wisdom which leads to better decisions than anything a student could learn to do from a book.

Many of the big promises and hopes in artificial intelligence and machine learning are that computers are far better able to learn patterns from large amounts of data, remember them without bias, and use everything learned (without selectively forgetting) to make better investment decisions than any human being or non-behaviorally enlightened program could do. AI is still in its infancy, and many applications as of early 2018 still mostly limited to well-defined, repeatable pattern recognition tasks, and it will be far harder to notice if robotic portfolio managers prevent the next crash than if they cause it. The program traders that caused the crash of 1987 and even the flash crash of 2010 did not even use the level of AI found in 2017-model smartphones, and it is important to differentiate between simple rules-based computer programs (e.g. "sell if a price reaches X") versus one that actually requires learning and decision (e.g. "estimate whether it makes sense to buy into this dip, based on all current and past data in the massive database"). While institutionalizing investing codified rather than eliminated behavioral volatility in financial markets, AI robots are not all supposed to run by the same rules in the same way as today's institutions, and have the unprecedented potential of making twenty-second-century stock markets behave like twentieth-century-textbook ideals of them.

11.6   FURTHER READING

Even many students of finance are likely to find more fascination in reading stories about how the rules of finance are broken than about the theory and definitions of how each type of financial instrument and market are supposed to work. Fortunately, there is plenty of literature that could broadly be categorized under behavioral economics.

University courses on behavioral investing often start with the papers of Princeton professors Daniel Kahneman and Amos Tversky, who developed the field of Prospect Theory to observe and model real-life choices people make in the face of uncertainty, rather than the optimizing choices classical finance theory is based on. Amos Tversky passed away in 1996, and in 2002, the Sveriges Riksbank Prize in Economic Sciences in Memory of Alfred Nobel (sometimes known as "the Nobel Prize in Economics" for short) was divided equally between Daniel Kahneman "for having integrated insights from psychological research into economic science, especially concerning human judgment and decision-making under uncertainty" and Vernon L. Smith "for having established laboratory experiments as a tool in empirical economic analysis, especially in the study of alternative market mechanisms" (Source: NobelPrize.org).

Around the time of the dotcom bubble of the late 1990s and early 2000s, Yale professor Robert Shiller published the book *Irrational Exuberance*, titled after a term used by then Fed chair Alan Greenspan about the mood driving markets to frothy valuations. This book returned to popularity in 2006 and 2007 when Shiller worked with Karl Case and Standard & Poor's to launch the S&P Case-Shiller index series of US home prices to measure the bubble in real estate prices across multiple American urban areas.

Behavioral finance reemerged as a top popular topic when the Nobel Prize was awarded to Richard Thaler in late 2017. Coverage of Thaler's prize highlighted his influential 2009 book *Nudge: Improving Decisions About Health, Wealth, and Happiness*, which describes situations from default retirement savings options to organ donation where small changes to an individual's environment or "path of least resistance" can change mass behavior for the better. Thaler's 2016 book *Misbehaving: The Making of Behavioral Economics* steps back from policy to the more classically micro fields of economics and psychology. A similar-sounding title more focused on the limits of mathematical models of a system where not all behavior is rational is Emanuel Derman's *Models.Behaving.Badly: Why Confusing Illusion with Reality Can Lead to Disaster, on Wall Street and in Life*.

Three practical guides on how to apply behavioral investing to an investment portfolio, based on his studies at Société Générale, are *Behavioral Investing*, *The Little Book of Behavioral Investing*, and *Value Investing* by James Montier.

Conclusion

This book aimed to cover, in 11 concise chapters, some of the most important things investors should need to know about some of the many different asset classes, strategies, markets, and mechanisms they are likely to encounter. Although the whole chapters can of course not be comprehensively summarized in one bullet point each, if this book were to be summarized in a "cheat sheet" for beyond the final exam, a summary of ten key takeaways for "beyond the final exam" might include:

1. Bonds are the benchmark for what fixed returns can be earned with little to no risk over relatively short periods of time (<30 years).
2. Buying credit risky and high-yield bonds is the first step to earning a higher rate of return for taking a calculated risk.
3. Real estate is tangible, easy to understand, and can provide income, inflation protection, and real appreciation, but beware of illiquidity, high transaction costs, and unique risks and costs with a specific property.
4. Stocks have provided the most scalable and flexible place to earn a 6%+ long-run real return, but also require attention to fundamentals, avoiding common behavioral traps, and limiting the bite of fees and taxes.
5. Alternative assets like art and collectibles, hedge funds, private equity, MLPs, BDCs, CTAs, and SPACs can provide returns from sources other than the traditional stock and real estate economic cycle, but it is still critical to know the underlying exposure and

© The Author(s) 2018
T. Dennison, *Invest Outside the Box*,
https://doi.org/10.1007/978-981-13-0372-2

what the fees are. Gold and silver are mostly speculative stores of value that may protect against a collapse in the financial system, but are otherwise unlikely to generate much real return.

6. The key to high returns is not getting one high return bet right, but rather diversifying across many different investments to keep risk low enough to lever up without blowing up.

7. Indices and ETFs track an increasing number of asset class benchmark and "smart beta" strategies that are scalable to invest in at very low cost. Investments related to an index or ETF but deviating from it must have a thesis on why they would beat the index on a risk-adjusted basis by a wide enough margin to cover cost and hassle.

8. Blockchain technology is likely to do for many applications involving signed documents what the Internet did for applications involving sharing information. The original cryptocurrencies have drawn price speculation on the future of networks based on little more than raw computing power, but the real value will come from the network effect of blockchain applications serving fundamental needs like any other business.

9. The hardest box for most investors to break out of is usually their geographic box, as many have the tendency to invest too much in one's home country and too little abroad. International diversification is still one of the best ways to improve risk-adjusted return and protect against a collapse of one's home country or economy.

10. Humans often don't act rationally. Investors can improve their outcomes both by knowing how to avoid behavioral pitfalls themselves and by understanding how to profit from the irrationality of others.

11. As valuable as it is to be a specialist and have deep knowledge on at least one thing, hopefully this book has shown the importance of knowing a little bit about at least ten things and allocating a little bit of one's fortune (financial or chronological) to each.

Hopefully at least one of these chapters has introduced you to a way or form of investing you didn't know as much about before, and helped you see and use financial markets in a new way.

Kind regards,
Tariq Dennison

INDEX